A Brief History of
COMMERCIAL
CAPITALISM

A Brief History of
COMMERCIAL
CAPITALISM

JAIRUS BANAJI

Haymarket Books
Chicago, Illinois

© 2020 Jairus Banaji

Published in 2020 by
Haymarket Books
P.O. Box 180165
Chicago, IL 60618
773-583-7884

www.haymarketbooks.org
info@haymarketbooks.org

ISBN: 978-1-64259-132-3

Distributed to the trade in the US through Consortium Book Sales and
Distribution (www.cbsd.com) and internationally through Ingram Pub-
lisher Services International (www.ingramcontent.com).

This book was published with the generous support of Lannan Foundation
and Wallace Action Fund.

Special discounts are available for bulk purchases by organizations and institutions. Please call 773-583-7884 or email info@haymarketbooks.org
for more information.

Cover photograph: Panoramic view of Istanbul and the Golden Horn tak-
en from the top of Seraskier (or Beyazit) Tower by the Swedish photogra-
pher Guillaume Berggren *ca.* 1870.
Cover design by Jamie Kerry.

Library of Congress Cataloging-in-Publication data is available.

10 9 8 7 6 5 4 3 2 1

CONTENTS

For Henry, Javed, M. J., and Sughosh

———————————————————

REINSTATING COMMERCIAL CAPITALISM

A NOTION OF CAPITAL

I have shown elsewhere (see appendix) that in Muslim trading circles capital was invariably referred to by the term *al-mal*, which could also have the more generic meanings of "property," "assets," and so on. On the other hand, in Italy terminology stabilized only gradually. In a Venetian commercial agreement (*collegantia*) dated August 1073, the notary Domenico uses no fewer than three distinct terms for capital: the sum invested by Giovanni, whose contract this is, is called *habere*, the total capital invested by him and his partners is called *capetanea* (in the formula "if the capital is saved," *capetanea salva*), and if he violates the agreement then he promises to return "everything in the double, both capital and profit" (*caput et prode*).[1] "The capital and the profit" became a standard expression in Italian commercial contracts of the medieval period and suggests a clear evolution since the ninth century, when a famous will (drawn up by a Venetian doge in 829) had referred to his investments in overseas trade (*navigatio*) less straightforwardly as "money put to work" (*laborantis solidis*).[2]

By the early fifteenth century, the Franciscan priest Bernardino could say that money which is "not simply money or a thing" but, over and above that, "is meant to generate a profit" is "what we commonly call capital" (*capitale*).[3] It was more or less at this time (ca.1433) that a leading Florentine of the Peruzzi banking family tells his debtors, "I have no more capital remaining in the shop; it is all in the wool manufacturing, and indeed both businesses are ruined. I have made nothing or very little in the last two years because all our capital is tied up in debts which can't be called in, because the times are so hard."[4] And certainly by the start of the sixteenth century, the term capital was becoming common elsewhere in Europe. The Portuguese investment in Malabar pepper was standardly described as "cabedal da pimenta." This could take the form of either goods or money, so that when the capital sent out to buy spices was dispatched in the form of cash, it could be described as "cabedal do dinheiro," as Simão Botelho described it in 1552, when he complained that not enough "money capital" was being sent from Lisbon.[5] So too in 1585 when the factor Sassetti stated that the "capitals" (*i capitali*) sent out to buy pepper consisted in *reales*. The same sense of the formal distinctions within capital is reflected in a Venetian report of 1603 where it is said, "capital has always returned from the Levant in the form of merchandise" (*mercancie*).[6]

That a notion of capital was present elsewhere as well is shown by the example of the weaver-poet Kabir who (in the fifteenth century) says about himself, "Kabir, the capital (*punji*) belongs to the sâh / and you waste it all."[7] (Bigger merchants of the *bania* caste were called *sāh* or *sāhu*.) In a late sixteenth-century work, the Ottoman intellectual Mustafa 'Ali writes about rich merchants "constantly enlarging their capital" as their associates travel to India and beyond and return with "precious rarities." About a Damascus merchant who had to rent an entire caravanserai to accommodate the goods he came back with, the same author says, "his capital had produced a multitude of goods and immeasurable profit."[8]

As Venice rapidly lost her commercial supremacy at the start of the seventeenth century, one observer wrote (in 1612), "It is not that we lack capital (*A noi non mancano i capitali*); our nobility wants no part in trade," adding, nowadays "the prosperous prefer to invest their money in the financial markets (*sui cambi*)."[9] A few years later, in a widely read directory of commerce published first in 1638, Lewis Roberts described the East India Company as "a great and eminent Company . . . imploying in a joint Stock a great Capitol, by which

Trade and Stock they have built many warlike ships."[10] And by the eighteenth century, when the French economist Turgot provided a clear description of the simplest form of capitalist accumulation (this in 1766), usage of the term "capital" was of course widespread.[11] In the late 1720s Bombay servants of the East India Company would complain that they had "no large capitalls to enable them to build large ships."[12] Again, in 1788 an English official notes that "It is a general complaint among Merchants that they are Losers upon the Capital invested in Shipping which they find it necessary to employ."[13] And in 1766 again, the same year that Turgot published his *Reflections on the Formation and Distribution of Wealth*, a French report on Portugal could refer to the Marquis de Pombal "scrupulously fleecing" Portuguese "capitalists" and shareholders.[14]

MERCHANT CAPITALISM, COMMERCIAL CAPITALISM

The Marxist reticence about merchant's capital stems not just from a failure to grasp Marx's method in *Capital* (the study of capital "as such" differs not just from "the study of capital in its reality,"[15] it differs also from what Marx in the *Grundrisse* calls the "real history of the relations of production"[16]), it stems also and even more perhaps from the polemical divide that was created in the postwar tradition by the decisive rejection of Pokrovsky's work in Russia in the early thirties and the concomitant stigmatization of any general category like "merchant capitalism."[17] But the transmission of this constructed orthodoxy was mediated, crucially, by Maurice Dobb whose influential *Studies in the Development of Capitalism* first appeared in 1946. Dobb himself was deeply ambiguous about the term. Thus, early on in *Studies* he told the reader he was willing to accept "merchant capitalism" in the specific sense of an "early period of capitalism when production was subordinated to the 'merchant manufacturer' under the putting-out system," but unwilling to see it as a characterization of the "existence of large capitals and specialized merchants in the sphere of trade" at any time before the later sixteenth century when, he claims, capital began to "penetrate production on a considerable scale."[18] Yet, in the book itself Dobb goes on to note that "In certain Flemish towns the capitalist merchant-manufacturer had already begun to make his appearance in the thirteenth century."[19] And a few pages later he goes on to say, "Evidence not only of a fairly extensive capitalist-controlled 'putting-out' system in the wool industry but also of manufactory-production is to be found *in the early part of the fourteenth century.*"[20] However, by 1950 when the debate on the "transition" was first aired in the pages of *Science & Society*, these nuances were entirely lost and merchant capitalism had, in Dobb's mind, degenerated into "the Pokrovsky-bog," that is, some hopelessly confused miasma that the great Russian historian had left half-lurking in left-wing historiography.[21]

Pokrovsky, of course, was forced to recant by 1931. Merchant capitalism, he said in the recantation, is an "illiterate expression" because "[c]apitalism is a system of production, and merchant capital produces nothing."[22] The prostration before Stalin could scarcely have been more complete. That its dismal legacy has survived for so long in Marxist scholarship shows how paralyzing the influence of political orthodoxies can be. In any case, a major upshot of this turn of events was that the whole field of "early capitalism" was left entirely vacant for other traditions of historiography to move into and occupy firmly. The best response to Dobb's work came not from other Marxists but from R. H. Tawney, who had just retired in 1949. Reviewing Dobb's book in 1950 he wrote:

> Mr. Dobb's limitation of the term [capitalism] to a particular system of production, under which labour is employed on the basis of a wage-contract to produce surplus-value for the owner of capital, might seem, at first sight, to escape some of the ambiguities inherent in less restricted interpretations; but it raises problems of its own. It is not merely that, as he would agree, financial and commercial capitalism have been highly developed in circumstances where the institution, as interpreted by him, has been a feeble plant, and that *to exclude these varieties on the ground that they do not fall within the four corners of a nineteenth-century definition* is to beg the

question. It is that, as his work shows, the origins and growth of the industrial species require for their elucidation to be considered in relation to other members of the family, some of which have been among its progenitors.

Tawney went on to ask whether the restricted sense of capitalism favored by Dobb had not "ceased to be the usage most convenient for the purposes of history." And in terms of English political history, he suggested that Dobb's definition of capitalism "leads at times to a misconception of the significance of the part played by *capitalist interests* in periods when an industrial wage-system was, in this country, in its infancy."[23]

In some ways the closest counterpart to Pokrovsky in the West was the non-Marxist Tawney. *Religion and the Rise of Capitalism* was published in 1926. If "no single concept was so identical with Pokrovsky as that of commercial capitalism,"[24] Tawney, too, "explained British economic development in the sixteenth and seventeenth centuries through the maturing of a specifically commercial form of capitalism."[25] In *Religion* the most general characterization he offers is when he refers at one point to "the phenomena of early commercial capitalism."[26] But Tawney's commercial capitalism embraced a very wide range of economic phenomena (unlike Pokrovsky and Dobb). "Then, in the late sixteenth and early seventeenth centuries, had come the wave of commercial and financial expansion—companies, colonies, capitalism in textiles, capitalism in mining, capitalism in finance—on the crest of which the English commercial classes ... had climbed to a position of dignity and affluence."[27] Again, "Foreign trade increased largely in the first half of the sixteenth century, and, as manufactures developed, cloth displaced wool as the principal export. With the growth of commerce went the growth of the financial organization on which commerce depends, and English capital poured into the London money market which had previously been dominated by Italian bankers." "*In industry, the rising interest was that of the commercial capitalist.*"[28] "The age of Elizabeth saw a steady growth of capitalism in textiles and mining, a great increase in foreign trade ... and the growth ... of a money market with an almost modern technique—speculation, futures, and arbitrage transactions—in London."[29] On the whole, Tawney tended to eschew any special terminology and decades later, when writing *Business and Politics Under James I*, he would refer to the "triumph of this commercial capitalism," but qualify the expression by adding, "to use the conventional, if ambiguous, term."[30]

With one precocious and brilliant exception, "commercial capitalism" simply failed to resurface in the English-language historiography till the 1980s. The exception was Eric Williams, who concluded *Capitalism and Slavery* (1944) with the argument, "The commercial capitalism of the eighteenth century developed the wealth of Europe by means of slavery and monopoly. But in so doing it helped to create the industrial capitalism of the nineteenth century, which turned round and destroyed the power of commercial capitalism, slavery, and all its works. Without a grasp of these economic changes, the history of the period is meaningless."[31] In the eighties, Geoffrey Ingham,[32] John Brewer,[33] and P. J. Cain and A. G. Hopkins[34] all invoked a notion of mercantile or commercial capitalism as essential to any understanding of modern British history. In *Capitalism Divided?* (1984), Ingham showed how in the course of the nineteenth century the City's commercial capitalism had functioned as "a prop for the economy as a whole," and how the country's ruling class survived on "essentially preindustrial forms of commercial capitalism which have persisted in the City."[35] In *The Sinews of Power* (1989), Brewer's seminal argument about the nature of the British state began with his own implicit acceptance that "Britain's aggrandizement was impelled by the powerful forces of commercial capitalism." And in *British Imperialism, 1688–2000*, Cain and Hopkins were willing to allow for various sorts of commercial capitalism ("an indigenous, Indian brand of commercial capitalism,"[36] "advanced forms of commercial capitalism such as the East India Company,"[37] etc.) in addition to their own overarching characterization of British capitalism as "gentlemanly capitalism."

In contrast to this disjointed evolution was a much tighter tradition of continental historiography where the major influences were those of the French. Vilar, a Marxist, was circumspect, referring only once to "European mercantile capitalism" in a *Past and Present* paper from 1956.[38] But Braudel's *Mediterranean* and his later work were very largely structured around a vision of commercial capitalism (in his later work mostly "merchant capitalism") fluctuating between trade, industry, and the money markets; of a "Mediterranean capitalism" driven by "a few powerful combines," and of industrial capitalism itself (the *Verlag* system) as largely merchant-dominated.[39] To Braudel, long-distance trade, *Fernhandel*, was "the very lifeblood of commercial capitalism."[40] In his famous essay "La longue durée" (1958), he suggested that merchant capitalism (*capitalisme marchand*) imparted a "certain coherence" to a whole four or five centuries of Europe's economic life down to the eighteenth century, and described the expression as a "model that we can disengage from Marx's work."[41] Mousnier's own conception of commercial capitalism seemed to stand halfway between Braudel and Tawney, both in underlining the interdependence between the *grand commerce capitaliste* and the absolutisms of the sixteenth century, *and* in seeing Calvinism as exerting a major influence on capitalism, even if capitalism itself predated the Reformation, as Tawney had argued.[42]

If we amalgamate these streams of historiography, then every decade since the sixties has produced substantial pieces of work in which "commercial capitalism" and "merchant capitalism" are in some way *central* to their argument: Manuel Nunes Dias's innovatory tomes on Portugal's "monarchical capitalism" (1963),[43] Charles Carrière's studies of the trade of Marseilles and of bills of exchange (1973, 1976),[44] Catharina Lis and Hugo Soly's monograph on the putting-out system (1979),[45] the works by Béatrice Veyssarat,[46] Peter Kriedte,[47] David Ormrod,[48] Bob Shenton,[49] and Joseph Miller[50] in the eighties, Bin Wong's comparative study of European and Chinese economic development[51] or Leo Noordegraaf's paper on the "new draperies" (both 1997),[52] down to more recent work like Sergio

Tognetti's monograph on the business groups involved in the silk industry of Florence [53] or Scott Marler's study of merchant capitalism in the US South.[54] All of the authors cited above refer explicitly to "commercial," "merchant," or "merchant and banking" capitalism. And beyond them lies an even greater mass of writers who refer in passing to "mercantile" or "commercial" capitalism and capitalists.[55]

Marxist reticence (Perry Anderson, Robert Brenner, and a host of others) is thus strikingly at odds with much of the historiography that has evolved and it can scarcely invoke orthodoxy when Lenin, for example, admired Pokrovsky's work and would himself use the term "private commercial capitalism" in the 1918 debates about the organization of Russian industry.[56] Left-wing academics and intellectuals who felt unconstrained by orthodoxies could posit forms of capitalism that Marx himself had never properly discussed. Among the historians listed in the previous paragraphs, only a handful were consciously working in a Marxist tradition. Bob Shenton is probably the best example of this group. A good example of an intellectual (*not* a historian) who made pointed references to "mercantile capitalism" is Sartre. In the *Critique of Dialectical Reason* he refers to "the apparatus and structures of mercantile capitalism" in the context of a discussion of Spain's struggle to retain its massive flows of American treasure.[57] Now one can always say that Sartre is merely summarizing Braudel's argument in *Mediterranean*, which is true, but the introductory essay *Questions de méthode* has Sartre describing the long-standing commercial rivalry between the British and the French as a "secular conflict of mercantile capitalisms," an apt description that stemmed purely from his own reading of history.[58]

CONSTRUCTING THE CASE FOR COMMERCIAL CAPITALISM

A historian of English commerce has noted that in the eighteenth century "London merchants invested in provincial manufacturing on a large scale."[59] What does one make of this? In *Capital*, Marx maintains an unbreachable separation between commercial capital

and the production of capital. This is because the capital that em-
bodies capital-*production* is what he calls industrial capital. The industrialist can always sell his own commodities, but if he chooses to
dispose of his commodity capital through a class of agents who specialize in the circulation of commodities, that is, through merchants,
then the capital of the merchant can (for the purposes of analysis)
be treated simply as a "transformed form" of a portion of the (industrial) capital in circulation.[60] The merchant is simply an agent of
industrial capital; other functions are irrelevant.

Yet there are clear indications scattered through the corpus of
Marx's own writings to suggest that he would *not* have reacted with
horror to the idea that merchant capitalists might "dominate production directly," that is, subject it to their own expansion as capital. In
the famous chapter of volume three called "Historical Material on
Merchant's Capital," statements like "commercial capital is confined
to the circulation sphere and its sole function is to mediate the exchange of commodities" or "Commercial capital simply mediates
the movement of these extremes"[61] generate the tautology "The independent and preponderant development of capital in the form of
commercial capital is synonymous with the nonsubjection of production to capital,"[62] but this is then almost immediately undermined
by his fascinating but unexplored reference to "the manner and form
in which commercial capital operates *where it dominates production
directly*." The two examples of this cited are: "colonial trade in general (the so-called colonial system)," that is, the vast transatlantic
commercial system which revitalized slavery as a modern-world development, and secondly "the operations of the former Dutch East
India Company";[63] in short, two very substantial trade sectors in
both of which Marx seemed to think commercial capital was active
in new, more "direct" ways. Again, in volume two, Marx refers to
the cottage industries in Russia that "are already being pressed more
and more into the service of capitalist production." "[F]or example,
merchants supply the weavers with warps and weft, either directly
or by intermediate agents," so that these "rural subsidiary industries"

become "points of vantage for the capitalist, who first intrudes in his capacity as merchant."[64] Even more explicitly, in the supplement that he added to volume three shortly before he died, Engels described the "merchant capitalist" "buying" labor power which "continued to possess for some time its instrument of production but had already ceased to possess its raw material." Since he could ensure regular employment for the weaver, the merchant could depress his wages and "appropriate surplus-value on top of his previous trading profit."[65] Both of these latter examples refer, of course, to the putting-out system which became widespread by the later Middle Ages.

In the same chapter where, fleetingly, he allowed for a more active role for commercial capital in the Atlantic and the Dutch trades, Marx went on to posit an overall contrast between forms of transition to capitalism by saying, either "the producer may become a merchant and capitalist" *or* "the merchant may take direct control of production himself."[66] Again, there was no sense here of an archetypal separation between production and circulation, since merchants *could* "take direct control of production." The example he cites is interesting. "Right up to the middle of this century, for example, the manufacturer in the French silk industry... *was a manufacturer only in name. In reality he was simply a merchant*, who kept the weavers working in their old fragmented manner and exercised only control as a merchant; *it was a merchant they were really working for.*"[67] The reference here was to the Lyons silk industry and is particularly interesting because it helps to tie up with more recent work which I shall come back to in a later chapter.[68] "A manufacturer only in name" was an implicit acknowledgment that the industry involved accumulation of capital by the silk merchants rather than by any class of industrial capitalists in a more obvious sense. This form of capitalist industry, Marx wrote, transformed the direct producers into "mere wage-labourers and proletarians" working under worse conditions than the workers in factory production and did nothing to alter the dispersed, domestic basis of production, that is, to "revolutionize" the "mode of production," that is, the way production was organized.[69] In fact, however, more recent work shows that while the weavers of Lyons were rapidly subordinated to big merchants and merchant firms in the early eighteenth century, the silk industry itself was more innovative, even technologically, than Marx allowed for.

There is no doubt that in most passages with statements of the form "the merchant becomes an industrialist directly,"[70] Marx tended to see the putting-out system as involving an actual "transformation of the merchant into an industrial capitalist." Thus in *Theories of Surplus-Value* he writes both that "The merchant as such becomes a producer, an industrialist" and that the "transformation of the merchant into an industrial capitalist is *at the same time the transformation of commercial capital into a mere form of industrial capital.*"[71] It was almost certainly this conflation that stopped Marx from positing a distinct form of accumulation that one could identify as *merchant* capitalism specifically, since putters-out were no longer merchants but industrialists. In this respect, at least, Dobb's own study moved beyond Marx. Not only did Dobb see the putting-out system as emblematic of a specifically merchant capitalism[72] and refer repeatedly to "merchant-manufacturers," "merchant-employers," and so on, but unlike Marx he was open to the idea that "the capitalist merchant-manufacturer had *an increasingly close interest in promoting improvements in the instruments and methods of production.*" "The very division of labor which is specially characteristic of this period prepared the ground from which mechanical invention could eventually spring."[73] This was a radically different perspective to Marx's, and one we owe to Dobb's theoretical perspicacity in disentangling the much larger process of the "subordination of production to capital" from industrial capitalism as such.[74] The French historian Georges Lefebvre restated this perspective in a more dynamic way in his contribution to the debate between Sweezy and Dobb when he argued that it was the "collusion between commerce and the State" that "promoted the development of capitalism," and that "merchants played a part in the historical mission of capitalism" by their role in "concentrating and rationalising production."[75] All this was decades ago, of course, and since then studies like the one by Sven Beckert have been able to demonstrate the ways merchants contributed directly to the emergence of industrial capitalism in industries like cotton textiles when mechanization began.[76]

The major breakthrough of theory, it seems to me, came with Chayanov in Russia. Responding to the accusation that his school looked at peasant farming in isolation from "world capitalist circulation," he made the fundamental point that the penetration of capitalism into the countryside took the form of "trading and finance capitalism" establishing an "economic dictatorship over considerable sectors of agriculture, which as regards production will remain as before, composed of small-scale family labor peasant undertakings subject in their internal organization to the laws of the labor-consumer balance."[77] This was said in the introduction to *Peasant Farm Organization* (1925). In chapter seven, Chayanov went on to expand on this idea by reiterating that, "while *in a production sense* concentration in agriculture is scarcely reflected in the formation of new large-scale undertakings, *in an economic sense* capitalism as a general economic system makes great headway in agriculture."[78] Agriculture "becomes subject to trading capitalism that sometimes in the form of very large-scale commercial undertakings draws masses of scattered peasant farms into its sphere of influence and, having bound these small-scale commodity producers to the market, economically subordinates them to its influence."[79] Chayanov then referred to large commercial firms like the Knoops using the advance system to convert the organization of rural production almost into a special form of the "sweatshop system."[80] Commercial capital penetrates the countryside through "trading machines" (viz., its commercial organization and networks) that Chayanov described as "leaving them [peasant farms] free as regards production" while "entirely dominating them economically ."[81] Finally, Chayanov allowed for an evolution of contract farming by suggesting that the same firms could "actively interfere in the organization of production, too."[82]

Chayanov's specific term for this form of capitalist penetration and control via commercial firms and their "trading machines" was "vertical capitalist concentration." Vertical concentration was how commercial capitals established a degree of control over rural households and their labor powers. The concept developed here strikes me as an innovation in Marxist theory, and I shall return to the way it worked in chapter six.

2

THE INFRASTRUCTURE OF COMMERCIAL CAPITALISM

TRADING COLONIES

The dispersion of networks was a major instrument of capital accumulation. If the characteristic mobility of capital is what Marx calls "circulation," then for centuries the circulation of capital presupposed the physical movement of commercial agents, which in turn would mean their ability to establish more or less stable settlements in locations abroad. The term for such a settlement was "factory." "'Factory' according to Dr. Johnson means 'a house or district inhabited by Traders in a distant country.'"[1] Thus, the "factory" was the community of merchants of this or that nationality. In the Levant in the seventeenth century, "the factories lived self-centred lives"; among other things this meant that "the Turks rarely appeared in the (European) quarters."[2]

The history of commerce is thus a rich tapestry of trading colonies that spanned the entire globe, wherever this was accessible. In Guangzhou (Canton) in the later eleventh century, "The foreign ward (*fanfang*) is where those from various countries from across the ocean congregate and live."[3] Muslim merchants had been trading here since at least the eighth century and were both numerous and prosperous. In 1216 there were some three thousand European merchants living in Alexandria.[4] Two and a half centuries later, the Dutch traveler Joos von Ghistele tells us, Alexandria "swarms with rich merchants who have come from all nations imaginable." "The

majority of these have their own *maison* which they call *fondigoes*,"
the Venetians having at least two establishments of this sort.[5] In the
twelfth century, Venetians were so numerous at Constantinople that
thousands of them were rounded up in March 1171 when the emper-
or Manuel Komnenos decided to curb their "insolence" after they
"attacked and plundered the newly established Genoese quarter" in
the city, "tore down its houses and left it in ruins."[6] The Venetian
Quarter occupied a whole stretch of the southern shore of the Golden
Horn, the district known as Perama, where there were three *scalae*
(places where ships could dock) and a long row of *officinae* and *ergas-
teria*, that is, commercial establishments, workshops, and retail outlets.[7] Venetians maintained trading colonies in all the major cities of
the Levant.[8] There were several thousand Venetians settled on Crete
in the fourteenth century, with the "greatest names of the Venetian
aristocracy" dominating the island's economy.[9] In Acre, "[t]he Italian quarters were very crowded," with "self-governing quarters for
the Venetians and the Pisans close to the harbour, and a substantial
Genoese section" tucked behind them.[10] Here, in the late thirteenth
century, after violent clashes with the Genoese, the Venetians decided to redevelop their quarter as a solidly fortified enclave, with
their "citizens and merchants" encouraged to reside strictly within its
walls.[11] By contrast, Palermo in the twelfth and thirteenth centuries
had a mixed quarter around the port, although in 1184/5 the Muslims
were said to live in their own suburbs, "apart from the Christians."[12]
(Ibn Jubayr also claims that "they do not congregate for the Friday
service, since the *khutbah* is forbidden.")

In Tunis, a suburb outside the eastern or "Sea" gate (the Bab el-
bahr) was the home of Italian and Catalan merchants in the early
sixteenth century.[13] When the French colonized the country in the
1880s, a more purely European city emerged next to the historic one,
with "a cathedral, markets, hotels, banks, and buildings of all sorts,"
sufficiently modern in character for one traveler to call it "un cachet
européen" as early as 1885.[14] In Istanbul, the old (pre-Ottoman, Byzantine) Genoese colony of Pera (on the northern side of the Golden

Horn) resurfaced in the nineteenth century as a purely European enclave dominated by Greek merchants and bankers, the nerve-center of a new, but still largely commercial, bourgeoisie.[15] There were also large colonies of Spanish Jews in Istanbul and "above all" Salonica in the sixteenth century.[16] In *The Merchants Map* Roberts described Salonica as a "rich and large City." "The present inhabitants are Greeks, Turks, and *principally Jews, who are here found to be very rich and eminent Merchants.*"[17] Further south, in Smyrna/Izmir "the houses of the Franks (Europeans, JB) were the best and most handsome buildings in the city. They were all in one street which ran along the shore."[18] The French botanist Tournefort described Smyrna in 1702 as "one of the richest cities of the Levant," but noted that "the Turks rarely appear in the rue des Francs."[19] Smyrna, one writer has said recently, "was both Ottoman and European."[20] There were thousands of Italian merchants in Lisbon toward the end of the fifteenth century[21] and a conspicuous colony of English merchants in the eighteenth century, when English capital was "very evident in the Brazilian and African trades."[22] (A French report even claimed "On peut regarder Lisbonne comme une colonie Angloise"!) In London by 1860, there were some eighty-six Greek merchant houses. "Almost all the London-Greeks lived in Finsbury Circus, where they had luxurious residences and the company headquarters."[23] Likewise, nineteenth-century Marseilles had a "very large number of Greek houses," and was next to London the other main recipient in western Europe of cargoes sent by Greek merchants from the eastern Mediterranean and the Black Sea.[24]

Finally, between the Mediterranean and China were ports like Sohar, Masqat, Calicut, and Malacca, all of which had substantial settlements of foreign traders. Sohar, on the edge of the Indian Ocean and the only town in Oman with any real urban development, was "closely linked with the Omani overseas community living in Basra."[25] The networks that extended across the Gulf to the east coast of Africa and to al-Mansura in Sind were inextricably religious *and* commercial, and dominated by religious dissidents known as Ibadis (al-Ibadiyya). Wilkinson has argued that "as a cosmopolitan centre with very close links with Basra," Sohar was the "centre of a number of 'vanguard' philosophies which displeased the reactionary *'ulama'* of the (Omani) interior" in the ninth century.[26] There were numerous Sirafi merchants at Sohar[27] as well as a "sizeable Jewish community."[28] The Gulf networks were characterized by high levels of internal mobility. "The merchants of these ports regularly moved around between them and often had residences in more than one."[29] Masqat's own commercial life later came to be dominated by a succession of Bania (Guj. *vaniyo*) communities. In 1765 when the Sindi Bhattias were still strong, the Danish explorer Carsten Niebuhr reported, "In no other Mahometan city are the Banians so numerous as in Maskat; their number in this city amounts to twelve hundred."[30] By 1840, with the ruling family moving house to Zanzibar, Kutchi Bhattias had emerged as the "principal economic power in Masqat" and the Bania population reached two thousand.[31] The Banias of Masqat retained a high degree of community solidarity. Accounts were kept in Gujarati, Indian dress styles were maintained, and, in general, "the Masqati Hindu made no attempt to assimilate."[32]

What was so striking about Calicut was the more or less stable presence of a substantial colony of foreign merchants from Cairo and the Red Sea ports as well as other parts of the Middle East from as early as the fourteenth century.[33] In 1502 it was claimed there were some "4,000 households of Muslims *just from Cairo and the Red Sea in Calicut.*"[34] Barbosa described them as "extremely wealthy" since they dominated the crucial part of the circuits by which spices traveled to Venice via Aden, Jedda, and Cairo.[35] Since Calicut was the chief base of Middle Eastern capital in the Indian Ocean, the Portuguese failure to turn the Zamorin, the (Hindu) ruler of Calicut, against them triggered a campaign of exceptional violence which caused a rapid flight of capital. "Many nations used to have great factories here," Tomé Pires could say in less than two decades of the Portuguese coming.[36] On the other hand, even as late as the start of the seventeenth century Calicut was still said to be the "busiest" port in the whole of India and to have "merchants from all parts of the world, and of all nations and religions, by reason of the liberty and security accorded to them there." The Zamorin, it was said, "permits the exercise of every kind of religion, and yet it is strictly forbidden to talk, dispute, or quarrel on that subject; so there never arises any contention on that score."[37]

East of Malabar, Malacca was "the richest seaport with the greatest number of wholesale merchants and abundance of shipping and trade."[38] The value of goods passing through the port *ca*.1511 has been estimated to be a staggering two million cruzados![39] Tomé Pires, who spent two and a half years there, claimed that "eighty-four distinct languages could be heard in the streets of Malacca" and estimates the number of foreign merchants in the city in 1509 to be about 4,000.[40] Thomaz has argued that Muslims from Gujarat were the most powerful community there and lived in a section of the rich merchant quarter (*kampong*) of Upeh. Next in importance were the "Kelings" or Coromandel Tamils who lived in Kampong Keling some distance away, near the sea.[41] Malacca's cosmopolitanism threw up a policy of "broad religious tolerance" under its fifteenth-century sultans, so much so that the famous Muslim navigator Ibn Majid would actually complain about the frequency of mixed marriages (marriages between Muslims and non-Muslims).[42]

Of course, trading colonies were not confined to port cities and were found in major inland centers as well. Isfahan in the 1640s was said to have "a large number of strangers who usually frequent this Persian Emporium on account of its flourishing trade and commerce." The Portuguese monk Manrique claimed that "more than six hundred caravanseries exist for these foreigners."[43] The suburb of Julfa contained a colony of "six to seven thousand Armenians," transplanted there by Shah Abbas I; "very wealthy" because its residents "follow trade in various parts of Asia and Europe."[44] Later in the seventeenth century, the Venetian-born writer Manucci describes Lahore as "crammed with foreign merchants."[45] And Cairo in the eighteenth century had a wealthy and highly organized community of Fasi merchants, merchants from Fez in the Maghreb. They were substantial traders in coffee and Indian textiles, and "tended to agglomerate in the same districts (of the city) for their businesses and lived in proximity to each other."[46]

WHOLESALE MARKETS

Wholesale markets with a global reach are attested in various sources from the seventh to the tenth centuries. "*Rešir i Parsan*, from which come fine pearls" was how an Armenian geographer described one market of this sort in the seventh century, referring to Rishahr on the southern coast of Iran.[47] Barda' west of the Caspian exported vast quantities of raw silk to Fars and Khuzistan in the south of Iran.[48] Busir in Middle Egypt was the leading wholesale market for flax.[49] In Kabul, the market for indigo was said to have an annual turnover of over two million dinars![50] Marsa al-Kharaz (La Calle) on the Algerian coast specialized in coral fishing. At any given time fifty boats were active, each with roughly twenty men.[51] "The coral is then polished in a special marketplace, and *sold in bulk*, at a low price."[52] Seville retained its dominant position as the chief European market for olive oil from the tenth to the fourteenth centuries,[53] and Barus in the far north of Sumatra was where merchants went to buy camphor.

By the twelfth century Ceuta was another major center of the coral trade. Al-Idrisi tells us it had a market "where one cuts and polishes the coral and makes jewellery out of it." This was widely exported, the bulk of it to Ghana and the Sudan.[54] Tabarca, too, had numerous coral reefs and again (al-Idrisi tells us) merchants came there "from all over the world" and "exported a great deal" of this precious commodity.[55] In fact, the Tabarca coral market is a striking example of how stable wholesale markets could be over time. In 1543 two major Genoese merchant houses acquired its coral island and by 1584 one of them, the Lomellini, was selling 100,000 ducats worth of coral in Lisbon. As late as 1633 there were no fewer than fifteen hundred Genoese still based there.[56] Alexandria, too, had a wholesale market which was called *souq al-murjaniyya*, where a whole street of coral workshops was plundered by King Peter I of Cyprus in 1365.[57] In the early thirteenth century al-Tifashi reports that a pound of raw coral cost five dirhams in the home ports, but the price could be three or four times as much once it was processed at Alexandria.[58]

Flax and spices were likewise wholesale trades dominated by medieval Alexandria. In the late eleventh century, it exported between five to six thousand tons of raw flax to markets in the Mediterranean,[59] and under Saladin and the Ayyubids it became the leading spice market of the East Mediterranean. A major wholesale market could generate secondary ones elsewhere; for example, Abulafia notes, "There was a famous market for Egyptian flax in Mazara" on the west coast of Sicily.[60] Further west, Venice was Europe's largest bullion market before the arrival of American silver,[61] which was doubtless the reason why the Florence merchant-bankers decided to make the Rialto Europe's pivotal exchange market from the early years of the fourteenth century and make Venice "the most predictable of Europe's banking places."[62] By the fifteenth century, Venice was also the "chief distributor of both high-grade and middling varieties of Levant cotton to European industries,"[63] and the key wholesale market for spices in the west.[64] Lisbon became the great spice market of Europe by the first decade of the sixteenth century, destroying the Venetian "monopoly." Antwerp was the great international money market of the middle of the sixteenth century. The total value of financial transactions concluded on the Antwerp Bourse in the course of a single year was estimated in 1557 at 40 million ducats.[65]

Danzig was a major grain market with massive shipments to the Iberian Peninsula. Almost eighty thousand tons passed through the town in 1562.[66] Gallipoli at the southern extremity of Puglia had a virtual monopoly over the export of high-quality olive oil.[67] It was said to influence olive oil prices as far away as Naples.[68] "This trade is entirely in the hands of the merchants at Naples and Leghorn, particularly the former who have their agents at Gallipoli, and by making advances to the poor cultivator, keep him constantly in their chains."[69] The same writer adds, "The orders for delivery of oil at

Gallipoli are treated like bills of exchange, and have sometimes five or six indorsements."[70] Thus, next to its silk industry, Naples could count on being the great olive oil market of the whole southern region.[71] Patras in the Peloponnese was the chief market for the currant trade, exporting 8 million pounds annually at the end of the eighteenth century.[72] Bayt al-Faqih in Yemen was described as "the greatest market for coffee in the world"; "coffee is always bought for ready Money."[73] The biggest buyers, the Turkish and Arab merchants, shipped the beans to Jedda using Yemen's northern ports, not Mocha where the European companies were active. Also, "Egyptian merchants rarely dealt directly with their Yemeni counterparts. Instead, transactions were made through Jidda."[74] The Jedda market is thought to have been ten times larger in volume than the Gulf market served by Mocha.[75] The size of this Ottoman trade can be glimpsed from the fact that by March 1720 the total Turkish capital amassed at Bayt al-Faqih came to one million Spanish riyals over a seven-month period.[76]

In Cairo the coffee trade involved some five hundred merchants importing roughly one hundred thousand quintals, of which half was reexported to markets in the Ottoman empire.[77] Muhammad al-Dada of the Sharaybi family was described by the French consul in 1708 as the most powerful coffee merchant in Cairo.[78] He had come to Cairo from Jedda following a plague that had wiped out most of his family. When he inherited management of the Sharaybi family fortune at the end of the seventeenth century, this stood at two and a half million para. By 1722 this sum had expanded to *ca.*37 million para, an "enormous capital" which was then rapidly fragmented in the division he arranged among younger Sharaybis of the fourth generation.[79]

In the second half of the sixteenth century most Iranian raw silk was traded in Aleppo. The wholesalers were Armenian merchants who recirculated the silver acquired from European buyers to finance purchases of high-quality indigo in the wholesale markets of Agra and Bayana.[80] Vast sums of capital poured into the Bayana region during the boom of the 1620s,[81] and Armenian and Mughal merchants were said to have advanced as much as 350,000 rupees as late as 1636.[82] Benares was the center of the North Indian diamond trade in the eighteenth century,[83] and the main money market for eastern India.[84] Mirzapur was "the great mart for cotton,"[85] and a "very considerable trade" in opium was carried on at Patna.[86]

Salonica was described as the "great mart for tobacco in the Levant."[87] In Europe the market was dominated by a handful of Glasgow firms who disposed of their Chesapeake cargoes in huge sales to French buyers in Scotland.[88] Kingston,[89] Kilwa, and Luanda were all major slave markets in the eighteenth century, the last of these "easily the greatest concentration of Portuguese commercial investment in western-central Africa."[90] In Kingston, Port Royal Street had extensive slave yards,[91] while Kilwa was described by the French as "*the* trade centre for slaves on the (east) coast of Africa."[92] In New Orleans, the "citadel of southern merchant capitalism," as Marler calls it, the city's slave markets were the largest in the US, contributing millions every year.[93] More crucially, slavery propelled Crescent City's rapid emergence in the early nineteenth century as Britain's largest supplier of cotton. Half of all the South's cotton production "routinely passed through the hands of News Orleans merchants on its way to textile manufacturers in the North and Europe,"[94] making it the fourth largest port in the world in terms of value of exports by the 1840s.[95]

Wholesale markets were as important as ever in the nineteenth century, which saw a new proliferation of commercial capitals as *industrial* accumulation massively increased the demand for industrial crops like cotton, silk, palm oil, teak, jute, and rubber, and for mass consumption goods like tea, coffee, sugar, cocoa, rice, wheat, and so on. The volume of international trade grew fivefold in the central decades between 1840 and 1870.[96] Liverpool imported around three-quarters of Britain's palm oil throughout the first half of the century,[97] and 70 percent of total British port stock of raw cotton was in Liverpool.[98] Odessa was rapidly colonized by Greek merchant firms to become the greatest commercial port on the Black Sea, pure replica of a modern European metropolis[99] with a strong representation of Jewish merchants,[100] all thanks to a sustained boom in the export of Russian grain. By 1846 the Odessa branch of Ralli Brothers "traded yearly in commodities worth more than 1.5 million roubles."[101] Le Havre was the epitome of commercial capitals linked to the colonial trades. In the early 1880s it controlled 72 percent of the stocks of coffee in France and was France's leading rubber importer and importer of US cotton by the end of the century.[102] By 1937 Le Havre imports accounted for nine-tenths of the country's total consumption of cocoa, four-fifths of its coffee, two-thirds of its raw cotton, two-thirds of exotic timbers, and half of the copper consumed in France.[103] On the other side of the Atlantic, the Buenos Aires and Rosario markets handled Argentina's humongous production of wheat at the end of the century. Sizeable grain transactions were concluded on the floor of the Bolsa de Comercio, which was largely controlled by the export firms.[104] As the boom intensified, a handful of large companies, "in reality branches of powerful European commercial interests," established a virtual monopoly of the export trade.[105] Like the biggest merchant capitals everywhere, the export firms were resentful of their dependence on the middlemen (the *acopiadores*) and sought to establish their own offices and agents in the Buenos Aires wheat zone, which only deepened tensions between the local grain merchants and the "Big Four."

Wholesale markets had always been characterized by a degree of specialization but in the nineteenth century this became more obvious than ever. Beirut was *defined* by its exports of raw silk, Alexandria of cotton, Karachi of wheat, Rangoon of rice, Foochow of tea. "The tea business in Foochow was generally on a *grand scale*."[106] Jardines made "vast purchases on the Foochow market" in the late 1850s and early 1860s.[107] "On the whole, Western merchants obtained more tea by purchasing on the Foochow market than by contracting with teamen," that is, with the big tea contractors.[108] Rangoon was described as "the world's premier rice port" toward the end of the century.[109] By 1900 Karachi was the biggest wheat exporter in the east, the "natural port" for the immense grain production of the canal-irrigated tracts in the Punjab.[110] Alexandria's fortunes were built on cotton, a trade dominated by a largely Greek business oligarchy,[111] and Beirut's silk exports were controlled by a partnership between French firms and the mainly Christian Lebanese commercial bourgeoisie.[112]

BILLS OF EXCHANGE

"In addition to bank notes, wholesale trade has a second and far more important means of circulation: bills of exchange," Marx writes in volume three of *Capital*.[113] Since banknotes only began to be issued from the second half of the eighteenth century, he was right to describe bills of exchange as the major means of circulation in wholesale trade. For example, from figures that he himself cites, the total sum of banknotes in circulation in Britain actually declined between 1844 and 1857, even though Britain's external trade "more than doubled."[114] In a stricter definition, of course, Marx always treated bills of exchange under means of payment, that is, as a form of credit, and specifically of (short-term) "commercial credit" as opposed to "bank credit."[115] Bills of exchange were the "very basis of the money market." This was as true of Venice in the fourteenth century as it was of London in Marx's day.[116]

Bills of exchange were widely used in Venetian trade in the Levant.[117] There are numerous references to them in the ledger or account book of Giacomo Badoer, a Venetian banker who lived in Constantinople from September 1436 to early 1440.[118] As in Venice, "bills in Constantinople were handled on current account in the local deposit banks."[119] In Europe the bill market was dominated by the Italians. Even in Bruges the exchange "was merely the daily Bourse assembly of the Italian merchants."[120] "Subjects of other nations usually had to apply to them, if they wished to buy or sell bills." In Venice, huge sums of money were kept in constant circulation on the exchanges, for example, "the Venetian branch of the Fugger firm is reported to have had a turnover of about 100,000 ducats in its exchange dealings *with Antwerp alone*."[121] By the late sixteenth century, the Piacenza fairs acted as a clearing house for the vast amounts of money circulating in bills of exchange.[122] If "[p]ure economizing on means of circulation appears *in its most highly developed form* in the clearing house, the simple exchange of bills falling due,"[123] then those fairs, dominated by a club of some sixty bankers, show us how advanced the financial markets still were under Italian (in this case, Genoese) dominance.

However, by the sixteenth century bills of exchange were widely used in the Ottoman empire as well (where they were called *suftajas*)[124] and by *ca*.1700 the enormous stocks of silver in circulation in the Mughal economy formed the basis for a massive system of credit transfers through both treasury bills and the commercial bills known as *hundis*.[125] And in Europe itself in the seventeenth century, the discounting and sale of bills of exchange became a lively business in Amsterdam. "In the trade of no other city in this period was the bill of exchange used so freely and flexibly." Amsterdam was described as the "theatre where all the world's exchanges are transacted."[126]

The eighteenth century was when bills of exchange came into circulation in a big way. Charles Carrière describes the bill of exchange as "the perfect instrument of commercial capitalism in the eighteenth century."[127] In other words, the bulk of money in circulation in the sphere of large-scale commerce took the form of bills of exchange. For example, in 1783, while Marseilles's maritime trade reached or even exceeded 200 million livres, the actual cash in the hands of merchants was estimated to be a mere 1.8 million livres at most.[128] This was a time when the more substantial merchants (*négociants*) numbered some six to seven hundred in France's leading port city.[129] By the end of the eighteenth century, bills of exchange were widely used in most trade sectors of the international market. In the British Atlantic, where the commission system began to be used from as early as the late seventeenth century, bills of exchange were "the key link between the planter and his commission agent."[130] Barbados planters bought slaves with bills and "sold their sugar not in the islands but by consignment to London."[131] In the so-called "cargo trade," local merchants in both South Carolina and the West Indies imported dry goods on credit from the London commission houses and made their returns, either wholly or very largely, in bills of exchange.[132] In India, sales of *hundis* had become so widespread in Gujarat by the eighteenth century that commercial payments were seldom made in cash.[133] A small group of Surat bankers known as "the Bengal shroffs" came to specialize in discounting and buying East India Company bills.[134] The Surat money market was a vital part of the financial operations of the Company. More importantly, the Court of Directors allowed the treasuries at its settlements to receive money "in return for bills of exchange payable in London at various dates at rates fixed by the Company."[135] The Company's bills thus became a major channel for repatriating fortunes from India, either directly from Calcutta or via Canton where capital was needed to finance purchases of tea. By the 1770s the Canton treasury was receiving very large sums from Calcutta, carried there by the "country" ships carrying opium and cotton.[136] Finally, in Britain itself the volume of inland bills grew from £2 million *ca*.1700 to £30 million *ca*.1775.[137]

Sterling-denominated bills drawn on London became the pivot around which international trade revolved by the main part of the nineteenth century. Liquidity was the key here, fueling massive commercial expansion. The City became "a short-term money market of unrivalled liquidity and security,"[138] a wholesale market in the financing of trade. Trade finance or the discounting of bills of exchange was the glue that held the system together, the London merchant banks *guaranteeing bills* by "accepting" them ("writing or stamping the word *accepted* across its face for a fee of 1 or 2 percent of its value"), the bill brokers *buying bills* at a discount to face value ("discounting" them), and the Bank of England acting as lender of last resort, prepared in extreme circumstances to *"rediscount"* the better-quality bills, thus enabling the discount houses to finance their massive bill portfolios with money borrowed from the banks as "call loans" secured on first-class bills.[139] Joint-stock bankers preferred commercial bills over government securities,[140] and, as the London banks built up their own liquid cash reserves, vast sums were held on call with the bill brokers.[141] By the 1850s it could be said, "The Bill brokers have been in the habit of holding probably from 15 to 20 Millions of Money at call" from one day to the next.[142]

The truly important innovation in the first fifteen years of the nineteenth century was the emergence of the manufacturer who exported *directly* to distant markets. In "consigning exports *on their own account*, with the assistance of Liverpool and foreign-based commission agents" who in turn relied on the London acceptance houses,[143] these British cotton manufacturers were the first signs, historically, of what Marx would later call the "subordination" of commercial to industrial capital. Marx himself telescoped this process massively, projecting it back to a much earlier period, whereas in fact even in the nineteenth century commercial capital remained largely dominant down to the later decades of the century when an entirely new breed of industrial capital, the capital-intensive vertically integrated firms, would finally emerge to eliminate the old-style merchants by organizing their own sales networks.

3

THE COMPETITION OF CAPITALS

Struggles for Commercial Dominance from the Twelfth to Eighteenth Centuries

BYZANTIUM: THE SUBORDINATION OF GREEK CAPITAL

In Constantinople the early modern world inherited an "urban monster,"[1] but one whose trajectory had involved *sharp fluctuations over the centuries*, with a history going back, of course, to late antiquity (unlike megacities like Cairo and Baghdad). On the eve of its conquest by the Ottomans in 1453, the city's population had stabilized around seventy thousand,[2] but at its early-Byzantine peak in the sixth century it had been probably well over half a million, and at the end of the twelfth century was again somewhere in the region of half a million, say, four hundred thousand.[3] Between those peaks came a downturn reaching a low point, forty thousand to seventy thousand, in the eighth century (following a plague in 747–8),[4] and then a sustained renewal or expansion from the ninth century down to the end of the twelfth. As the political base of an empire, however, the massive expansion of the internal market that occurred from the ninth to twelfth centuries was true not just of the metropolis but to some degree of the whole empire including its various secondary urban centers as well as the islands.[5] What was in play here was a huge *common market*, the biggest in the world in the twelfth century (if we except China, of course), and it was bound to exert considerable force as a commercial magnet.

Constantinople is sandwiched between the Golden Horn to its north and the Sea of Marmara to the south. In the sixth century, as one scholar has argued convincingly, the plague of 542 triggered a major relocation of business and residence to the southern (Marmara) coast, because bodies were being dumped in the sea and any dumped in the Golden Horn would not have been washed away.[6] The Golden Horn had been abandoned well before the late seventh century[7] and it was the south coast that was more actively used in the seventh to tenth centuries.[8] The sustained expansion of the ninth to twelfth centuries, however, saw a succession of Italian city-states starting to trade with the empire in a big way, and it was essentially their presence in Constantinople that revitalized the Golden Horn into the major commercial hub that it became from the eleventh century down to early Ottoman times[9] and then again, with the renewed colonization of Pera (Galata, on the European side of Istanbul), in the main part of the nineteenth century. All the major Italian colonies (Amalfi, Pisa, Genoa, Venice) were clustered in the lower Golden Horn, with jetties or landing-stations (*skalai*) where seagoing vessels could load and unload. The city center and the seashores were "heavily built up with three- or even five-story houses."[10] In the twelfth century Constantinople was a densely populated cosmopolitan city, sharply divided in social terms, and prone to violent, uncontrollable fires.[11] John Tzetzes boasted he could speak to local residents in no fewer than seven languages, including Persian, Arabic, Russian, and Hebrew.[12] Eustathios of Thessaloniki counted sixty thousand "Latins" in the city,[13] and a keen observer, the Jewish traveler Benjamin of Tudela tells us, "They say that the tribute of the city alone amounts every day to twenty thousand florins, arising from rents of hostelries and bazaars, and from the duties paid by merchants who arrive by sea and by land."[14] It was the greatest commercial center of the eastern Mediterranean,[15] with a population by then not far short of half a million.[16] Finally, even as late as 1192 the native, Greek, merchants of Constantinople were a "large, influential, rich" group.[17] Oikonomidès cites the example of Kalomodios, a banker who accumulated a vast fortune through successful operations in large-scale trade, financing commercial trips undertaken by others.[18]

Yet the most extraordinary fact about Byzantine commerce from the end of the eleventh century to the thirteenth century and later was the severe discrimination Greek merchants were subjected to vis-à-vis foreign competitors *by their own state*. By the terms of the treaty of 1082, "Venetian merchants could buy and sell in every part of the Empire, free of duty or customs examination." Many ports were opened and "vast territories made accessible to them for free trade."[19] "These privileges, renewed by the emperors of the twelfth century... rendered the Venetians virtual masters of the commercial life of the empire."[20] By the thirteenth century, when the Genoese came into Byzantine economic life in a big way and similar wide-ranging concessions were granted, "Italian merchants, whether Genoese or Venetians, became so entrenched in Constantinople that they controlled the economy of that city."[21] And by the end of the thirteenth century, the islands of the Aegean (the Archipelago) were being divided between Genoese and Venetian control,[22] the Aegean's east coast becoming the heart of Genoa's maritime domain. Greek merchants, meanwhile, continued to pay a duty of 10 percent and Byzantine access to markets in the west remained severely limited. Greek merchants rarely gained access to Italian markets.[23] The Italians discouraged Byzantine expansion west of the Peloponnese,[24] so that Greek capital was effectively shut out of the long-distance trade.[25]

A major upshot of entrenched Italian economic dominance was the endemic hostility that grew up between the Italians and large sectors of the local population.[26] The violent crusader occupation of Constantinople in 1204 and the long-standing division between the churches did nothing to abate that, of course. Every attempt to bring the two churches together was seen as a "national betrayal" and sparked riots.[27] Greeks living in territories under Latin control were looked down upon as a "conquered people" and suffered the economic and social consequences of that even to the point of being denied the right to have their own bishops.[28] "They treated citizens like slaves," wrote one twelfth-century chronicler. "Their boldness and impudence increased with their wealth until they not only detested the Romans [Greek-speaking Byzantines] but even defied the threats and commands of the Emperor."[29] On the other hand, as the left-wing historian Nicolas Oikonomidès emphasized, none of this prevented Greek business circles from entering into partnerships with Italian capital. There was extensive collaboration, and Greek merchants even sought Genoese or Venetian nationality to enjoy the same benefits.

The emergence of a Byzantine commercial "middle class" was a remarkable feature of the eleventh-century boom in the economic and cultural life of the empire, and its most striking political outcome was the three decades in the middle of the century when a strictly aristocratic model of government split wide open to allow the popular classes and commercially active strata (literally, "those of the market place") access, for the first time ever, to the senate and higher administration.[30] No less interestingly, the same rulers who brought about this revolutionary change responded to the *economic* needs of the middle class (*mesoi*) by allowing for a controlled devaluation of the gold coinage—a measure *not* of crisis but of the economic boom reflected by a growing demand for means of circulation and payment as Byzantium's markets were becoming more deeply integrated into the expansion occurring in the west.[31] What emerged briefly in the eleventh century was a fascinating alliance of the absolutist power with a middle class hostile to the aristocracy. It was this "capitalist" dream of the eleventh century that was shattered in 1081/2 in the violent reaction of a strongly pro-aristocratic dynasty (the Komnenoi) that set about curbing the growing affluence and power of the Greek mercantile class by abolishing "all the privileges the businessmen had just acquired"[32] and (just as important!) granting extensive concessions to Venetian capital, effectively allowing a wholesale takeover of Byzantine markets by Italian merchant capitalists, with the major exception of the Black Sea which in any case failed to attract much attention till the later thirteenth century. The French Byzantinist Lemerle described Alexios I Komnenos's *chrysobull* of 1082 as a "massive economic capitulation," the point being that though a Byzantine merchant class survived and continued to be active down to the end of the twelfth century, it had lost control of the empire's markets.[33] Going by later experience, it is possible that the vast majority of local merchants worked as brokers for the Italian firms.[34]

The last two and a half centuries of the Byzantine empire (1204–1453) were characterized by the catastrophe of the Venetian occupation of Constantinople, which permanently dismembered the empire and left the city itself depleted and impoverished;[35] by ferocious struggles between Venice and Genoa for control of the leading trade sectors, once Byzantine rule was restored (in 1261) and Genoa established a major presence through its alliance with Michael VIII Palaiologos (those struggles erupted in the last quarter of the thirteenth century and began with the Black Sea); by the civil wars of the 1340s which saw the aristocracy contending with rebellions based on a loose coalition of urban classes that included sailors and longshoremen; by the aristocracy's decisive turn to commercial investment as landed assets were progressively lost to the Ottoman advance from the middle of the fourteenth century; and finally, by the overwhelming grip that Genoa even more than Venice had now established over much of the truncated empire's trade. Indeed, the Genoese had close relations with the Turks throughout the fourteenth century, and a very substantial part of their business was done in the Ottoman territories.[36]

The idea that ancient and medieval writers were oblivious to the play of economic forces in the history of their respective societies and civilizations does not stand up to scrutiny. To Byzantine writers like George Pachymeres and Nikephoros Gregoras it was fairly obvious that Genoa's exploitation of Byzantine markets was the basis of her prosperity.[37] Pachymeres himself has some remarkable passages on the kind of dominance the Genoese had established over the empire and about the fierce struggles between them and the Venetians for the domination of Greek markets. In one of these he writes, "the Venetians and their community (in Constantinople) formerly greatly surpassed the Genoese in wealth... because they made greater use of the [narrow] waters (the Aegean) than did the Genoese and because they sailed across the high sea (the Mediterranean more widely) with long ships (galleys), and they succeeded in gaining more profit than did the Genoese in transporting and carrying wares. But once the Genoese became masters of the Black Sea by grant of the emperor (Michael III) and with all liberty and franchise, they braved that [sea], and sailing in the midst of winter in ships of reduced length... they not only barred the Romans (Byzantines) from the lanes and wares of the sea *but also eclipsed the Venetians in wealth and material [goods]*. Because of this they came to look down not only upon those of their own kin (other Italians) but also upon the Romans themselves."[38] Here Pachymeres describes two broad periods in the commercial history of the empire, in the first of which, according to him, the Venetians established their primacy through a strategy of cabotage or coastal trading in the purely Greek parts of the empire (a Byzantine version of what in India the British would later call the "country trade"). The Genoese later surpassed them by making the Black Sea the renewed focus of their commercial operations. This strikes me as a remarkably coherent summary of over two centuries of Byzantine commercial history.

In both cities, Venice as well as Genoa, the aristocracy itself was very substantially involved in the trade with "Romania."[39] The investments at stake were those of the leading families in both centers. But commercial capital was still widely dispersed among the *alberghi*. On the Genoese side, the six leading families accounted for 29 percent of all investment, a degree of concentration scarcely comparable with the much higher levels characteristic of later centuries.[40] In *ca.*1170 the Venetians had vastly more capital tied up in Byzantium than any of their competitors. They had a stronger hold on the islands, and this was extensive by the second quarter of the twelfth century.[41]

When the Genoese first sought to establish themselves in Constantinople, their newly established quarters were repeatedly attacked and even demolished—in 1162 by a mob consisting mainly of Pisans, then again in 1170 by the Venetians themselves, and a third time, in April 1182, in a dreadful local pogrom against all Italians (except that the Venetian quarter lay vacant at this time).[42] On all these various occasions, claims for compensation were submitted by the main aggrieved parties, and from these one gets at least a crude impression of the scale of their respective investments. Genoese estimates of the losses they sustained in 1162 and 1182 respectively suggest that in the previous decade or so there had been very rapid enrichment of Genoese merchants trading to Byzantine markets.[43] It seems entirely likely that the disruption of Venetian business following the reprisals against them in 1171 worked strongly in Genoa's favor.

That the Latin conquest of Constantinople was largely a function of the endemic rivalry between the two main commercial powers is shown by the fact that Genoa was *not officially represented in Constantinople* during the occupation.[44] Venice's territory in the city expanded substantially soon after the conquest.[45] The restoration of Byzantine rule in 1261 turned the tables dramatically as Genoa became the dominant economic power in Constantinople and secured access to the Black Sea, where a colony was established at Caffa that was thriving by the 1280s.[46] The whole period from 1270 to 1340 saw substantial Genoese investment. In 1348, according to the chronicler Gregoras, revenues from the customs collected at Genoa's colony at Pera were almost *seven times bigger* than the collections at Constantinople.[47] These fell sharply in the later fourteenth century, which saw a prolonged recession that only lifted in the early part of the fifteenth century. Competition was sharper than ever in these decades, since there were no fewer than three "colonial wars" between Venice and Genoa for control of the Aegean, the upshot of which was a division, a "de facto carve-up," of the sea between them.[48]

Thus the "colonization" of the Byzantine empire probably counts as the most striking example of a "colonial-style" economy before colonialism. The parallel has been drawn repeatedly, and Oikono-midès himself would speak of the "economic imperialism of western merchants."[49] An attempt in the middle of the fourteenth century to reestablish greater parity in the duties paid by Greek and Italian merchants led to a violent reaction which forced the emperor John VI Kantakouzenos to reverse his decision.[50] (The Genoese reacted by burning Byzantine merchant ships and warehouses!) The treaty of 1352 included a clause "severely limiting the access of Byzantine merchants to Tana and the Sea of Azov."[51] The *mesoi* who were active in the rebellions of the 1340s included a layer of Greek capital that both resented its subordination to more powerful competitors *and* depended on them for its own survival. In Thessaloniki, the most radical faction, those known as the Zealots, even controlled the city's government for some seven or eight years and were led, in part at least, by the city's harbor workers.[52] Angeliki Laiou argued that the civil war was "an abortive effort to create a state quite different from what had existed in Byzantium, *one where the interests of the commercial element would be paramount.*"[53] In any case, by the latter half of the century a more substantial kind of involvement emerged as members of the Greek aristocracy compensated for falling incomes from their estates by turning to large-scale trade and banking. As Oikonomidès showed, the highest levels of the aristocracy were involved in this,[54] with the number of aristocrats involved in trade growing dramatically. "The urban upper class of Byzantium was at last united in purely capitalist aspirations," he wrote,[55] and the previous distinction between the *mesoi* and the aristocracy eventually disappeared.

A final word. None of the leading Italian trade centers that traded with Byzantium simply replicated the pattern of their competitors. In the eleventh century, Amalfi (where, again, the aristocracy were key drivers of external investment, unlike the other southern nobilities)[56] had specialized in luxury imports from Constantinople for markets in Rome and Naples, integrating its trade with the southern Mediterranean by using the gold from the Sahara acquired in the Maghreb ports and in Egypt (in exchange for grain, timber, linen cloth, and so on) to finance purchases from the Byzantines. In Constantinople the Amalfitans were buyers, not sellers.[57] In the eleventh and twelfth centuries, the Venetians had traded in the local produce of the Greek mainland and Greek islands and of southern Italy, in items such as olive oil, cheese, wine, wheat, raw silk, and raw cotton. About sixty percent of Venice's trade with the empire is said to have been transacted in Greece.[58] Southern Calabria was a major producer of raw silk[59] and this must also have reached manufacturing centers such as Thebes in Venetian ships. Olive oil came from the Peloponnese.[60] A Venetian by the name of Vitale Voltani, who settled in Greece in the 1160s, was said to have "dominated the oil market in Corinth, Sparta and Thebes."[61] For their part, the Genoese combined the bulk trades of the Black Sea region, Phokaia, and Chios (grain, alum, leather, cotton, etc.) with the importation of expensive fabrics, "many different types of European cloth,"[62] the export of Anatolian carpets,[63] Russian furs,[64] and so on.

VENICE TO PORTUGAL

Unlike the rulers of Byzantium, it was Mamluk policy not to intervene in the conflicts between Venice and Genoa. In 1294 the commercial battle between them had spilled over into the far end of the eastern Mediterranean. The Syrian chronicler al-Jazari notes that in 1294 "witnesses reported that large numbers of Franks came by sea to Ayas for purposes of trade and that they belonged to two nations (*taifa*). One lot were called Venetians, the other Genoese." As acts of hostility escalated between them, they got into a bitter fight and "on one day alone over 6000 people were killed." "The Genoese got the better of the Venetians."[65] Al-Jazari was describing a crucial part of the prelude to the major war that developed two years later, which began and ended with the Venetians setting fire to Pera and the Genoese retaliating by massacring large numbers of them in their quarter of the city.

In the twelfth and thirteen centuries, the expansion of Italian business interests in the Levant ran *parallel* to a rapid growth of Muslim trade and settlement on the Malabar coast.[66] The Levant cotton trade was dominated by the Italians, so that by the late fifteenth and sixteenth centuries "in peak years the total volume of Venetian cotton imports from all sources could exceed 4,000 tons."[67] They had substantial interests in the Levantine sugar industry, for example, in the villages around Tyre where the most important sugar plantations of the Syro-Palestinian coast passed into Venetian hands in 1123 (between the first and second Crusades).[68] With the fall of Acre in 1291, Venetian sugar interests were relocated to the islands. In Cyprus in the later fourteenth and fifteenth centuries, the Corners, a powerful Venetian family, built a thriving enterprise in sugar.[69] In 1183 the Spanish traveler Ibn Jubayr saw innumerable loads of pepper being shipped to the Sudanese port of Aydhab and transported from there in numerous caravans.[70] Barely seven years later, the value of goods exported by Christian merchants trading through the Nile ports was estimated to be "well over 100,000 dinars," and this at a time of considerable political tensions (Saladin had captured Jerusalem in 1187).[71] The number of merchants from the west trading in Alexandria in 1216 was (as I noted earlier) put at three thousand by the historian al-Maqrizi.[72] In *ca.*1260 Venetian sources indicate "large cotton shipments from Acre."[73] Candia in Venetian-controlled Crete became a major spice market in the early fourteenth century. The sugar and cotton exported there from Alexandria were reexported to Italy in Venetian galleys.[74] By the middle of the century the papers of the Venetian notary Bresciano reflect *massive* imports of Italian and Flemish textiles into Candia, something that was doubtless true of other Venetian colonies.[75] By the end of the century the volume of Italian business had increased dramatically. Investments could run as high as 450,000 dinars with the Venetians in the 1390s, and between 200,000 and 300,000 dinars every year between 1394 and 1400 in Genoa's case. (The Catalans came third with an annual average *ca.*200,000.)[76] And by the fifteenth century when, as Braudel says,

"Venice was unquestionably the vigorous heart of the Mediterranean,"[77] thanks largely to its trade with the Levant, merchant galleys with goods worth one million ducats plus 400,000 in cash were sailing from Venice for Alexandria and Beirut.[78]

The Levant trade was the middle segment of a circuit that extended to the ports of Malabar in South India and beyond them into Southeast Asia. Here the great counterpart to the crusading period's "creation of numerous Latin trading colonies in the Near East with their own consuls, hostels, warehouses, marketplaces, and churches"[79] was the expansion of Islam, which, similarly, begins in the twelfth century and reaches its commercial zenith in the fifteenth. The oldest reliably datable mosque on the Malabar coast was founded in 1124, at Madayi.[80] By the end of the thirteenth century Muslim settlements were well established both there and on the Coromandel coast,[81] reflecting an expansion across the entire western half of the Indian Ocean. Even in the early thirteenth century, it has been claimed, the East African coast was largely Islamic,[82] and certainly by the end of the century the evidence from Kilwa implies a "very large Muslim resident population."[83] By ca.1331 Ibn Battuta describes a "vast network of Muslims all around the periphery of the Indian Ocean."[84] These were essentially commercial networks drawn from many different parts of the Near East. Calicut's Muslims who tendered their allegiance to the Rasulid sultan al-Ashraf II in 1393 reflected a multiplicity of geographic origins,[85] and the same is suggested in Barbosa's report that by the second decade of the sixteenth century these cosmopolitan merchants "departed to their own lands abandoning India and its trade,"[86] following the dramatic and violent way in which the Portuguese made their entry into the Indian Ocean trade with Vasco da Gama insisting on the expulsion of the Muslims from Calicut and bombarding the town when its ruler refused.[87]

That the crushing of the Venetian spice monopoly was the premeditated goal of Portugal's maritime expansion in the fifteenth century can, of course, be ruled out. The strategy of Atlantic expansion evolved only gradually.[88] There was, as Luís Filipe Thomaz has argued, no *coherent* imperial project till the last two decades of the fifteenth century and what he calls the "calculated imperialism" of a model that was "imperial, globalizing, and state-driven."[89] From the reign of Dom Ferdinand (1367–83), Portuguese royal power had found its strongest support in the population of the ports,[90] where the Portuguese merchant class grew in strength.[91] But in the partnership that evolved over the following century between the monarchy and private capital, the state can scarcely be described as a passive agent of the latter. Financially, it depended on the resources of big Lisbon merchants like Fernão Gomes *ca.*1469 and, later, of powerful syndicates of German and Italian businessmen, but it was the crown that both drove and monitored the process, and (just as important) there was never any "clear-cut demarcation between the finances of the State and its commercial capital."[92] All commercial capitalisms of the sixteenth to eighteenth centuries would come to be *inextricably bound up with the state*, but in Portugal's case the relationship was posited as immediate. It was the crown that would act as a merchant company on the west coast of India, "setting up *feitorias* (trading posts, factories) in various key ports, buying up pepper, spices and other precious commodities, which they would ship to Europe and sell there at a huge profit."[93]

The Portuguese, of course, were quite clear who their competitors were. Trying to convince the members of his council of the need to capture and retain Malacca, Albuquerque wrote, "Since we gained control of the Malabar pepper trade, Cairo has not received any except what the Moslems have been able to take from this region (the Straits)... I am very sure that, if this Malacca trade is taken out of their hands, Cairo and Mecca will be completely lost and *no spices will go to the Venetians except those that they go to Portugal to buy*."[94] The target here, in 1511, was the entire Red Sea route, a circuit dominated by a sort of massive joint venture between Venetian capital, Cairo merchants, and the suppliers in Calicut. But moving back along the chain, the majority of his captains agreed with Albuquerque, it was essential to "take the city of Malacca, *to expel the Moslems*, and to build a fortress there."[95] Portugal's "commercial and religious war against Islam"[96] occupied the greater part of a century and was never completely successful, but in Calicut the effects of her intrusion were felt almost immediately. Already by 1507 one traveler, the Italian Ludovico di Varthema, was writing, "Calicut was ruined by the King of Portugal, for the merchants who used to come there were not there, neither did they come."[97] It was Cochin that became Portugal's economic base in the region and the bulk of Portuguese pepper from Malabar was exported from there.[98] By 1512 Albuquerque was telling King Manuel that the *net* value of shipments from India was now "worth a million *cruzados*."[99] If so, these levels were never subsequently sustained. The majority of actual cultivators were St. Thomas Christians.[100] Pepper was sold to the Portuguese factory in Cochin by merchants from their community and by Cochin Jews.[101] Apparently, the king had asked officials to deal with Christian and Hindu traders (Nairs were used as brokers) "and to *keep the Muslim merchants away from trade activities*."[102] Dom Manuel's "royal capitalism"[103] was a curious mixture of mercantilism and messianism[104] where hardheaded business decisions and a Mediterranean-style economic war were cloaked in religious zeal and a great deal of both ignorance and bigotry.

The *habitual* use of force as an acceptable part of the competition between substantial *blocs* of capital was now, for the first time in the history of either sea, transposed from a theatre where it had flourished for centuries (since Venice's devastating attack on Comacchio in 932, say) to the Indian Ocean, where its major targets were the powerful Muslim commercial networks that straddled the entire ocean from Kilwa and Sofala in East Africa to Sumatra and the southern Philippines. In Cochin itself the principal merchants of the port (Muslim converts of the Marakkar family) relocated to Calicut by the 1520s, forced out by what one historian calls an "atmosphere of coercion and violence."[105] Ahmad Zayn al-Din's late sixteenth-century history, *Tuhfat al-mujahidin*, has graphic descriptions of the violence inflicted on Malabar's Muslim communities. He writes of the burning of the *jami' masjid* in Calicut in 1510, the earlier demolition of the Cochin mosque, the seizure of ships, destruction of property, and so on. There was also the repeated personal humiliation Muslims were subjected to, and of course bloodshed. Zayn al-Din had an acute sense of the history of his own lifetime, knowing that the advent of the Portuguese had been ruinous for the prosperity of Muslim commerce in the Indian Ocean. The Portuguese, he writes, had sought to "secure for themselves a *monopoly of this trade*" (the spice trade).[106] They had established themselves "in the greater part of the sea ports of this part of the world."[107] They had even "found their way to the Chinese empire, carrying on trade in all the intermediate and other ports, in all of which the commercial interests of the Muslims have been in consequence consigned to ruin." The Portuguese "rendered it *impossible that any others should compete with them*" in the trades they sought to dominate.[108] The Muslims of Malabar had seen the bulk of their international commerce massively disrupted and were left only with the coasting trade of India. They had become "impoverished and weak and powerless."[109]

There is a fascinating reference in these passages to a self-financing model that became characteristic not only of Portugal's trade in Asian waters but, even more crucially, of the better-organized Dutch expansion that would later replace it in the seventeenth century. The Portuguese monarchy was chronically short of cash and sought to sustain the European side of its monopoly of the spice market by involving the biggest German and Italian capitalists as investors and encouraging governors like Albuquerque to finance the royal share of purchases from profits generated by Portuguese trading *within* Asian markets.[110] At the Malabar end, there was never any real monopoly, since exports to Lisbon never seem to have exceeded about 40 percent of the total output of pepper even in the early sixteenth century and fell dramatically by the end of the century, when Francisco da Costa reliably estimated that of a total production of 258,000 quintals, exports to Portugal were a meagre twenty thousand to thirty thousand quintals.[111] In 1587 Ferdinand Cron, Cochin agent of the Fuggers, wrote that although *ca.*

three hundred thousand quintals of pepper were produced annually in southern India, only a very little of this came into the hands of the contractors to be taken to Europe.[112] Thomaz has argued that "Portuguese commerce in the sixteenth century developed predominantly in the Indian Ocean, *over a network of short and medium range routes* which actually encompassed almost every coast of Asia... The main reason which drove the Portuguese to apply themselves to the local trade seems to be that the Cape route to Portugal was often a loser."[113] In short, Portugal's Asian trade cross-subsidized the trade to Lisbon, since overheads were so high in the latter.

Pepper was grown on literally thousands of gardens in Malabar.[114] The Portuguese simply did not have the logistical set-up to deal with producers directly and certainly had no way of controlling the producers.[115] Therefore, price domination had to be enforced through agreements with the ruler of Cochin and other local rulers. A low fixed price was vital to the whole enterprise as king Dom Manuel had conceived this initially. In 1503 the price of a *bhar* of pepper (that is, of a batch of *ca*.166 kg) was fixed at less than half the market price prevailing in Calicut three years earlier.[116] Prices would remain fixed for decades. But Malabar pepper was a highly competitive market with over a dozen regional centers where merchants bought the produce wholesale. Competition was fierce in those markets.[117] This accounts for the purely theoretical nature of the Portuguese monopoly, since, as Cesare de Federici noted, probably in the 1570s, the bulk of good-quality pepper was being shipped to the Red Sea because merchants connected with that trade *paid more and got a better quality of produce*, "cleane and dry and better conditioned."[118] This is the essential reason behind the resilience of the Mediterranean route that Braudel constantly drew attention to.[119]

If the "royal capitalism" of the early sixteenth century was eventually abandoned for a "more straightforward semi-Absolutist conception of the state's relationship to trade,"[120] Portuguese colonial enterprise, or the Asian thalassocracy that formed its core, became even stronger as a magnet for an agglomeration of capitalist interests that is probably best described in Henry Bernstein's idea of "classes of capital." At the top were the biggest German and Italian capitalist houses (the Welsers, Fuggers, Höchstetters, Affaitadi, Bartolomeo Marchionni, Giovanni Rovelasca) who combined in powerful syndicates to finance the actual expeditions to India, such as the one in 1505 in which the Welsers had a very substantial investment of twenty thousand cruzados, or agreed to handle sales in Europe, with pledges to buy a stipulated quantity of pepper at an agreed price. Both arrangements were fraught with tensions bound up with the volatility of this market, with the crown quite capable of reneging on contracts. Florentine merchants were well-entrenched in Lisbon and many of them "financed and joined the Portuguese on the earliest ventures to the Indies during the first quarter of the sixteenth century."[121] The South German commercial houses had strong organizational structures and worked through cartel arrangements with one another.[122] They "amassed capital far beyond the capability of any Florentine merchant-banker,"[123] so that even at this rarefied level there were interesting differences. Considerably below these giant capitalists were the richer *casados* of Cochin, settlers of Portuguese origin, who at various times acted as financiers to the *Estado* and dominated Cochin's coastal trade.[124] Between 1570 and 1600 the *casados*, "a powerful mercantile group with considerable capital resources," "virtually turned Cochin into one of the biggest entrepôts of Asia."[125] Their interests extended all over the Indian Ocean.[126] However, from the second decade of the seventeenth century, there was a mass exodus of *casado* traders from Cochin to the opposite coast, as the latter part of the sixteenth century saw dwindling supplies of pepper thanks to mass disaffection among St. Thomas Christians who had seen their bishop arrested twice (and die in Rome in 1569) and "begun to cooperate with the traders of the ghat route" in retaliation.[127] Finally, Malabar's own native Muslims, the Mappilas, were among the "largest financiers of Portugal's imperial project in Asia"[128] and were doubtless active in much of the trade that escaped Portuguese control, the vast amounts of pepper that crossed the ghats to make its way to the east coast, from where it was widely exported.

In economic terms, the fragile basis on which Portugal's armed thalassocracy rested was obvious to members of its élite. In 1563 the Ottomans offered the Portuguese a free trade agreement, with the latter being given the right to "establish trading houses in Basra, Cairo, and Alexandria and to trade freely in all the Ottoman-controlled ports of both the Persian Gulf and the Red Sea," in return for similar freedoms for Ottoman merchants to trade throughout the Indian Ocean, with the right to establish commercial agencies of their own "in Sind, Cambay, Dabul, Calicut, and any other port they desired."[129] Against this quite remarkable proposal one *fidalgo* is supposed to have argued, "if the Turks were allowed to travel freely to India, and establish factors, and trade in merchandise wherever they wished, not only would Your Majesty's own profits suffer greatly, but the rest of us would be left completely empty handed, because *all of the business [handled by the Portuguese] would immediately fall to the Turks.*" There was a clear reference here to Portuguese *private* capital. He went on to say, "As for [the state monopoly in] pepper and other controlled spices, this would also be threatened by allowing the Turks to establish factors in India. *Even now, when they have not been allowed to openly compete against the Portuguese,* it is known that they conduct a trade in secret, carrying spices to Hormuz, to Basra, and to Bengal, Pegu, China, and other lands, and especially to their own markets, despite the great risks involved. Thus, [if allowed to operate freely, their ties with] local Muslims would *leave them even better informed and better organized,* such that by means of the [Red Sea and Persian Gulf] they could send as much [pepper] as they wanted, *and become masters of the lion's share of the trade in spices.*"[130] Here it was an entrenched network of trading communities that was seen as the biggest potential "competitive advantage" the Ottomans would have if commerce was completely free, that is, not deterred by the permanent threat and actual use of violence from the Portuguese side.[131]

In his great *History of Italy*, Francesco Guicciardini saw Portugal's breaking of the Venetian spice monopoly as "the most memorable thing that has happened in the world for many centuries."[132] This was written late in the 1530s and was a remarkably accurate assessment, not only because commercial positions that Venice had built up over *centuries* were (momentarily) plunged into depression and drastically affected by the new trade regime,[133] but more obviously because Portugal's opening of the Atlantic reconfigured the whole shape of commercial capitalism as the world had known it till then. It opened the way for a new capitalism which would soon be reflected in the commercial dominance of the Dutch in the seventeenth century as well as England's expansion in the same century. In 1519 the Venetians were perfectly aware of Portugal's devastating impact on the Levant pepper trade, and for the next ten years they were totally at the mercy of the Portuguese as global supplies of pepper were cornered by the latter.[134] But Braudel rightly insisted that Venice remained a formidable economic force throughout the sixteenth century. As late as 1585 there were still some four thousand Venetian families "scattered throughout the cities and lands of Islam" as far away as Hormuz.[135] Nor was the Red Sea route ever completely stifled. In 1560 the Portuguese ambassador at Rome received reports that enormous quantities of pepper and spice were arriving at Alexandria.[136] In 1593 the Fuggers were similarly told that Alexandria was supplying Venice with as much pepper as Lisbon received.[137] However, by the second decade of the seventeenth century Venice's primacy in the Mediterranean was finally over.[138] The Italian crisis of the seventeenth century has been characterized as a "gradual introversion of the northern Italian bourgeoisie," a "progressive closure to the world beyond Italy."[139] If so, Guicciardini's judgement was even more prophetic.

DUTCH PRIMACY

The fall of Antwerp in August 1585 triggered a vast exodus of refugees from the southern provinces of the Netherlands to the North, with major consequences for Amsterdam and Dutch commerce. Amsterdam's prosperity after 1600 was built by *émigrés* from Antwerp.[140] Over half the Dutch East India Company/Vereenigde Oostindische Compagnie or VOC's starting capital of 6.42 million guilders was subscribed in Amsterdam, but among Amsterdam investors the biggest individual investments were made by men like Isaac le Maire and Balthasar Coymans, all *émigrés* from Antwerp.[141] They were Walloon or Flemish exiles and provided close to 40 percent of the Company's total capital.[142] It was their "vast wealth and international connections"[143] that enabled Holland's rapid breakthrough into the rich trades of the Mediterranean and Asia.

The seventeenth century was dominated by the competition between English and Dutch capital. The trajectory of Dutch capitalism runs from its rapid expansion in the early seventeenth century to its decline in the second quarter of the eighteenth century, with a peak in the decades around 1647–72, described by Jonathan Israel as the zenith of the Republic's "world-trade primacy."[144] Dutch trade with Asia had far outstripped that of the Portuguese possibly as early as 1601.[145] The clash with England for mastery of the Mediterranean trade exploded in the late 1640s, prompting the first of several "Navigation Acts" by which English capital sought to curb Dutch dominance. In 1661 Colbert assumed the direction of commercial affairs in France, and by the late seventeenth century the French had emerged as a major commercial power,[146] with the last quarter of the century dominated by a confrontation between them and the Dutch.[147] The 1680s was also when the VOC was at the peak of its success as an Asian power.[148]

The crushing Italian supremacy of the twelfth to fifteenth centuries had encapsulated a capitalism of *networks*, the only kind indigenous to the Mediterranean countries and the wider world of

Islam. The new capitalism of the seventeenth century was driven, in contrast, by *joint-stock companies* that emerged from the maritime fringe of northwestern Europe and enjoyed the strong backing of the state (as, indeed, Venetian capital had). They were capitalist enterprises of a higher power than the imperfect "royal capitalisms" of Iberia, but like them they retained a public or *semi-public* character that embodied a quasi-formal delegation of sovereignty that made them formidable competitors.[149] The main East India Companies (English, Dutch, and French) were the most powerful of the joint-stock companies in the seventeenth and eighteenth centuries, and the competition between them was such that David Hume, in an essay published in 1742, could famously say, "Trade was never esteemed an affair of state till the last century."[150] The head-on clash between the English and the Dutch generated the doctrine that came to be called "jealousy of trade."[151] Toward the end of the eighteenth century Adam Smith agreed with Hume that trade had changed European politics in the seventeenth century. In *Wealth of Nations* he refers to "mercantile jealousy" which "inflames, and is itself inflamed by the *violence of national animosity*."[152] State and capital now had a unifying "national" interest in securing or retaining commercial dominance. In "Of the Jealousy of Trade" (1752) Hume wrote "Nothing is more usual, among states which have made some advances in commerce, than... *to consider all trading states as their rivals*."[153] In the late nineteenth century Gustav von Schmoller expressed this more forcefully. "Commercial competition, even in times nominally of peace, degenerated into a state of undeclared hostility: it plunged nations into one war after another, and gave all wars a turn in the direction of trade, industry, and colonial gain...."[154]

To Josiah Child who became governor of the English East India Company in 1681, the essential characteristic of the Dutch model was its peculiar integration of state and capital. At the top of Child's list of reasons for Dutch economic success "was the fact that Dutch Councils of State, the law-making bodies, were composed of trading merchants who had lived abroad most of their lives and who had great practical and theoretical knowledge of commercial matters."[155] In *Observations upon the United Provinces of the Netherlands* (1673), Sir William Temple would likewise note this particular feature of the Dutch Republic; among its strengths, he claims, was "[a] Government manag'd either by men that trade, or whose Families have risen by it, or who have themselves some Interest going in other men's Traffique, or who are born and bred in Towns, The soul and beeing whereof consists wholly in trade."[156] In other words, the VOC and its predecessor companies "typified the *high degree of interaction of ruling oligarchy with private enterprise* which characterized much, if not most, of Dutch overseas commerce."[157] The VOC was "the creation of the Dutch state as much as of the merchants who had actually opened up the East India traffic,"[158] and, like its later, Atlantic, counterpart, the West India Company, "intimately entwined" with the country's "regent oligarchy."[159] In short, the nexus between state and commercial capital was altogether more direct here than anything reflected in the "strong social and commercial ties between the merchants and financiers of the City of London and the British state and aristocracy"[160] that were coeval with it.

The sheer *efficiency* of Dutch capital stemmed from the remarkable efficiency of its shipping industry, the massive concentration of capital in Amsterdam's exchange-bank, established in 1609 (one early eighteenth-century estimate put the bank's holdings at around three hundred million guilders),[161] the technical sophistication and flexibility of the Dutch fine-cloth industry,[162] and the "sophistication of Dutch methods and technology"[163] more generally. But beyond these factors, all essential, was a *commercial strategy* defined by its single-minded concentration on the rich trades of Europe and Asia, by far-reaching vertical integration into source-markets and, most strikingly, by the sheer scale of its Asian trade network[164] (unmatched by the English)[165] and the way the VOC was able to integrate its local, inter-Asian trade into a largely self-contained if expanding circulation of capital that minimized the need for payments in silver.[166] In most ways, it was the Asian part of this strategy that showed just how much the Dutch entrepôt was harnessed to the actual machinery of the Dutch state,[167] since Dutch commerce in Asia was "heavily armed" from the outset.[168] By 1623, the Dutch had ninety ships in the East Indies and two thousand regular troops posted in twenty forts![169]

Ralph Davis explained why Dutch shipping was more efficient. Before the seventeenth century Dutch shipbuilders did not have to look out for the defensibility of their ships but simply carrying capacity and cost of operation. "They evolved hull forms that maximised cargo space in relation to overall dimensions." Because they were flat-bottomed, "they drawe not soe much water as our ships do," wrote the English explorer George Waymouth in 1609, "... and therefore must have less Masts, Sayles, Tackling and Anchors, than ours have; *and are therefore able to sayle with one third part of men less than ours, or ther abouts.*" "Thus, by the advantage they gayn of us in burden, and by the charge they save in marriners wages, and victuals, they are able to carry their fraight better cheap than wee."[170]

Within Europe and large parts of the Mediterranean, barter was widely used as a mercantile strategy because it was *always* "more profitable to traders to export goods rather than money."[171] However, in Asia the crucial constraint on European trade, as the Portuguese rapidly discovered, was Europe's "inability to supply western products at prices that would generate a large enough demand" to provide the necessary revenue for the purchase of Asian goods. "The only major item that Europe was in a position to provide Asia [with] was precious metals."[172] (Even down to the end of the seventeenth century, "treasure" accounted for 70 to 90 percent of the English East India Company's total exports.)[173] The resurgence of economic conflict between Spain and the Dutch in 1621 and the embargo on Dutch shipping in Iberian ports[174] were therefore potentially disastrous to continued Dutch expansion in Asia, because they choked the transfer of Spanish American bullion to the Netherlands and created an endemic shortage of specie there; the VOC in particular required "an immense regular input of bullion to settle its balances in the East Indies."[175] Instead of seeking infusions of capital from Amsterdam, the VOC's governor-general at Batavia, Jan Pieterszoon Coen, evolved a commercial strategy or "master plan" that encouraged the Dutch to participate *extensively* in the trade of the Indian Ocean.[176] No other European commercial power did this on quite the same scale or with the sophistication and ruthlessness demonstrated by the Dutch through most of the seventeenth century. With their precocious base in Taiwan, they commanded a major share of the Nagasaki trade (basically, an exchange of Chinese silk yarn for Japanese silver), which meant that a large part of their Asian operations could be financed with Japanese silver and, to a lesser degree, Chinese gold. "In 1652, for example, the VOC exported from Nagasaki 1,555,850 guilders (equivalent to 17,022 kgs.) of Japanese silver" of which less than 9 percent arrived at the Company's headquarters in Batavia, the remainder ending up in China.[177]

Yet bullion stocks were never enough to resolve the problem of financing commercial accumulation in Asian markets, and the VOC would eventually create a vast continental system of barter which, *reduced to its simplest elements*, embodied an exchange of Indonesian spices for Indian textiles. This is the sense in which "the sales of spices formed the basis of Company expansion in other spheres of trade in Asia"[178] and the reason why the directors could state in 1648, "The country trade and the profit from it *are the soul of the Company which must be looked after carefully*."[179] The Company became an Asian trader on a large scale,[180] with major positions at one time or another in everything from Chinese sugar and Japanese silver to Japanese copper, spices from the Archipelago, indigo from Bayana and Gujarat, cotton cloth from the Coromandel, pepper from Malabar, cinnamon from Ceylon, raw silk, Dacca muslins and opium from Bengal, silk from Persia, coffee from Mocha, and so on. In 1619 when Coen sent his blueprint of the Asian trade to the directors in Amsterdam, the Company already had a "permanently circulating capital" of between *f*2.5 and *f*3.5 million in the East Indies and Coen wanted more.[181] After 1647 the resumed flow of Spanish silver to Amsterdam reversed the decline of bullion remittances to the east,[182] and by the middle of the century the East India fleet was returning home with cargoes worth between fifteen and twenty million guilders, roughly equivalent to the combined value of the Cadiz and Smyrna fleets![183] By 1673 Sir William Temple would refer to the "vastness of the Stock turn'd wholly to that Trade" and to the VOC "engrossing the whole Commerce of the East-Indies."[184]

Renewed access to Spanish silver in the late 1640s and a boom in Leiden's textile industry triggered by conversion to the expensive fabrics known as camlets and *laken* meant rapid Dutch domination of Mediterranean markets,[185] with Turkey now absorbing a third of Leiden's output. For the English this spelled a sudden crisis as "massive quantities of fine goods began to be loaded on to Dutch vessels at Livorno for the English as well as for the Dutch market."[186] It was this "sudden maritime crisis" that formed the "background of the first thoroughly worked out piece of English protective legislation—the Navigation Act of 1651—and of the First Anglo-Dutch War."[187] The ordinance of 1651 established a model for the tighter Navigation Act of 1660, which "remained at the heart of English maritime policy for nearly two centuries," providing that "all goods imported to England should come directly from their place of production (thus eliminating the Dutch entrepot)" and that "no foreign (i.e. Dutch) ships should trade with English colonies."[188] The years from 1651 to 1672 have been described as "the peak of Anglo-Dutch commercial rivalry."[189] However, from the mid-1660s Colbert's mercantilism became the pivot of a new struggle for Mediterranean dominance, this time between France and Holland, with the French tariffs of 1667 unleashing a commercial war in which Colbert's "clear objective was to capture the rich trades," wresting control from the Dutch.[190] By the 1690s the French could make rapid inroads into the Ottoman market, and by 1701 were selling more fine cloth there than the Dutch.[191] The Dutch had dominated Smyrna for most of the seventeenth century.[192] As late as 1680 silver remittances to the Levant were running at well over two million guilders a year.[193] In 1675 the majority of Europeans in Smyrna were reported to be Dutch.[194] However, between 1688 and 1719 the number of Dutch merchant houses there fell drastically from *ca.* twenty-five to only six,[195] clearing the way for the overwhelming French domination that characterized the Levant for the greater part of the eighteenth century. Richelieu and Colbert reflected ideas that overtly aligned the interests of commercial capital to those of the state. In the words of the French diplomat Nicolas Mesnager, Richelieu "did not find any means more effective to increase the power of the king and the wealth of the state than to increase navigation and commerce."[196]

Much of the précis above is based on Jonathan Israel's tightly-argued history of the Dutch commercial system, which ends by suggesting that "the basic reason for the decisive decline of the Dutch world-trading system in the 1720s and 1730s was the wave of new-style industrial mercantilism which swept practically the entire continent from around 1720."[197] A "comprehensive interventionism" took hold of northern Europe, with fatal consequences for Dutch export markets and industries.[198] Within Europe, the Dutch rich trades were "devastated" during those decades, and in India the English East India Company "had decisively overtaken the Dutch" in most parts of the country where they were present by 1740.[199] The essential vitality of the seventeenth-century entrepôt had been largely destroyed by the middle of the eighteenth century.[200]

ENGLAND'S RISE TO DOMINANCE

In England the "conscious use of state power for commercial ends"[201] first came to the fore in the revolutionary decades in the middle of the seventeenth century, roughly a whole century *after* the Elizabethan commercial expansion began. That expansion, as Brenner showed, was driven by the rapid growth of the import trades and had nothing to do with English cloth merchants looking for new markets.[202] The remarkable feature of the import trades of the late sixteenth century is their interlocking structure, with the same groups of entrepreneurs dominating the various companies floated between 1573 and 1592.[203]

English overseas commerce was thus highly concentrated and of course remained so as long as it was organized as a cluster of commercial monopolies ruled by a handful of big London merchants. A "close-knit group of Venice Company merchants with widespread operations" helped organize the Levant Company in 1592, and the East India Company in turn, when it was founded in 1599, "was dominated by the Levant Company merchants." Seven of the original fifteen directors were Levant Company merchants.[204] "Levant Company members provided between one-fourth and one-third of the total fund invested in the first, third, and fourth joint stocks" of the East India Company.[205] By 1630 the total combined value of Italian, Levantine, and East Indian imports was £527,000, in 1634 £689,000, and in 1669 £1,208,000, showing where the dynamism of England's trade lay for much of the first half of the seventeenth century into the early years of the Restoration. Nothing better demonstrates the dominance of the import trades (in both England and the Netherlands) throughout the seventeenth century than the fact that *exports* were very largely a function of the need to finance these substantial and rising levels of imports; for example, English merchant importers "increased their cloth exports *in order to pay for increased imports*, and they generally fell far behind."[206] It was this that caused major concern about the balance of trade in England.

The import boom of the second quarter of the seventeenth century[207] fueled a steady increase in *reexports* from the 1630s onwards.[208] In fact, the growth of a reexport trade was the chief innovation of the later Stuart period[209] and bound up both with the monopoly created by the Navigation Acts as well as the new mass production industries linked to the colonial trades in plantation produce.[210] Between them imports and reexports sustained a new, gigantic wave of expansion of English merchant shipping, especially in the years 1660–89.[211] Not only did the Levant trade rank high in the overseas commerce of Restoration London,[212] but the same years saw a near-doubling of England's plantation tonnage (the deadweight tonnage of this shipping sector).[213] Tobacco imports had registered a fivefold increase between 1620 and 1640, leading the way to sugar.[214] London's sugar imports trebled between the 1660s and 1680s, with six hundred importers active in the trade in 1686.[215] In the same year there were 1,283 merchants trading to the West Indies, of whom twenty-eight, with turnover exceeding £10,000, accounted for just over 50 percent of total imports by value.[216] They were *among* the biggest colonial merchants and could "accumulate sufficient capital to diversify investment around their core business into ship-owning, joint-stocks, insurance, wharf-leases, and industry."[217] London accounted for 80 percent of colonial imports and 85 percent of all reexports *ca.*1700, and in the last decades of the seventeenth century "England established a larger stake in the Atlantic than any other country in Northern Europe."[218] Tobacco, sugar, and Indian calicoes accounted for the bulk of England's reexports and prefigured the mass markets of the eighteenth century.[219] By 1700 the English planters in Barbados, Jamaica, and the Leewards were supplying close to half the sugar consumed in Western Europe.[220]

Of the 170 London merchants classified by Zahedieh as "big colonial merchants," two-thirds are said to have had a "substantial trade in the Caribbean."[221] That would make around 110 merchants with substantial stakes, which makes the Atlantic trades vastly more accessible than any of the trades to the east, Levantine, or East Indian. By its charter of 1592, the Levant Company was restricted to fifty-three persons, and recruitment to the Levantine trade required both wealth and family connections.[222] The richest and most active traders were, in Brenner's words, "joined in a ramified network of interlocking family relationships, the members of which controlled a major share of the trade."[223] In the East India Company, the largest of the joint-stock ventures, twenty-four directors "claimed that they held more stock than four hundred of the generality."[224] Again, it is useful to conceptualize London's commercial capital in terms of "classes of capital," with the eastward-trading combine that formed the heart of London's commercial establishment[225] forming a substantially more powerful layer than the "middling stratum" from which the vast majority of colonial merchants derived.[226] On the other hand, in terms of commercial concentration, the two trade sectors were not vastly different. During 1627–1635, when the trade to the Levant ran between £200,000 and £300,000 a year, some twenty-four Levant Company merchants controlled 54 percent of the trade,[227] which is not dramatically higher than the 50 percent share controlled by the biggest twenty-eight merchants trading to the West Indies who were mentioned previously. Regardless of whether trades were reserved or open, economic concentration worked in the same way.

In the Mediterranean in the early part of the seventeenth century England's main commercial rivals, the Venetians and the French, both lost ground rapidly. The Venetians were "undersold and driven off the stage," their agents complaining of the low price of the cloth sent out by the English.[228] By the 1620s Livorno had emerged as the prime commercial base for England's trade with southern Italy and the Levant. "In 1629," Wood reports, "there was said to be four million crowns worth of English goods lying on the quays of Leghorn (Livorno)."[229] In *The Treasure of Trafficke* (1641) Lewis Roberts noted that a million ducats in cash were exported from Livorno annually.[230] The "most modern and fully equipped port in the Mediterranean,"[231] it played a crucially important part in the Levant trade as a center where English exports and reexports could be converted into currency.[232] That the Levant Company could repeatedly attack the East India Company for its export of bullion to India suggests that the Levant trade itself was largely a barter trade, that is, one where the bulk of imports was financed by the export of cloth, tin, spices, and so on. Thomas Mun claimed, "Of all Europe this nation drove the most profitable trade to Turkey by reason of the vast quantities of broad cloth, tin, &c., which we exported thither; *enough to purchase all the wares we wanted in Turkey—whereas a balance in money is paid by the other nations trading thither.*"[233] On the other hand, in the "currant islands" where the English purchased about two-thirds of the crop, there was "practically no market for English goods and payment had to be made in ready money."[234] In 1629 the Venetian

ambassador reported that the Levant Company, "having a considerable capital, *buy up beforehand* the produce of the poorest of the
inhabitants of these islands . . . so that for them *the prices are almost
always the same*."[235] Advance payments were used to ensure low stable prices. In Italy, English merchants ran a deficit on the trade in
goods with all Italian states through most of the seventeenth century,
which they could successfully transform into a *trade surplus* thanks
to the surplus on "invisibles," that is, net earnings from shipping,[236]
insurance, and the commissions charged on English exports.[237] It was
this commercial strategy that would later form the heart of the City's
economic dominance in the nineteenth century.

The Levant Company was not a joint-stock, members traded
independently on a "regulated" basis.[238] Factors were recruited as
apprentices on seven-year terms, after which they were paid a commission on all goods they handled that varied from 2 to 4 percent.
Of course, as with the East India Company's servants in India, "factors made a good deal of profit from their own personal trading."[239]
Wood's *History of the Levant Company* suggests that the three factories at Constantinople, Smyrna, and Aleppo "reached their greatest
prosperity and size in the latter half of the seventeenth century."[240]
However, the bulk of the commerce was concentrated only in those
factories and there was a strong tendency to discourage expansion at
other trading stations.[241] By the 1680s both the East India Company
and the French had become major sources of competition. The Levant merchants would complain bitterly about the import of Indian
raw silk and silk goods by the former, but "the crown consistently
backed the East India Company against its critics."[242] Meanwhile,
Colbert's revival of the Languedoc cloth industry made the French
even more formidable rivals, as they proved to be for the Dutch as
well. By the end of the century, French imports from the Levant were
soaring, and by the 1720s signs of a rapid decline became visible in
the fortunes of the English company.[243]

The eighteenth century saw the *decimation* of English trade in
the Levant,[244] the result both of France's domination of the textile

market and of the Company's own fatal policy "to curb attempts at expansion and to discourage the opening of new markets."[245] It was left to the East India Company to note, in 1696, "it has always been observed that the particular traders in a regulated company content themselves to go to a certain known place in trade, ever taking a measure of their profit and loss before they go out...."[246] In addition to which, throughout the late eighteenth century trade was hampered by a Company regulation forcing merchants to make all purchases in the Levant by the barter of goods exported from England and forbidding the export of coin or bullion to Turkey, whereas French and Dutch merchants "carried large quantities of coin to the Levant," where local traders preferred outright sales to barter.[247] By the 1730s only some fifty or sixty Levant Company merchants remained active traders, "and it was widely believed this handful of monopolists deliberately curbed all initiative, enterprise, and expansion in pursuit of high profits on a limited business."[248] Again, the Company's factors were crucially dependent on Jewish brokers in the Ottoman markets, but the fear of potential competition from them sustained strong resistance to the admission of Jews to the Company. When they finally were admitted (in the 1750s) Jewish members of the Company were banned from employing fellow Jews as factors in the Levant![249]

In the eighteenth century well over half the seaborne trade between Europe and the Middle East came to be controlled by the French merchants of Marseilles,[250] and French competition was widely acknowledged to be the main cause behind the collapse of the Levant Company. If the Mediterranean had been the seminal ground of England's commercial expansion in the latter part of Elizabeth's reign, by the eighteenth century the decisive centers of gravity had firmly shifted to the Atlantic and the East Indies. By 1750 almost half of England's merchant fleet was engaged in the transatlantic trade.[251] From the 1730s there was a huge increase in the volume of capital advanced to the colonies by specialist groups of commission agents.[252] Jamaican estates tripled in value and planters like Peter Beckford could die leaving fortunes worth £300,000.[253] Sugar began to be financed by longer-term lending on mortgage, and when Henry Lascelles died in 1753, he had *ca.* £194,000 (sterling) out on loan to clients in Barbados and Jamaica.[254] Lascelles had financed his loans by borrowing from London bankers, which shows us that New World slavery was tightly integrated into financial and commercial webs centered in London.[255] By around 1770 the total sum owing to London merchants by West Indian sugar planters was in the region of several million pounds.[256] Doubtless the same was true of American planters. In 1784 Thomas Jefferson described them as "a *species of property annexed to certain mercantile houses in London*"![257] By the 1770s the American colonies provided 40 percent of British imports and took over 40 percent of Britain's domestic exports.[258]

The transformation of the East India Company from a purely commercial organization into a "political power"[259] was of course its most distinctive feature historically. However, an inordinate stress on what John Brewer has called the "privatized imperialism of the East India Company"[260] runs a double risk, both of distracting attention from the fact that the Company was always run "by a group of extremely rich capitalists"[261] *and* of failing to see, or not seeing sufficiently, that its transformation from a purely commercial entity into an imperialist one redefined the framework within which new forms of commercial capital proliferated from the end of the eighteenth century to spawn the powerful commercial lobbies of the nineteenth, such as those which lay behind the Opium Wars. In the pages that follow the focus is thus on the purely commercial or capitalist aspects of the Company's operations similar to those that K. N. Chaudhuri foregrounded in his substantial monograph *The Trading World of Asia and the English East India Company*.

The English East India Company was a tightly centralized business organization where the investment decisions were made by the Court of Directors working through the central managerial committees in London. Capital sums were assigned to individual "factories" *from London*.[262] The business model was of course import-driven, which in turn implied (a) a massive export of capital to finance

imports and (b) the vital part played by the re-export trades "in closing the gap that would otherwise have opened up in Britain's visible
trade balance."[263] In the EIC's case, capital exports took the form,
overwhelmingly, of precious metals, which were purchased initially
in London from the goldsmith-bankers and later, from the eighteenth
century, on the continent (in Cadiz and Amsterdam).[264] The Company's Asian import portfolio was "so finely differentiated that it took
more than two hundred pages in the Ledger Books to list them,"[265]
but by and large imports were dominated by a few key commodities
such as cotton and silk piece goods, raw silk, pepper, tea, and so on.
Distribution at the London end took the form of quarterly sales at-
tended by individual members of the Company who were themselves
substantial exporters as well as by wholesale dealers from Holland,
Germany, and elsewhere,[266] with orders for future supplies being adjusted on the basis of the actual prices received at those auctions.

At the Indian end, the advance contracts had to be made in antic-
ipation of the exact orders and financial resources that were to come
from England. The post-Restoration period saw calicoes rapidly
gaining in popularity, and by the 1680s the Company was importing more than a million and a half pieces, with the textile share of
total imports exceeding 80 percent by value.[267] To secure this vast
supply the Company relied on substantial local merchants acting as
brokers with the power to ensure that orders would be fulfilled on
time. "[T]he Company's servants advocated the use of middlemen on
the ground that if *they* dealt directly with the weavers, 'att the yeares
end, when we expected to be invested of our goods, we should un-
doubtedly come shorte of half our quantitye.'"[268] In other words, the
risk of default by the weavers was shifted to the shoulders of the merchants. Chaudhuri notes, "All commercial risks were to be borne by
the Indian merchants, and if the latter made a loss on the Company's
business they were still expected to carry on contracting for goods
as before."[269] Weavers, of course, refused to work without substantial advances which Chaudhuri confusingly calls their "working
capital,"[270] when the advances, the *capital* laid out on labor and on

raw materials, came from the Company. The "working capital" was strictly that of the Company, since the disbursements of cash made through their brokers (and later, more directly through the agents called *gumashtas*) involved a circulation of that part of the Company's capital which went into enabling the labor process, including reproduction of weavers' labor power.

In the 1720s Alexander Hume noted, "The English and Dutch, who are the greatest Traders in this country (Bengal), do their business wholly by their Brokers, who are their principal Merchants."[271] Forward contracts with large wholesale merchants were the rule both in the Coromandel and in Bengal,[272] with merchants who contracted for the investment frequently borrowing "large sums of money to carry it on" and wealthy bankers acting as their guarantors.[273] The Company wouldn't always secure such guarantees. "The wealthy merchants living in Hugli or Kasimbazar habitually refused the Company's demand for financial security as their credit and business status were unimpeachable."[274] Hume states in the same memoir that the greater the advance the more certain the Company was of receiving the goods on time, which is probably why in Bengal the group known as *dadni* or *dadan* merchants were usually paid as much as 50 to 75 percent of the contract value in advance.[275] From the 1750s, with large parts of India reeling under the impact of the Maratha incursions and the damage inflicted on mercantile fortunes, the substantial merchants who acted as brokers for the Company found it less and less possible to guarantee delivery and the system broke down. The *dadan* merchants withdrew from the Company's trade, thus forcing it to establish more direct control over producers, a drive that culminated in a series of regulations (between 1773 and 1793) that sought to reduce weavers to the status of Company employees, with restrictions on their mobility, tighter supervision of looms, and a more overtly coercive use of debt.[276] Indebtedness became an "integral part of production for the Company" in the final decades of the eighteenth century, and absconding workers were pursued remorselessly.[277]

Dutch exports from the Coromandel ran at almost two million guilders by the late 1660s,[278] while total EIC exports were often in excess of £1 million a year a century later.[279] Volume production meant that the European companies dealt with whole clusters of weaving villages, either on their own or more usually through their brokers ("principal merchants"), on a model broadly similar to the widely dispersed *Verlag* networks that South German commercial firms like the Fuggers had built their prosperity on in the thirteenth to sixteenth centuries.[280] For most of the seventeenth and eighteenth centuries the Companies were crucially dependent on local merchant capitalists[281] who had the resources to run their own commercial networks and even finance production on behalf of the Company. Both the English and the Dutch used the big merchants of Kasimbazar for their silk buying in North Bengal.[282] Bengal silk, Coromandel calicoes, Agra and Bayana indigo, etc. were all, like Malabar pepper, highly competitive markets; for example, "the contract price for silk was an object of intense bargaining between the (Bengal) merchants and the European trading companies."[283] However, by the eighteenth century the competition of *private*, mostly English, merchants injected a new dimension into the commercial dynamics of the East India Company. British private capital and its involvement in the commerce of India saw a steady expansion in the early part of the eighteenth century and then a bigger and more rapid expansion in the later eighteenth century, following developments that quickly opened the inland trade of Bengal to private capital and saw the contemporaneous capture of Surat in 1759.

Already by the later seventeenth century (the 1660s, in fact) the Company extended a "wide measure of official toleration" to the private shipping that emerged in Indian ports with sizeable European trading communities over which the British had some control.[284] Masulipatnam (not a British settlement but a cosmopolitan port),[285] Madras and Calcutta became, in turn, the major hubs of a burgeoning "country trade" that was progressively dominated by private capital. In the context of Company dominance, the term "private capital" is of course ambivalent, since it would have to cover the private trading activities of officials like the Governors of Madras who were big-time private traders at the start of the eighteenth century, other Company servants with commercial interests of their own, as well as the greater mass of so-called free merchants who were entirely outside the Company. In 1681 came the Company's "dramatic and sudden decision to withdraw from the local trade of the Indian Ocean,"[286] and a potentially vast field opened up for the expansion of non-Company commercial capital, where the main competition stemmed not from the Company itself but from indigenous Asian capitals trading to the Red Sea and to markets like Acheh and trading between the main coastal regions of India. In the trade between Surat and Bengal, the free merchants who eventually gained control of Calcutta's shipping faced "formidable competition from Asian shipowners."[287] Yet British dominance of India's carrying trade was swift, and by the 1730s Asian-owned ships had largely ceased to trade between Bengal and Surat.[288] By the 1780s free merchants were growing rapidly in numbers and wealth,[289] began to supply a large part of the Company's exports of textiles (in the Dhaka *arangs* vastly more than either the Company or its Commercial Resident),[290] and took the lead in opening up new areas for trade.[291] One upshot of this surge of private commerce was that as much as *ca*. £15 million could be sent home in remittances over the twenty-seven years between 1757 and 1784.[292] By the 1790s the massive expansion of Bengal indigo, much of which came from Awadh and further afield, was dominated by private merchants.[293] Their chief contribution to the commercial history of both Britain and India were the "houses of agency" which Calcutta-based free merchants were largely responsible for establishing. It was this layer of capital that helped to destroy the monopoly of the East India Company early in the nineteenth century.[294]

The transatlantic trades were roughly a century ahead of British private enterprise in Asia in innovating the commission system as the chief method of trading typical of commercial capitals in that sector. The reason should be obvious: private capital was dominant in the

colonial trades by the main part of the seventeenth century, indeed
it never faced the challenge of the big "Company merchants" except
for the Royal African Company's short-lived monopoly of the slave
trade. This precocious development of non-monopoly, private enterprise was significant because already by the 1660s the colonial trades
were "among the greatest of English trades."[295] In India, Houses of
Agency only evolved from the 1770s and then more rapidly from the
1790s, following Cornwallis's ban on servants of the East India Company engaging in private commercial enterprise.[296] But the Calcutta
agency houses are the most palpable link between the two main periods or "epochs" of British commercial capitalism, whose dividing
line lies at the start of the "long nineteenth century" (1784–1914), in
the years after 1784 which saw the ending of the American War of
Independence, a boom in new commission houses,[297] and a radically new economic conjuncture that saw banking revolutions on both
sides of the Atlantic, a dramatic expansion of the cotton industry in
Britain, and a surge in manufactured exports to the US and other
international markets. Meanwhile, the EIC's trading monopoly was
formally terminated in 1813, that of the Levant Company in 1825.

4

BRITISH MERCANTILE CAPITALISM AND THE COSMOPOLITANISM OF THE NINETEENTH CENTURY

AGENCY HOUSES TO MANAGING AGENCIES

In Aden in 1927, a young French socialist by the name of Paul Nizan found a microcosm of the mercantile capitalism of the late nineteenth century, but here stripped to its bare elements, devoid of the cosmopolitan cultural façades of Beirut or Alexandria. "There was no news except what came in cables from the agencies." European newspapers piled up unopened in the corners of bedrooms.[1] "No theatres, no publishing houses, no libraries... all the décor was forgotten and temporarily abolished."[2] "Every second of time that they passed—or rather, that passed them by—was *subject to the pressure of the world market...* In Aden, this pressure was an immediate presence, there were no intermediaries."[3] "Every heart *hung on the electric waves that traveled under mountains of sea at a rate of speed which no shareholder of Shell tried to imagine.*"[4] "These men were replaceable parts of an invisible mechanism that slowed down on Sunday, because of religion, and was periodically jammed by the violent accidents of economic crises. This whole mass of machinery, bolted together, without safety valves, vibrated like a structure of sheet iron."[5] "They were men obsessed, and they were dying by inches in the service of anonymous capital."[6]

If Nizan is to be believed, the most powerful capitalist in Aden at the time was a leather merchant from London, the chief of a "great company" whose offices "wield[ed] more power between Suez and Kenya than any European ministry."[7] Mr. C, as Nizan called this businessman, "possessed what three-quarters of the individuals most liberally endowed with a sense of their own importance do not have: cable addresses in Bombay, New York, Marseille, and London, and a private cable code."[8] The telegraph had revolutionized communications between Europe and India in 1865, and Nizan's references here are a distant echo of the transformations that were bound up with that change and with the laying of the first transatlantic cable in 1866. The 1860s were a watershed in numerous other ways. In Syria silk production expanded from just under 1 million kgs of cocoons to 3.4 million kgs in 1866, then fell sharply again by the end of the decade.[9] In Egypt the cotton harvest expanded four times in size in the boom of 1861–66.[10] Vagliano Brothers established the first and largest Greek shipping office in London.[11] The introduction of steamships increased competition in the shipping market.[12] There was frantic activity among British trading companies in India. The agency houses now first evolved into what would come to be known as "managing agencies."[13] The Sassoons, Iraqi Jews who had moved to Bombay shortly after 1830, fleeing persecution, cornered the Indian opium market, forcing the biggest opium trader, Jardines, to move out of commodities into services.[14] Large financial institutions like Crédit Lyonnais and Société Générale began to specialize in the business of lending to Middle Eastern governments.[15] In 1862, Egypt's ruler, Sa'id, turned to a syndicate of English and French banks, agreeing to borrow £3,292,800 (by 1875 the country's foreign debt stood at £91 million!).[16] In 1862 it was estimated that the Government of India (now removed from the hands of the Company) earned a net income of £4 million from the sale of opium to the commercial firms that exported it to China.[17] 1863 saw a major bull market, with some seven hundred new companies registered in London.[18] In 1864 Wallace & Co. floated the Bombay Burmah Trading Corporation, extending British commercial interests beyond eastern India.[19] On May 11, 1866, the Bank of England was forced to lend £4 million to banks, discount houses, and merchants on what was described as a "day of the severest credit panic."[20] And November 1869 saw the official opening of the Suez Canal.

The blurring of lines between commercial and industrial capital was nowhere more evident than in the evolution of the agency houses into "managing agencies" and "investment groups" in the final decades of the nineteenth century. The managing agencies would become the backbone of British business in Asia, consolidating their hold over entire sectors of the economy. But the early history of the agency houses was defined by a chronic overaccumulation of capital (thanks in part to the sudden influx of private capitals into the East India trade) that created a constant pressure to diversify. Among the earliest agency house merchants, John Palmer was described as "an indiscreet, fussy, petulant, and indecisive man," "obsessed with status," "gullible" and "naïve."[21] Already by 1820 he had to write off bad debts to the staggering sum of *ca.* £1.25 million (the sterling equivalent of 100 lakh rupees).[22] In 1823 he was complaining bitterly that Calcutta was "crowding out" with competition.[23] His chief creditors in the City became progressively disillusioned and eventually abandoned the company toward the end of the decade.[24] In the 1820s, it seems, the established agencies found it impossible to sustain profitability to cover the interest they had to pay to depositors without recourse to "imprudent speculations."[25] This was code for indigo, which had seen frenetic expansion in the 1820s and the price of which had begun to slide by 1826, when England was in the midst of a trade depression. Around 80 percent of the indigo grown in the Presidency was financed by six agency houses, among whom Palmer & Co. and Alexander & Co. had the largest stakes, £5 million and £3½ million respectively.[26] It was estimated that nearly three hundred indigo factories were part of this financial web.[27] In 1827 John Palmer was boasting that "his house enjoyed a degree of confidence on the part of Indian merchants unmatched by the other houses," but by late 1829, when it was obvious to them that Palmer & Co. was in serious trouble, the company's credit among Indian moneylenders simply collapsed.[28] The failure of the company in January 1830 has been described as "a fatal blow for the *system of mercantile capitalism which had operated since the 1780s*."[29] Within four years all the other major Calcutta agency houses crashed as well, opening the way to a reordering of the commercial capitals active in the East India trade.

William Jardine became the leading figure among the Country traders in Canton as China was flooded with cheap opium in the 1830s.[30] Exports from India reached the enormous level of forty thousand chests by the end of the thirties.[31] By 1832 Jardine and James Matheson had taken over Canton's leading opium firm, Charles Magniac & Co., renaming it Jardine Matheson & Co., some eight years after Magniac died.[32] Both partners were Whigs and avid supporters of a showdown with the Chinese authorities, denouncing the EIC's conduct as one of "subservient timidity" and lobbying furiously through their paper *The Canton Register*, through petitions to the House of Commons, and through private conversations at the top level in the Foreign Office.[33] As the government in Peking swung into action to stop the traffic, Jardine in 1838 would complain to Jamsetjee Jeejeebhoy, Jardine Matheson's biggest trade constituent with whom they were transacting more than £1 million worth of business annually,[34] that the "persecution" of the opium dealers had now spread to every province in China.[35] A year later, now back in England and asked for advice by the foreign secretary, Jardine suggested a show of force.[36] The main upshot of the first of the Opium Wars was Britain's acquisition of Hong Kong, about which Matheson told Jardine, in January 1841, "So independent will Hong Kong be that it will even be allowable to store opium on it as soon as we build warehouses there."[37] It was no exaggeration for one scholar to write that William Jardine had "masterminded British strategy in the Opium War" or "literally masterminded the government's approach towards China and the Opium War."[38]

In the middle decades of the century, Jardines had more than 150 correspondents in Calcutta, Bombay, and Madras, but this was essentially an information network, important though that was.[39] The most important of their Bombay associates acted as brokers only, refusing either to buy or advance on crops.[40] When the Chinese legalized opium in 1858 and all dealers in China faced similar competitive conditions "so that prices and costs in India became crucial to continued success in the trade,"[41] Jardines would lose out hugely to a competitor with much higher levels of vertical integration on the supply side. In a brilliant monograph, Edward Le Fevour argued that "the real strength of the Sassoon group lay in their practice of advancing as high as three-quarters of costs to Indian dealers willing to consign shipments on a regular basis. Jardine's associates in India attempted the same but, as their advances were provided through large agency houses in Bombay and Calcutta, they failed to affect the producing areas where Sassoon purchased unharvested poppy crops through experienced agents."[42] "Sassoon's methods were so successful that by 1871 Jardine's had only one considerable account... and had ceased to invest its own capital regularly in opium."[43] "Early in 1871, the Sassoon group was acknowledged to be the major holder of opium stocks in India and in China; they were owners and controllers of 70 percent of the total of all kinds."[44] Beaten out of opium, Jardines diversified into shipping, railway-construction, banking, and insurance, and later bought out Matheson & Co. which was probably the biggest managing agency in China, with its own interests in mining, insurance, and railways.[45]

Strong capital growth became characteristic of many of the agency houses that developed into managing agencies in the late nineteenth century. Jardine, Skinner, & Co., a firm founded by one of Jardine's nephews, saw its capital expand from £100,000 ca. 1845 to £660,000 by 1860 and £1.3 million in 1890.[46] By the First World War it was "one of the biggest managing agency houses in Calcutta," with interests in trade, industry, and shipping.[47] Another Scottish firm, James Finlay & Co., expanded its capital by £2.21 million over the years 1861–1910, that is, at an average rate of *ca.*£45,000 a year.[48] Harrisons & Crosfield (H&C), a small firm of tea merchants that evolved into a global (or, as it called itself, "Eastern") plantations and trading company, saw the total book value of its assets grow from £564,436 in 1908 when it became a limited liability company to £2,867,168 ten years later![49] Much of this sort of expansion was fueled by agency houses diversifying into control of joint-stock companies in the jute, coal, tea, and rubber industries, showing how problematic the distinction between "mercantile capital" and "industrial capital" had become under this transformed form of merchant's capital.

From the 1870s on, commercial firms became active promoters of joint-stock companies. The techniques they evolved to enhance control over capital were every bit as modern as that ascribed by Hilferding to the financing of the American railway system. In *Finance Capital*, Hilferding posited "a distinctive financial technique, the aim of which is to ensure control over the largest possible amount of outside capital with the smallest possible amount of one's own capital."[50] When the Calcutta agency houses "floated numerous jute, tea, and coal companies on the British and local capital markets, retaining a percentage of the equity and a managing agency contract,"[51] they were of course doing precisely that. Chapman notes that "from a dispersed shareholding of perhaps £2–3 million, Birds and Heilgers were able to direct an investment of £20 million. Yules' capital was only £1.2 million, and it looks as if the firm controlled an even larger capital investment than Birds."[52] The disproportion between owned capital and effective control over a larger mass of capital mobilized from the market was a key feature, indeed the very basis, of the managing agency system. On the eve of the Second World War sixty-one foreign agencies were managing more than six hundred rupee companies; "of the ten major British houses or groups, Andrew Yule managed 59, Bird-Heilger 37, Martin Burn 34, Begg-Sutherland 27," and so on, and of the agencies listed here Andrew Yule, Bird-Heilgers, and Martin Burn were among the ten largest corporate groups in India in 1951.[53] Yet Kidron points out that by the late forties "foreign managing agencies held, on average, under 15 percent of the paid-up share capital of their managed companies."[54]

Other features are worth underscoring. Late nineteenth-century managing agencies had the strong backing of the City firms they were connected with, established substantial interests in individual sectors so that between them the leading agencies dominated the main sectors they were active in, and were often highly diversified concerns. To illustrate these aspects briefly—among the rupee companies (those raising their capital locally), seven managing agency houses "controlled 55 percent of the jute companies, 61 percent of the tea companies, and 46 percent of the coal companies," this *ca.*1911.[55] Indian jute manufactures remained "almost completely dominated by British... businessmen right up to the end of the Second World War."[56] The involvement of agency houses (H&C in London and Guthrie's in Singapore) in the great rubber boom of the 1900s[57] would eventually mean that in Malaya as late as the mid-1960s "over 180 British companies owned in excess of 800,000 acres of rubber trees."[58] Andrew Yule & Co. which managed over sixty companies in India by 1917 and had a strong presence in the jute industry also described itself as "the largest producer of coal in the private sector" in 1963.[59] Most jute and tea companies were in turn trade-financed by the City. In 1871 James Finlay & Co.'s "Glasgow head office advised the Calcutta and Bombay branches that the Royal Bank of Scotland would cover acceptances to the extent of £100,000."[60] In 1890 Finlays's Calcutta manager reported "that he was running as much as £40,000 or £50,000 of bills with different banks for each of the two major (tea) companies."[61] Finlays built a very substantial stake in the tea industry at the end of the decade, when it controlled a capital of £4,458,400, had seventy-four thousand acres under cultivation and as many as seventy thousand workers in India and Ceylon.[62] Finally, Forbes and Forbes in the 1930s "had over a score of interests as exporters and importers, bankers, brokers, shipping and insurance agents, merchants, commission agents, and engineering and building contractors."[63] Balmer Lawrie, a Calcutta agency house of London parentage, had interests ranging over "the production, warehousing, and marketing of tea; heavy and light engineering; steel fabrication, including a wide range of containers, and the manufacture of switchboard and other electrical equipment."[64] The London house of Steel Brothers & Co. were into "timber extraction, paddy buying, oil drilling, cotton ginning, cement making, tin dredging and rubber planting."[65] Between the wars Steels became the largest of the rice-milling and exporting firms in Burma, "with a total milling capacity of 5,500 tons of cleaned rice daily" *ca.*1915 and control of close to half the country's paddy crop by the Second World War.[66]

The point worth retaining from all this is that the managing agencies were pure emblems of Britain's mercantile capitalism, reversing the relationship between trade and industry in the sense that control of industrial enterprise was here subordinated to what were essentially trading companies that still earned a major part of their profit from commissions. Amiya Bagchi's statement that "the managing agency houses with large industrial interests continued to have strong interests in trade"[67] understates the case, since the agencies remained merchant houses and commercial firms and can hardly be compared with the industrial enterprises that had emerged both in the UK itself and elsewhere in the world by 1914.[68]

CITY COSMOPOLITANISM: "THE WHOLE SURFACE OF THE GLOBE"

To Marx and Engels who linked the idea of cosmopolitanism to the trade expansion of the mid-nineteenth century, it seemed self-evident that capital would scour the "whole surface of the globe," "nestle everywhere, settle everywhere, establish connections everywhere," in an endless search for markets and for raw materials.[69] In fact, confining ourselves to the Scottish and English families that dominated most managing agencies in India runs the serious risk of underestimating the distinctiveness as well as the real *strength* of British mercantile capitalism in the nineteenth century. At one level, Victorian capitalism was strikingly cosmopolitan in that London and the industrial towns in the north of England acted as magnets for commercial firms from all over the world. The number of German merchant houses in Manchester alone grew from twenty-eight in 1820 to ninety-seven *ca*.1850.[70] The more successful of them included N. M. Rothschild at one level (he was already a millionaire by the 1820s) and Engels's father at another. The number of Greek firms settled in Manchester rose dramatically in the late 1840s and 1850s, and exceeded the number of German houses by the mid-sixties.[71] Among the richest of these, Spartali & Co., based in both Manchester and London, was probably typical of the UK-based trading houses that pioneered Britain's commercial penetration of the Middle East in the mid-nineteenth century, given that almost no native British firms were resident in Beirut in these years. In 1855 British imports to Syria were estimated to be about £1,200,000.[72] In an official report from that year, one of the key factors in the recent surge of British trade was described as "rivalry amongst the Levantine merchants in London engaged in the Syrian trade, especially the firms of Spartali and Lascaridi, *who have given unusual facilities to their correspondents, thereby enabling them to sell British goods in Syria* nearly as cheap as in England."[73] The striking fact here is that "the increase in British trade seems to have been carried out mainly by Lebanese firms engaged in direct trade with England," and that the twenty-nine Lebanese houses that dominated this trade (in fact, dominated Lebanese trade and finance down to World War II) used a handful of Greek and Lebanese firms as their agents in England, among them Spartali & Lascaridi in London.[74] In 1857 this firm was said to be "worth £100,000,"[75] which would make it one of the wealthiest merchant houses in Britain at the time. Again, when David Sassoon swore allegiance to the Queen in 1853, he spoke not a word of English, "signing his naturalization certificate in Hebrew."[76] The Sassoons of course had their headquarters in Bombay, but their head office in London (at 12 Leadenhall Street, which also housed the offices of the Cuban sugar merchants, Fesser & Co.) was "almost entirely manned by co-religionists recruited mainly from Baghdad and Persia."[77] When the family-patriarch David's eldest son Abdullah (later Sir Albert) finally moved to England in the 1870s, London became the firm's "nerve-centre, with all major policy-decisions and directives originating from Leadenhall Street."[78] And the Greek merchant houses in England were no different. The Ralli Brothers' head office in London was almost entirely staffed by Greeks from Chios, where the family originated.[79] By the end of the nineteenth century Rallis surpassed both Jardine Matheson and Finlay & Co. in terms of size of capital.[80]

At another level, British capitalism drove trade expansion for much of the nineteenth century, even in the decades when Britain's chief manufactured export, cotton piece goods, was rapidly losing market share in Europe and America, and Britain's share of world trade in manufactures declining markedly after 1870.[81] *The volume of international trade grew fivefold in the years between 1840 and 1870,*[82] and much of this was the work of British commercial firms. At mid-century, according to data compiled at Palmerston's request, the distribution of British mercantile houses worldwide was as follows: in north & central Europe, 501; in the Mediterranean and Middle East, 281; in North America (excluding Mexico), 142; in South America, 460; and in India and China, 111.[83] These figures tell us nothing about the scale of commercial investment in these various regions, since houses varied considerably in size, but they do convey a clear impression of the sheer spread of British businesses, which dominated international trade in India, South America, and China for most of the nineteenth century. To take one example, there were forty-one British houses in Buenos Aires in 1836, more than all the other European countries combined.[84] In particular, the prodigious commercial expansion of the Victorian era saw a very wide range of commodities trading at increasingly massive levels. Palm oil, raw cotton, opium, wheat, tea, teak, rice, coffee, cocoa, jute, rubber, and groundnuts all saw major periods of expansion in the mid-to-late nineteenth century or in the early twentieth century. Thus the value of UK's palm oil imports rose from £58,286 to £1,755,982 over the years 1817–1854.[85] These, as Lynn says, were "massive volumes for the export market."[86] The volume of cotton exports from Egypt grew from an annual average of 65,160 *cantars* in 1822–24 (1 cantar = 94 lbs) to 6,982,000 *cantars* in 1910–13.[87] India's opium exports to China climbed to a staggering level of over 90,000 chests or 5,715 metric tons a year by the 1870s and 1880s (from a reported figure of 24,000 chests in the mid-1830s).[88] Brazil's export of coffee rose from 9.7 million sacks in the 1830s (1 sack = 165 lbs) to 26.2 million sacks in the 1850s.[89] Teak exports from Burma went from an average of 85,000 tons in 1857–64 to 275,000 tons in 1883–4.[90] Colombia's coffee production grew from 114,000 sacks in 1874 (1 sack = 60 kg) to 3,453,000 sacks in 1932.[91] Rice exports from Saigon increased from 284,000 tons in 1880 to 1,548,000 tons in 1937.[92] By 1895 Siam was exporting 61,800 tons of teak, virtually all of it felled by British companies.[93] The value of Gold Coast cocoa exports rose from £27,000 in 1900 to £10,056,000 in 1920.[94] And Senegal's groundnut exports more than doubled from 227,000 tons to 504,000 tons in 1910–30.[95] The spasmodic nature of some of this commercial growth meant that some commodities saw short bursts of expansion in particular years. Thus there was a "vast expansion" of tea cultivation in Assam in the years 1856–60;[96] the raw jute consumed by Indian jute mills rose from 2,248,000 bales (1 bale = 400 lbs.) to 4,459,000 bales in the 1900s;[97] there was an unprecedented boom in rubber in 1909 and 1910;[98] and the new rail connection from Kano to the Niger saw an "enormous expansion" in Nigeria's groundnut crop in 1912–14.[99] Moving perspective slightly, the tonnage clearing Black Sea ports grew from 228,000 tons in 1831 to almost 12 million tons by 1910;[100] there was a threefold increase in the value of Britain's total trade with Latin America in 1865–1913;[101] India's export values "increased nearly five times between 1870 and 1914";[102] and Karachi's trade expanded by a factor of four between 1882–83 and 1904–5.[103] With the exception of Saigon and Senegal, almost all of these movements of expansion were bound up with British commercial interests. For example, Liverpool was the center of the British palm oil trade; Britain was the main consumer of Egyptian cotton and exercised direct control of the Egyptian economy after 1882; opium was a government monopoly first established by the EIC and remaining so throughout the nineteenth century; British export houses like Phipps Brothers & Co. dominated the Brazilian coffee trade in the 1870s (when exports were valued at £2 million);[104] modern Karachi was a purely British creation, Burma teak was controlled by the Bombay Burmah Trading Corporation (BBTC) which had a 65 percent export share by the 1890s;[105] and so on.

Because the computed real value of imports into the UK was apparently "not ascertained" until 1854, when it was it became obvious that Britain had run up what J. Y. Wong has called a "phenomenal global trade deficit" (on Wong's calculations, £41.67 million by 1857),[106] and the gap "widened markedly during the period 1875–1900," as exports slowed and manufactured imports began to rise sharply, the trade deficit with industrial Europe and the US growing very rapidly after 1870.[107] Yet the balance of payments on current account (that is, inclusive of net services income and net income from foreign investment) remained positive throughout the latter part of the nineteenth century,[108] thanks to the growth in "invisible" exports or Britain's dominance in world shipping, insurance and other commercial services, and to the gigantic surge in British investments overseas,[109] in short, to the primacy of British *mercantile* capitalism conceived in the broad sense of the entire range of commercial and financial interests bound up with the City.

Thus, the late-nineteenth century "Gladstonian Treasury" model depended *crucially* on invisible exports and Britain's ability to sustain those in the face of widening trade deficits. In 1898, when the country's visible trade gap swelled to £194 million, Edward Hamilton had to allay fears by pointing out: "In the first place, we supply foreigners every year with a huge amount of capital... the aggregate amount may be put at £2,000,000,000. The interest on this at 4.5% would be £90,000,000 which is being paid in the form of imports without any corresponding exports. In the second place, there are also 'invisible' exports to be taken into account in the shape of freights and profits on our vast shipping trade... [which] may be put at £90,000,000. When therefore the excess [of imports over exports] goes on increasing, there is no reason to suppose that it is due to other causes than interest due on the increased capital invested abroad and an augmented carrying trade."[110] The upshot of being able to sustain such a regime down to its catastrophic collapse in 1913–1937 was that "in 1913 Britain was the only nation whose interests were global" or, more accurately, truly global.[111]

The liberal cosmopolitanism of the City, which described itself as "free trade," reflected the rapid internationalization of the British economy from the mid-nineteenth century. On the other hand, it never precluded imperial aggression when this was required in the strict interests of bondholders, bankers, and the agency houses. Numerous commercial lobbies were strident in their support for Palmerston's government during the second Opium War.[112] Similar interests prevailed in the annexation of Sind in 1843,[113] or in the annexation of Burma in 1886 which had been preceded by demands for "decisive government action" to forestall the French treaty with King Thibaw which would have given the French extensive rights in Upper Burma.[114] Here Wallace Brothers played a key role in coordinating a wave of protests by Chambers of Commerce all over Britain, leading the "mercantile pressure for British intervention," given that the huge forestry interests of its subsidiary, Bombay Burmah Trading Corporation, were at stake.[115] However, Britain's occupation of Egypt in 1882 was by far the most extreme case of an economically-driven intervention. Here both French and British economic interests were at work. Wilfrid Blunt, diplomat-turned-anti-colonialist, wrote that Gambetta was "closely connected with the *haute finance* of the Paris Bourse, and was intimate with the Rothschilds and other capitalists who had their millions invested in Egyptian Bonds."[116] The Anglo-French regime of joint control "looked solely to finance and troubled itself hardly at all about other matters."[117] David McLean, London manager of the Hongkong and Shanghai Bank, is supposed to have said, "I want to see England take Egypt and hold it."[118] Gladstone himself "had an exceptionally large holding in Egyptian government bonds: £40,567, or 37 percent of his entire portfolio. Sixty-five other MPs also had investments in Egypt."[119] The bombardment of Alexandria in the second week of July 1881 was, as Kynaston has called it, a "turning point" in Gladstonian Liberalism.[120] By July 20 there were about thirty-eight hundred British soldiers, sailors, and marines in the city.[121] Yet Egypt already had over ninety-thousand Europeans living in the country, and it was certainly the emergence of a popular, national movement in 1881 and 1882 that triggered the call for occupation by British troops.[122]

GREEK DOMINANCE IN THE LEVANTINE BOOM

The origins of the Greek Levantine dominance have to be sought in the dramatic decline of French trade in the Mediterranean toward the very end of the eighteenth century. Down to the 1780s France accounted for the biggest share of Ottoman trade with western Europe,[123] but in the 1790s French trade in the Mediterranean was almost totally destroyed.[124] By the end of the eighteenth century Greek-owned ships were entering the western Mediterranean ports in groups of four, six, eight, ten vessels, or more.[125] By 1798 one out of every three ships arriving at Marseilles from the Levant was Greek-owned.[126] Further east, Greek-owned ships represented over half of all entries to the port of Alexandria in 1780–1821 and close to 60 percent of all entries in the port of Odessa in 1801–21.[127] By then Greek commercial houses had also taken over a large part of Smyrna's trade and the richer ones among them had correspondents all over western Europe.[128] By the 1810s Greeks from the Ottoman regions were settling in Odessa, Marseilles, and Livorno to set up commercial networks for the burgeoning trade in Ukrainian grain.[129] By the early 1820s both of the leading Greek houses, Rodocanachis and Rallis, had settled in Odessa.[130] The years around 1850 were the heyday of the Greek merchant houses exporting from Odessa.[131] By 1863 the owner of one of the most important firms in Odessa was telling the

French consul: "We can no longer compete with American grain in the English market... the means of transport remain expensive and the distance great."[132] Rallis adjusted to the slump in Russian grain by expanding globally, establishing branches in Calcutta (1851), Bombay (1861), and New York (1871).

The rise of Greek-owned shipping and the resurgence of Greek nationalism in the eighteenth century were both powerful factors in consolidating a mercantile Greek diaspora. This included both political refugees and "members of the old commercial houses of Constantinople, Salonica, and Smyrna, sent out to set up branches abroad and extend the operations of the parent firm."[133] As early as 1812, one observer noted, "Some branches of the migrating families... are always left in Turkey... from the convenience to both parties in a commercial point of view. Thus by far the greater part of the exterior trade of Turkey, in the exchange of commodities, is carried on by Greek houses, which have residents at home, and branches in various cities of Europe, mutually aiding each other."[134] Of the main ports of the eastern Mediterranean, Constantinople had the largest concentration of Greeks, while Smyrna had a very large number of Chian merchant houses by the end of the eighteenth century.[135] The Greek upper class of Istanbul contained two sectors of very different origin, on the one side an Ottoman-bureaucratic élite of provincial origin that lived in the old quarter of Phanar which was the seat of the Orthodox Church and a repository of the educated Greek dialect of Constantinople,[136] hence known as "Phanariots"; on the other, a larger mass of merchants active in textiles, banking, and shipping who were "almost all from Chios," as a mid-eighteenth century French report put it.[137] The bulk of Chian families who were settled in Pera were decimated in the massacres of 1822.[138] They were all strong supporters of the struggle for Greek independence and included the most important business families of the diaspora that would now develop an even wider radius in the commercial centers outside the Ottoman empire—the Calvocoressi, Rodocanachi, Ralli, Schilizzi, Baltazzi, and other families. By 1860 over half of all tonnage entering British ports from the eastern Mediterranean and Black Sea was handled by Greek merchants of Chian origin (Harlaftis' "Chiot network").[139] Among them the Rallis and Rodocanachis were the biggest Greek commercial houses in Odessa in the 1850s,[140] were strongly represented in ports like Liverpool and Marseilles, and "probably had the *largest organisations and capitals of any merchants operating in London*" at the time.[141] Intermarriage was extensive, so Schilizzi & Co., the biggest shipping brokers in Liverpool, were simply the Liverpool branch of Ralli Brothers.[142] The Baltazzi, in a rather different pattern of evolution, rose rapidly in the world of international finance and became leading bankers of Istanbul, with banking networks that straddled all the main financial markets of Europe and the Mediterranean.[143] Another banking family, the Zarifi, of local (Fanar) origin, likewise stayed in Constantinople, acting as bankers and diplomats to Sultan Abdul Hamid.[144] Dimitrios Vikelas's autobiography *My Life* tracks the complex trajectories through which Greek merchant families affected by the struggle for independence found themselves having to reassemble businesses both in Istanbul and in the wider networks that now included London as a leading hub of the diaspora. Both his grandfathers were from Istanbul families which experienced massive disruption in the 1820s, but survived and prospered economically. Vikelas himself was sent to London in 1852 to work as a clerk in the family business there and eventually became more famous as a writer and as the first president of the International Olympic Committee.[145]

As the Ottoman empire was opened up economically between 1838 and 1843, starting with the Anglo-Ottoman commercial treaty of Balta Limani, Pera in Constantinople saw a massive influx of Europeans. In 1839–79 a hundred thousand Europeans moved to Pera, which became Constantinople's predominantly Christian diplomatic and commercial district.[146] Anastassiadou claims that the Greek population alone grew five or six times in the late nineteenth century. But next to Istanbul, or more precisely Beyoglu (Pera), it was Izmir/Smyrna that was described as the true commercial capital of the empire.[147] Here the Greek presence grew very substantially, so that Greeks outnumbered Turks by the 1870s.[148] Most banks and bank managers were Greek, half the top merchants, lawyers, and doctors in Smyrna were Greek, and the buildings on the Cordon were mainly Greek-owned.[149] These developments were part of the wider economic boom that engulfed the Levantine ports in the nineteenth century and apply with modifications to Beirut (where a purely Lebanese, and largely Greek-Catholic, "commercial/financial oligarchy" played the equivalent role)[150] and of course to Alexandria. Beirut's population grew from *ca.*6,000 around 1820 to 150,000 in 1905,[151] while Alexandria's growth, given the bigger size of the city, was just as formidable: from 181,000 in 1865, 232,000 in 1882, 319,000 in 1897[152] to almost 600,000 (573,063) in 1927![153] By the 1920s foreigners made up 17.4 percent of Alexandria's population, and of those almost 50 percent (48.9 percent) were Greeks.[154]

Beirut and Egypt were convulsed by the silk and cotton booms of the 1860s. In Mount Lebanon "the silk industry was restructured and industrialized to the benefit of" French capital,[155] while Alexandria's rapid expansion as the main east Mediterranean port saw the number of Europeans quadruple in the nine years of Sa'id's reign (1854–63). By 1864 there were fifty to sixty thousand Europeans in the city, mostly Greek, Italian, and French.[156] Alexandrian families of Muslim origin had almost no share in the "fantastic enrichment that characterized certain Greek or Syrian families" in the 1860s.[157] As early as 1839, when foreign mercantile firms, the so-called *"maisons de commerce,"* had been expanding rapidly, twelve Greek merchant houses, Ralli included, had already "captured 33 percent of the Alexandria cotton export market, with the largest Greek house, Tossizza Frères et Cie, exporting 11 percent of Egypt's cotton."[158] In these early years, two Greek friends of Muhammad Ali (Michel Tossizza and Yanni Anastasi, later "Jean d'Anastasy") were said to be among the richest merchants in Alexandria; both "cosmopolitan merchants with agents in other Mediterranean ports such as Marseille and Livorno."[159] By 1872, when expansion resumed with more than 200 million pounds of raw cotton being shipped to European markets,[160] the Greek hold on the export economy was more entrenched than ever. What finally clinched it and secured its dominance for the next four or five decades was the defeat of Egyptian nationalism by the display of military force in 1882.[161] Britain's occupation of Egypt ushered in the "heyday of cosmopolitan Alexandria,"[162] the palmy years from 1882 to 1936, when the size of the cotton harvest more than doubled in the years before the outbreak of the war.[163] Britain transformed Alexandria into a trading station (*comptoir*) where cotton was "amassed, controlled, sorted, weighed and despatched." The agents of large international firms *had* to be based there.[164] But the trade was tightly controlled by the big cotton exporters, of whom the biggest were Greek firms linked to the Benachis, Choremis, Salvagos, and so on. These large Greek exporters formed "the wealthiest and most powerful group within the Greek community."[165] In *less than a year* of the British taking over, the bigger export firms would move to establish the Alexandria General Produce Association, which exerted a firm grip on the city's cotton exchange (next to Liverpool, the second biggest in the world)[166] and which native Egyptian growers would come to look upon as a cartel of sorts.[167] "Of the twenty-four founding members of the Association, fifteen were Greek with Theodore Rallis as president and Emmanuel Benakis as vice-president."[168] Ilbert writes that between 1885 and 1934 the "power of the Association was such that no one could touch it."[169] By 1890 Alexandria's business élite numbered some hundred and fifty individuals, with a smaller circle of sixty capitalists controlling the largest share of assets.[170]

The biggest of the Greek-owned firms was Choremi, Benachi & Co. Again, the founder of this firm, Emmanuel Benachi, came from a Chian family that had fled the massacres of 1822 to start up a textiles business, importing Lancashire goods, on Syros.[171] He belonged to the second generation of the Greek diaspora, the *defteroclassati*, whose fortunes were closely bound up with the British. The Choremi/Benachi business had dozens of branches in the Egyptian interior, in rural towns like Zagazig which thrived on the cotton trade. They employed only Greeks in their Alexandria office. Following the occupation, the Greek commercial bourgeoisie of Alexandria built an entire quarter to the east of the city called "Quartier Grec." The Benachis moved here in 1884, living in a villa opposite Theodore Rallis. Here was a group with a fierce sense of its own class location, fervent Anglophiles, fluent in English and French, and almost totally ignorant of Arabic. Emmanuel Benachi himself preferred Greek to other languages and exuded a strong nationalism. The Benachis were passionately interested in political developments in Greece and became avid supporters of the ultra-nationalist Venizelos. Benachi himself left Alexandria in 1911 to become the Greek minister of finance and then mayor of Athens.[172]

Kitroeff underscores the cosmopolitan origins of the Greek capitalists who dominated Alexandria's cotton trade and many of its insurance, banking, brokerage, and import businesses.[173] But this was a cosmopolitanism that allowed for both racism (toward Egyptians)[174] and a sometimes visceral Greek nationalism. Trimi states that the Benachis were "cosmopolitans," yet "their more intimate relations were almost entirely confined to Greeks."[175] Mansel suggests that they became "Greek nationalists as well as cosmopolitan Alexandrians."[176] Alexandria's upper-class residential areas were less mixed ethnically than, say, the old *hara*, the Jewish quarter, where Greeks, Italians, and Syrians lived side by side.[177] Business cosmopolitanism required no level of interaction beyond those dictated by the pursuit of accumulation. "The Benakis knew little of Egypt except how to exploit or—depending on the point of view—develop its economy."[178] A description of Alexandria *ca.*1909 recalls Nizan's portrait of Aden. "All considerations of science, art, and archaeology are choked by the city's strenuous commercial activity," it states. "Affairs of commerce, the state of trade, the movements in stocks and shares form the staple of the daily round of conversation in the clubs, in the streets, on the wharves, on the trams, in the trains, in short, everywhere in this city... now wholly and whole-heartedly given to the worship of the modern deity Mammon, who exacts the most exclusive devotion from his followers."[179]

Alexandria exerted a peculiar fascination on its Levantine residents. The celebrated poet Cavafy whose father's firm P. J. Cavafy & Co. had traded in cotton and grain, with branches in Cairo, London, and Liverpool, and failed in 1876 when he was thirteen, forcing his brothers to take "what jobs they could as clerks and managers with other Greek companies,"[180] knew he would never be able to leave.

> You said: "I'll go to another country, go to another shore,
> find another city better than this one."

Cavafy then tells himself:

> You won't find a new country, won't find another shore.
> This city will always pursue you.
> You'll walk the same streets, grow old
> in the same neighbourhoods, turn grey in these same houses.
> You'll always end up in this city.[181]

5

COMMERCIAL PRACTICES

Putting-Out or the Capitalist Domestic Industries

Marx's own recurring characterization of commercial capital as inexorably subordinate to industry and to industrial capital obscures the fact that historically a wide range of industries worked *for* merchant's capital. The chief but not the only form this took was what historians writing in English call the "putting-out system." Hilferding referred to industrial sectors organized in this way as "capitalist domestic industries." [1] Next to large-scale commerce, which Marx was willing in one passage to describe as a "form of capitalist production," [2] the capitalist domestic industries were probably the most widespread form of capitalism for centuries together. John Clapham regarded capitalist outwork as "still the predominant form" of industrial organization in Britain in the 1820s. [3] When the spinning of cotton began to be mechanized in the last two decades of the eighteenth century, "a vast amount of extra weaving capacity was required ... to work up the vast quantities of machine-spun yarn now being turned out," and this extra capacity "was supplied by an enormous expansion along traditional outwork lines, as a whole new army of men, women, and children were recruited to the handloom." [4] Thus "outwork was not some dying pre-industrial dinosaur, but ... a perfectly rational, viable, and adaptable form of organization in many industries." [5] It showed remarkable powers of survival throughout the nineteenth century in the wholesale mass-production of cheap ready-made clothing. [6] With the coming of the railways, London wholesale houses in the shirt trade sent their work into the country as well as to the East End.[7] In fact, London remained "the largest single centre of outwork production" anywhere in Britain in the nineteenth century.[8]

Carlo Poni offered a convenient definition in 1985: "Production that was essentially domestic, and therefore dispersed, was organized and dominated by *entrepreneurs who were traders* and exported to near and distant markets… In its 'classic' form the workers (often spinners and weavers who still owned their instruments of work) received the raw material from the *merchant-entrepreneur* and were paid by the piece when they handed over the finished product." He went on to say, "According to Sombart, this cottage industry is already a 'manifestation of the modern capitalistic mode of production,' the essential characteristic of which was 'the laborer's dependence on the capitalistic entrepreneur.'"[9]

In German this "dispersed" or decentralized form of organization is usually referred to as *Verlag* and the merchant deploying it as a *Verleger*, in English as the putting-out system or as "outwork" or "homework," and the merchant as a "putter-out" or just as often as a "merchant-manufacturer." Capitalist *production* in the strict sense may be said to have begun with the putting-out system.[10] The essence of the system was that the subjection of labor to capital occurred in a form that did not presuppose its simultaneous subordination through the labor process. (Marx called the latter the "real subsumption of labor to capital.") It was not embodied in the structure of the labor process or reflected in its "technical characteristics." As Marx says repeatedly, "At the outset it (capital) takes it (the labor process) *as it finds it.*"[11] "It does not therefore directly change the mode of production,"[12] where "mode of production" simply means the labor process itself. On the other hand, and this is crucial, it was essential that the merchant *controlled, managed, and coordinated production itself,* that is, the interconnected labor processes through which the commodity was finally produced. The dispersal of living labor was re-totalized in the final commodity thanks to the merchant's control and integration of production. Poni's definition contains the essential elements of this paradox: the dispersed nature of production, its organization and control by "entrepreneurs" who are basically merchants, the merchant's control of the raw material and designs, the widespread use of piece rates, and finally, from Sombart, the subjection of labor.

From its broad origins (in Europe anyway) in the twelfth century, the putting-out system reached a crescendo in the seventeenth and eighteenth centuries. Even after its heyday, it showed astonishing resilience. When the option of factory production became available to manufacturers in the nineteenth century, they could still prefer outwork because of its lower overheads, higher rates of exploitation (greater intensity of labor linked to low piece rates), and greater flexibility in hiring and firing labor.[13] These were all characteristics of the system that favored the countryside over urban locations, so that by the early eighteenth century "the bulk of all wool, linen, cotton, and blended cloth in Europe was produced in the great *rural* districts of England, France, Germany, the Low Countries, and Switzerland."[14] The crucial constraint was the availability of homeworkers, and where employers had the option of cutting costs by moving to cheaper labor in the countryside, they did so. When they did so in a big way in the eighteenth century, what evolved was the kind of capitalism that has been labeled "proto-industry," that is, concentrated industrial regions that specialized in mass production for export markets,[15] what Lis and Soly have called "industrial mass production in the countryside."[16] In the Beauvaisis in northern France, a typical region of this sort, textile production was widely dispersed through the countryside, with enormous levels of output even in Colbert's day and sales outlets controlled by powerful merchants.[17] But as Poni pointed out, proto-industry was not a purely rural system.[18] The Flemish woolen industry of the thirteenth century was a largely urban industry. So was the wool industry of Florence from its inception in the thirteenth century to its decline in the early seventeenth. And when concentrated in the towns, as it largely was initially, the skein of

Verlag could give medieval and early-modern cities the appearance of "great manufactories" (*grandi manifatture*),[19] of "one vast factory," as Eleanora Carus-Wilson described the great clothing towns of Douai, Ypres, and Brussels as they were in the thirteenth century.[20] In both periods (medieval as well as early modern), and regardless of whether production occurred in towns or in the countryside, when the putting-out system was used in a regular, systematic way it always implied mass production, "sales to a general market," in Marx's expression.[21] In England by the eighteenth and nineteenth centuries, "outworkers were producing at the behest of capitalists for a mass market, not for individual customers."[22] Some industries "relied heavily on outwork."[23] Bythell notes that "at the beginning of the nineteenth century ... several industries (in England) were to a large extent organized on these lines: the spinning and weaving of basic textiles, much of the manufacture of personal consumer goods such as clothes, boots, and stockings, and the making of certain common items of hardware, of which nails were the most important." These were "mass markets" in consumer goods which were supplied by "large capitalists"[24] variously described as "big urban manufacturers and merchants" or "merchant-manufacturers" or "large wholesale houses,"[25] while the workers were wage earners working with their own tools in their own workshops and homes.[26]

The basis of the merchant's dominance was a dual one, the first lying in a monopoly of the raw material, which was either inaccessible locally and thus too expensive or, where accessible, the focus of a ferocious struggle between merchants and artisans. In a very fine study of the Cholet linen industry Tessie Liu argues that "Successful putting-out required merchants to buy up as much yarn as possible to deprive direct producers of independent access to raw materials."[27] Putters-out "could only achieve their goals by monopolizing raw materials," "buying up the yarn before it reached the market, and forcing weavers to sell to or take commissions from them exclusively."[28] The other foundation of mercantile control over artisan labor was the merchant's ability to *organize* the overall production process in ways that would have been impossible for isolated groups of workers within it.

The following pages summarize some of the historical work that concerns industries that made extensive use of the putting-out system. The key fact to note is that merchant firms were the main owners of capital and employers of labor in each of these industrial sectors.

MERCHANT MANUFACTURING

"The great Florentine fortunes were made in banking and trade, never in manufacturing," wrote Raymond de Roover. He noted that only a minor part of the Medici capital was invested in the wool and silk industries.[29] However, Sergio Tognetti has since shown that the rapid expansion of the silk industry, especially from the later fifteenth century, was very largely financed by the city's great *casate*, the banking and commercial houses that were at the cutting edge of north Italian capitalism.[30] It is hard to say how far the same was true of the woolen industry. In the 1480s, for example, one of the biggest commercial houses, the Strozzi, had a total of twenty-one wool firms.[31] This was probably far higher than the average investment of other families from the Florentine banking and commercial élite. Braudel's view of a vertically integrated industry where "one end of the chain would be represented, for example, by the possession of a wool wash-house in Old Castile; the other end by piles of textiles in a store in Alexandria"[32] is largely contradicted by more recent accounts of the industry, notably Goldthwaite's, which suggests instead both that "No one firm had a significant share of the market"[33] (the industry was characterized by extreme fragmentation), and that "a firm sold its products immediately to any merchant-exporter who would buy them."[34]

The most important woolen industries of the later middle ages grew up in regions where there was an abundant supply of cheap labor. In Florence wage costs amounted to 60–65 percent of total manufacturing costs in the industry.[35] When top-quality English wool began to be used by the 1320s, the sector saw rapid reconversion to better-quality wool and grew rapidly in terms of value of output. The merchant-chronicler Giovanni Villani tells us (writing about the years 1336–38 specifically),

> The workshops of the *Arte della Lana* were 200 or more, and they made from 70,000 to 80,000 pieces of cloth, which were *worth more than 1,200,000 gold florins*. And a good third [of this sum] remained in the land as [the reward] of labor, without counting the profit of the entrepreneurs. And more than 30,000 persons lived by it. [To be sure,] we find that some thirty years earlier there were 300 workshops or thereabouts, and they made more than 100,000 pieces of cloth yearly; but *these cloths were coarser and one half less valuable*, because at that time English wool was not imported and they did not know, as they did later, how to work it.[36]

The firms that ran the wool industry in Florence were short-term partnerships between investors and managing partners, where the managing partner dealt with production,[37] showing that even when the city's big merchant-bankers (*grandi mercanti banchieri*, in Tognetti's description)[38] did invest in industry, they cannot be described as "industrial entrepreneurs," much less "magnates," as Alfred Doren imagined them to be in his classic, quasi-Marxist, monograph.[39] A more realistic picture of the industry should have divided it broadly into (1) "rich owners of large factories," (2) a larger mass of small entrepreneurs, and (3) the great mass of cloth workers.[40] Dyers, fullers, stretchers, and menders operated their own shops and apparently "chafed under their subjection to the Wool gild," wanting freedom to bargain with the manufacturers.[41] The production organizers who functioned as middlemen in the putting-out system were included among these *sottoposti*, below whom came the workers proper, the "thousands who lived by wages."[42] Similar divisions characterized the labor force. Beating, carding, and combing were operations performed on the employer's premises (the shops known as *botteghe*). These were "menial and tedious tasks" and the workers doing them were among the "most downtrodden and the most poorly paid."[43] It is therefore interesting that these groups (beaters, carders, and combers) played a leading part in the Ciompi revolt of 1378, when a large mass of workers in the industry (nine thousand on one estimate)[44] seized the government in the summer of that year and (briefly) won the right to form their own guild.[45] Spinning and weaving were home-based operations, and here too the major difference was that firms relied on labor contractors called *fattori* to recruit and pay the thousands of women involved in spinning but made sure weaving was closely supervised.[46] Weavers were piece-rated, owned their own looms, and did not stay long with the same employer.[47] They were often forced into debt so that firms were sure of having reserves of labor available in the future. Given that the likely average payroll size of most wool firms was anywhere between, say, fifteen and fifty,[48] the bulk of the labor force consisted, clearly, of the workers employed in the putting-out sectors of the industry. Interestingly, the weavers themselves played no significant role in the Ciompi Revolt.[49]

Thus, in the textile industries "putting-out" was hardly ever a stand-alone system, but was usually integrated into total production processes characterized by their "combined" nature. In the manufacture of wool, some operations were performed centrally on the employer's premises, some subcontracted to other, independent firms (this applied to wool-washing and dyeing), and the rest (spinning and weaving) "put out." In keeping with this, the wool itself kept moving back and forth between locations and between the city and areas in the *contado*. Gérard Gayot's study of the woolen industry in Sedan (in France) shows the same complicated movement.[50] Next to monopoly of the raw materials (wool of different qualities, dyestuffs, alum), integration of control over all these separate processes was the true basis of the merchant's dominance in capitalistically organized domestic industries.[51] Federigo Melis calculated that in the wool business run by the Prato merchant Francesco di Marco Datini, the production of 222½ pieces of woolen cloth over a three-year period required the employment of no fewer than one thousand persons who in turn were involved in 6,088 distinct or "partial" operations.[52]

The bulk of a wool firm's capital was tied up in raw materials and in the outlay for wages, mostly advance payments to spinners and weavers. What predominated in production was circulating capital. (The big exceptions to this among the *Verlag* industries were mining, iron-making, and shipbuilding, all of which involved substantial amounts of fixed capital.) Goldthwaite argues that none of the fixed capital used in the industry came from the firms; for example, the massive tentering sheds scattered all over the city or the fulling mills located in large mill complexes outside the city, along the Arno, belonged either to the Wool guild or to landowners.[53] This may explain why de Roover himself derived the *capitalist* nature of the industry more from its subjection of labor than from any ostensible "giant" enterprises of the kind Alfred Doren rooted for. "Although the wool workers for the most part were employed in their own homes and used their own tools, they were not independent artisans but wage-earners who worked on materials supplied by their employers."[54] "The employers, subject to severe competition in everything else, were united in a gild and *used its machinery to keep wages down and to prevent workers from organizing*."[55] The chief advantage of "outsourcing" the bulk of production to outworkers was the flexibility it gave the firms themselves, in other words, the ease with which they could curtail production by laying off workers whenever managers needed to.

Silk was a massively competitive market characterized by volatile demand (rapid changes in fashion) and a huge variety of fabrics.[56] From the early fifteenth century it became the leading sector of the Italian economy for the next several centuries.[57] As competition mounted rapidly in the sixteenth century, Florence, a leading producer, drastically reduced production of higher-quality silks, "downscaled" to simpler fabrics, and basically retained vitality throughout the seventeenth century by adapting to the nature of the English market.[58] By the 1660s "the city's silk industry was almost entirely geared to meeting the demands of the English market"[59] and England herself accounted for over half of Florence's total production of silks,[60] until an indigenous (English) silk industry began to take over the domestic market in the final decades of the seventeenth century.[61] But by the start of the eighteenth century it was the Lyons silk industry that emerged as by far the most advanced in Europe.

The twenty-odd years between 1712 and 1732 saw rapid concentration of capital in Lyons' *Grande Fabrique*, as the network of putting-out firms in the silk industry was called. In his monograph on the industry Justin Godart cites a *mémoire* dated 1712 that gives the total number of big merchants (or *maîtres marchands*, as they were called) as around two hundred and the number of homeworkers employed by them on piece-rates as between three thousand and four thousand.[62] Between those poles lay a mass of weavers working "on their own account" (*pour leur compte*), who were described as "merchants and workers rolled into one" and for whom no figure is given. In 1732, by contrast, a later *mémoire* cited by Poni puts the number of big merchants or *marchands fabricants* ("putting-out entrepreneurs") at *ca.* seventy and the number of workers at *ca.* eighty thousand.[63] Thus there was a substantial reduction in numbers at the capitalist end of the industry and a doubling of the mass of weavers at its base. Between those dates, the city authorities had gone on a major drive to eliminate the independent weavers as part of a concerted "subordination of labor to capital" that was being enforced at a social, collective level by the representatives of capital. The campaign involved allegations that the independent weavers, unable to afford the services of designers, were stealing designs from the big merchant firms with the active collusion of the workers employed by those firms.

The *Grande Fabrique* has been described as a "huge industrial and commercial complex" employing *ca.* thirty-five thousand workers by the 1780s, nearly a quarter of the city's population and almost half its labor force.[64] Its basis remained the dispersion of labor in domestic units controlled by capital. Sewell has argued that the master weavers themselves are better seen as subcontractors than as pure wage laborers, since they "hired and supervised their own journeymen."[65] But he also notes that "[t]he merchant simply paid the weaver, his subcontractor, enough to keep his family unit going."[66] The family labor that was essential to this form of capitalist organization was of course unpaid. This only adds to the irony of being told that Lyons' silk industry was "the most innovative of the eighteenth-century French textile industries in design, marketing, and technology." "In terms of value of product, it was *easily the most important industrial complex in eighteenth-century France*."[67] Lyons dominated the "very lucrative high end of the European and transatlantic silk market."[68] Against the claims of its weavers that the success of the industry was due to "the high professional quality of their work," the merchants chose to argue (in 1759) that the weavers were more like masons on a construction site, whereas they themselves were the architects without whom no building would have been possible.[69] What the analogy points to is the totalizing role of merchant's capital in putting the industry together and securing its dominance through a thorough knowledge of the market. The Lyons silk merchants "were the first... to use annual product differentiation as a strategic weapon to create barriers to entry, to capture important shares of the international market and to outmaneuver firms in competition with them."[70] This presupposed substantial investment in the production of new designs[71] and the "extraordinary flexibility" with which information was used to respond to rapidly changing market conditions.[72] The use and training of first-class designers was crucial to the way the industry retained competitive dominance. Young designers would continue to spend long periods in Paris every year, visiting the most famous silk warehouses in the area around Châtelet and Palais Royal. "These visits gave rise to substantial interaction between the producer firms and the needs and expectations of the market."[73] Back in Lyons, designers would "work in cooperation with a weaver and specialized technicians to transfer the designs from paper to loom before they were put out to the weavers."[74] Designers were well paid and pivotal to the whole commercial strategy to keep ahead of and actively shape the Paris fashion market. "Innovations had to be not only rapid but also appealing,"[75] and it was only in Lyons, or in Lyons and Paris, that this programmed "production of novelty,"[76] "chang-ing designs from one season to another," became a ruthless market strategy that defeated even the imitation industries. On the other hand, none of this would have worked without what Poni calls the "flexibility offered by the artisan or putting-out organization of pro-duction," which, as he says, the Lyons merchants were "the very first to exploit fully and systematically."[77] A major aspect of that flexibili-ty was the fact that outwork was, as Bythell described it, "eminently capable of rapid expansion, given an abundance of cheap labor."[78] In Lyons, industrial capacity almost trebled in the decades between 1720 and 1788.[79]

The Oriental Carpet Manufacturers Limited (OCM for short), finally, is a concise illustration of the *combination* of relatively ad-vanced forms of modern commercial capitalism with domestic indus-try. OCM's carpet manufacturing used both factories and domestic production in widely dispersed networks that were put together by a remarkably energetic field staff ("carpet men") across a vast region from Anatolia through Iran to Mirzapur in northern India.[80] Ottoman trade data shows there was a dramatic growth in the carpet trade at the end of the nineteenth century, with a large share of exports being sourced from traditional weaving towns like Ushak on the plateau *ca.* two hundred miles northeast of Smyrna.[81] In these towns, Smyr-na merchants "had agents who were paid 3 or 4 percent of the pur-chase price to supervise the manufacture and to accept the finished carpets." "The Smyrna dealers were either agents of European firms working for commissions of 3 to 5 percent, or selling direct to their overseas customers on FOB basis."[82] Competition was fierce, and, in 1907, a group of Smyrna-based Levantine merchants, "the most important and wealthiest carpet manufacturers of Smyrna," as they described themselves in the prospectus,[83] amalgamated to form what soon became Oriental Carpet Manufacturers.[84] OCM, which began essentially as a combination of these Levantine carpet traders and the London firm of G. P. & J. Baker, was from its inception a "complete-ly vertically integrated" concern, with "an immense trading capital of £400,000" and branch offices in London, Paris, Constantinople, Cairo, Alexandria, and New York.[85] "After three years of trading, the company had earned huge profits, amassed strong reserves and paid handsome dividends to its shareholders" and was "responsible for the export of 90 percent of Turkey's carpets."[86] By 1912 OCM had branches all over Europe, in Cairo, Sydney, and Buenos Aires, and was said to employ "some forty thousand weavers and factory workers in Anatolia alone," and was seeking shareholder approval for a doubling of their capital to £1 million.[87] Expansion was rapid and "[t]o increase production as fast as possible" OCM had "sent agents out to towns and villages across western Anatolia to establish looms in private houses to weave for them under contract."

Most of the weavers were Greek or Armenian Christians, since they were less "shy about letting men from outside the family into their houses."[88] The company's biographer Antony Wynn writes that "[e]normous effort was expended on getting both the quality and designs right."[89] "The design house in Smyrna employed skilled draftsmen to produce and copy designs on squared paper to send out to the weavers."[90] Weavers were paid piece wages, with rates declining and the intensity of labor growing as one moved to the outer concentric circles of production sites which shared their common center in Smyrna. Thus the number of knots required to earn one piastre or *kurush* was seventeen hundred for weavers in Smyrna but as high as three thousand in Bursa and Sivas.[91] On the other hand, rapidity of labor was not always an advantage: a company official would say later, about the weavers in Tabriz in the north of Iran, "They are very precise and clever weavers, but they give the carpet such a precision job that it looks too much like a machine made carpet." These weavers, both men and women, were said to be able to weave "at the rate of just over one knot per second" on stretches of single color.[92] At the time OCM entered the Persian market, a large colony of Tabrizi merchants in Constantinople exerted a virtual monopoly of the Persian carpet trade. American firms first broke this monopoly by paying much higher prices.[93] "Finance was the key to the carpet trade," writes Wynn. "Anyone who could pay cash for ready-made rugs, or pay advances to weavers for carpets to be delivered later, had a huge advantage over the local merchants," who paid weavers in promissory notes payable several months later.[94] Also, a "much better price was to be had if advances were given to the weavers," 25 percent lower than the price of the ready-made carpet.[95] Advances consisted of a combination of raw materials and wages. In Hamadan in 1917, when food was scarce, three-quarters of the advance was described as being "in materials, which the weaver cannot eat and dare not sell."[96] Cecil Edwards, who laid the foundations of the OCM operation in Iran, worked rapidly so that by the end of 1912 "[p]ractically no carpet-weaving area of Iran and the surrounding countries was left uncovered," and the company was thought to control about a third of all Persian export production.[97] In Iran anyway a substantial part of this was actually based on child labor.[98]

OCM introduced an altogether more advanced organization into the industry, concentrating on large-size carpets, rigorous quality control,[99] the accumulation of a huge library of designs that were "drawn up in minute detail on squared paper and sent out to Turkey, Greece, Persia, and India to be copied and given out to the master weavers,"[100] intense training of the OCM buyers,[101] forward integration into major retail outlets in New York, Constantinople,[102] etc., and so on. The Turkish disaster of 1922 saw a large-scale exodus of Constantinople carpet merchants (Jews, Armenians, and Greeks) to London,[103] which became the international wholesale market for medium-grade and specialty carpets from the East. By the end of the 1920s, "85 percent of the Oriental carpets imported into London. . . were re-exported to Europe, the USA, South America, and South Africa."[104]

In India OCM worked largely through E. Hill & Co., which it acquired fully only in 1944. Hill's was based in Mirzapur and ran an entirely home-based industry, "with no factories and no heavy overheads."[105] The Mirzapur villages were "company" villages weaving for one or other of the carpet companies.[106] In 1969 OCM was sold to Ralli Brothers and merged, along with other companies, into Ralli International. A Ralli company history describes the way production was organized in Mirzapur.

> Carpet manufacture is still very much a cottage industry in the Mirzapur district but it is *closely regulated by E. Hill who remain responsible for quality and production*. Though the actual weaving is done in loom houses in the weavers' villages, E. Hill buy the yarn, dye it to the required shades and produce the loom drawings. These are issued to the villagers with the weaving instructions for stitch and size and the cotton for the warps and wefts ... *Carpets are inspected regularly during the course of weaving by members of the company* on visits to the various villages ... The finished carpets are then packed and transported by road some five hundred miles to Calcutta where they are shipped to London, New York and Canada.[107]

The carpet made for the Morning Drawing Room, Holyrood House (the royal palace in Edinburgh) was commissioned to Hill's (that is, OCM), which had the weaving done in one of the villages near Mirzapur. The massive loom on which it was made was worked by twelve workers, all males, aged between sixteen and thirty, each paid about six hundred rupees a month (equivalent to *ca.*£24 a month in 1988 when the carpet was made). The size of the carpet was 10.3m x 7.6m, with a knot density or refinement of 210,000 knots per square meter. "The time taken from completion of the design of this monster in November 1987 to delivery to Holyrood in May 1989 had been seventeen months."[108]

6

THE CIRCULATION OF COMMERCIAL CAPITALS
Competition, Velocity, Verticality

The drive to monopolize markets, vertical integration, concentration of capital, and a striving for flexibility are features typical of capitalism that likewise run through the history of the bigger commercial firms. Scale and flexibility were linked. "Lesser merchants... lacked sufficient capital to move rapidly from one branch to another,"[1] while another historian tells us that "[t]he trade of the smaller merchants differed from that of the larger ones in being highly specialised."[2] *The bigger capitals were both diversified and vertically integrated.*[3] By compressing the chain of circulation, what Chayanov had called the "trading machine," vertical integration increased its velocity and re-appropriated a part of the surplus-value that otherwise accrued to middlemen. Thus Peirce Leslie described the business of South Indian coffee by saying, "Whereas we were expected by London to depend entirely on what we could buy on the Coast in Tellicherry and Mangalore, Volkart Bros. had a network of upcountry agents, and consequently were able to buy a large part of their requirements up-country at prices cheaper than those ruling on the Coast: thus having secured the cream of the market, they were able to dictate the price on the Coast, and were in a position to outbid us... It took a long time to convince the London office that we would have to follow suit, largely because... nobody in London had any knowledge whatever of conditions in India."[4] Big capitals were also more diversified. The leading London merchants of the early seventeenth century had portfolios characterized by "multiple investments"; for example, in Rabb's study about twenty-five of the leading merchants were invested in nine or more companies.[5] Of the silk enterprises run by Milan's commercial houses Stefano Angeli tells us the biggest houses shunned specialization. He refers to an "intense diversification of sectors and markets" as typical of their economic behavior.[6] Even within core businesses, the same striving for diversification was evident. Thus, Molà points out that "Venetians diversified their output of every single type of (silk) fabric, producing it in distinct varieties at higher or lower prices."[7] And one of the ways in which the English textile industry began to dominate the markets of Spain and Italy in the second quarter of the seventeenth century, turning the table on the Italians, was through the sheer assortment of different textiles it churned out.[8]

International trade was in any case *always* characterized by a high degree of concentration. In his classic monograph on the Venetian state and its big merchants, Giorgio Cracco laid out the axiom: to compete *effectively* on the international scale required a "concentration (both) of capitals and of mercantile structures."[9] As in large-scale industry and banking, concentration was driven by competition among the big players (although Marx correctly saw competition itself as merely "externalizing" the law of accumulation). Here are a few examples of this. At the end of the thirteenth century, at the start of the reign of the Mamluk ruler Nasir al-Din Muhammad, there were over two hundred Kārimī merchants in Egypt, each employing dozens of commercial agents in various markets overseas.[10] The Karimis were well-organized maritime traders who dominated the spice trade from its Egyptian end, trading to the Malabar coast via Aden. Yet a century later, by the end of the fourteenth century, a large part of Aden's traffic with Egypt had become concentrated in the hands of a much smaller group of Karimi families who were said to have close ties with the Mamluk rulers.[11] At the close of the sixteenth century, some sixty Genoese bankers dominated the Piacenza fairs, the great financial clearinghouse of European capitalism where "huge sums of money changed hands."[12] In the Atlantic trades, in 1686, forty firms had handled 86 percent of London's tobacco imports; by 1775 when London tobacco imports had trebled in value, 90 percent of the trade was handled by twenty-eight firms.[13] In the West India trade in the eighteenth century, twenty leading commission agents engrossed nearly two-thirds of a hugely lucrative business.[14] Of the total iron imported into Hull in 1751, 87 percent was handled by ten merchants, and almost sixty percent by the top two.[15] The olive oil trade of southern Italy was likewise "to a large extent" in the hands of a "relatively small group of big Neapolitan merchants and foreign merchant houses" for much of the eighteenth century.[16] For most of the early nineteenth, about two-thirds of the private trade in opium was controlled by just two agencies, Dent & Co. and Jardines,[17] and by 1871 a newcomer, the Sassoons, had acquired control of 70 percent of Indian opium of all varieties.[18] In the West African palm oil trade between 1830 and 1855, a half-dozen mainly Liverpool firms controlled over half the market each year.[19] Between 1895 and 1910 six or seven firms, American and German, exported up to sixty percent of the Brazilian coffee crop.[20] Around 1900 five French houses at most were responsible for purchasing two-thirds of Beirut's silk exports.[21] In Argentina the "Big Four" grain traders massively controlled the export market in wheat "and strongly influenced local markets."[22] In the 1925–26 season, the top five shippers, three of them Japanese, accounted for two-thirds of all raw cotton exports from Bombay.[23] By 1928 West Africa's trade was dominated by just four large firms, two of whom would merge a year later to form Unilever's trading arm UAC.[24] Among this handful of giants, the French firms CFAO and SCOA were, on one description, "vertically integrated trading and shipping combines."[25] In Indochina by 1938 five French banking groups controlled 70 percent of the land planted to rubber.[26] And in Burma by 1939, 1.7 percent of the rice mills handled around 44 percent of the paddy crop.[27]

All of the nineteenth/early twentieth-century examples here come from what are called the "produce trades." These were fiercely competitive, both among the handfuls of big merchant firms that were active in them and between them and the brokers they relied on. By the late nineteenth/early twentieth centuries, "[c]oncentration and centralization (of capital) were the only means of commercial survival," Bob Shenton has argued.[28] When Sir George Goldie headed an amalgamation of British merchant firms trading in the Niger Delta region and formed the United African Company in 1879, the express purpose of this, Shenton explains, "was to circumvent the Delta middlemen and to *trade directly with palm-oil producers* on the Niger River proper."[29] But the drive for vertical integration was never completely successful. In the decades that followed, a spate of acquisitions gave Lever Brothers direct access to oilseeds. But this was a soap manufacturer-cum-margarine producer gaining access to markets in British West Africa through trading companies, of which the biggest was the Niger Co. (Goldie's original 1879 company, recast as a chartered company called the "Royal Niger Company, Chartered and Limited").[30] William Lever acquired the Niger Co. in 1920 for a price exceeding £8 million, funded, evidently, through the market.[31] When this was then merged with its closest rival A&E (itself an amalgamation of Liverpool firms) in 1929 to form the United Africa Company (UAC), the commercial arm of Unilever which now assembled some ninety-three separate companies, it was UAC's experience in Africa that best demonstrated the limits to the vertical integration of a merchant firm.

THE "RELATIVE AUTONOMY" OF BROKERS

By the early part of the twentieth century the biggest merchant firms had reached enormous scales of operation. In British West Africa alone UAC paid £12.3 million for produce in the year ended September 1933.[32] Even as late as 1952 the value of all produce bought by it in Nigeria and the Gold Coast was over £42 million.[33] The produce trades depended on substantial volumes of working capital that were circulated as advances, and even if firms exercised tight control over the prices paid to producers, the advances only circulated via brokers and middlemen. In palm oil UAC had a "large and complex" organization. In Nigeria in the late 1940s "there were five main administrative centres... thirty-four local centres, and some two hundred outstations" that dealt with African or "Syrian" middlemen and employed African produce-buyers.[34] In groundnuts in 1948–9 "it had 150 buying points in Northern Nigeria and 55 in the Benue area, divided between main local centers and outstations. In the Kano area it dealt through twenty-eight contractors, seventy-nine middlemen, ten factors and 102 outstation clerks."[35] (Overall, by 1939 it employed twenty-seven hundred middlemen!)[36] Contractors, writes Fieldhouse, "were an essential feature of the system, but they presented one problem: because of their very size they were highly independent and were *liable to use UAC commissions to finance their own operations or purchases for other trading firms*."[37] Thus the "really big abuse and also the most debated issue between the firms was the advance made to middlemen and factors."[38] Yet the system of advances "remained virtually unchanged so long as the foreign firms continued in the produce trade,"[39] which demonstrates the "structural" impossibility of doing away with brokers for firms that traded outside family trading networks of the kind characteristic of the big Italian firms in the later middle ages or of the Greek commercial houses of the nineteenth century. Extending networks inland rather than "relying on African middlemen to bring produce to the main collecting centres" would have meant having to maximize purchases to cover the overheads of those additional buying points, which would further increase competition and strengthen the position of the brokers.[40] One response to this dilemma was pooling agreements or buying pools which, as a CFAO annual report explained, were directed specifically at middlemen and created to "remedy" their "abuses."[41] In Burmese paddy, four of the largest rice-milling and exporting firms (Steel Brothers included) formed the notorious Bullinger Pool in

1921, directed, again, against the sellers of paddy, that is, against "brokers, speculators, traders, and other middlemen."[42] The Entente Sénégal was likewise a combination of this sort, formed in 1889 by the export houses in Bordeaux to control the price of groundnuts.[43] Frédéric Bohn, founder of the Marseilles giant CFAO who was part of this buying pool, had strong views on the African brokers, describing them in one letter from 1894 as "our worst enemies."[44] All the *maisons de commerce* in French West Africa were in principle opposed to the advance system, "even as they knew it was the very basis of their economic transactions."[45]

Brokers were an endemic feature of the way capital circulated in vast sectors of the wholesale trade, and the economies of scale of dealing with large brokers created a strong tendency for firms to rely on bigger middlemen. When Venetian merchants moved inland from Alexandria to Cairo in 1552, with the reviving trade in pepper, "the move was motivated by the desire to dispense with intermediaries, the Jewish wholesalers and traders of Cairo" whom Braudel describes as "opulent rivals" of the Venetians. "In fact European merchants were usually *obliged to work in collaboration with them.*"[46] About Calicut the traveler Varthema wrote, "The merchants always sell by the hands. . . of the broker."[47] In Bengal textiles in the early eighteenth century, the total number of merchants dealing with the English East India Company varied from twenty to forty, and they were "certain to be men of substance."[48] The EIC's Bengal associates Khemchand and Mathuradas who dominated the commerce of Balasore and Hugli at the end of the seventeenth century in turn were said to have the backing of powerful financiers in Dhaka, "men of very great Estates[,] moneyed men."[49] In the palm oil trade, trade goods would be "advanced to brokers by European traders; brokers would then use these goods to purchase oil in the interior markets."[50] "[T]he brokers of West Africa cut impressive figures. . . the leading figures of the trade made huge sums from their skills in transporting large volumes smoothly and efficiently to the coast."[51] And Lynn notes, "The capital required to enter the oil trade was too great for small-scale traders effectively to challenge the existing oligarchy of brokers."[52] Economies of scale in transport especially gave large-scale African brokers "considerable advantage vis-à-vis smaller-scale ones." A Rallis Brothers handbook dated 1888 states that the company used to buy rice in India "from Mussulman dealers, but as their means are small it was difficult in advancing markets to obtain delivery of our purchases, and it often happened that we were unable to complete our shipping arrangements." The solution was to "buy only from a rich native merchant, *who makes advances in the interior*, and can secure large quantities at a time."[53] Here the cost of financing was shifted to the broker, in a move similar to Volkart Brothers' use of so-called "guarantee brokers" to finance purchases of raw cotton in Bombay's up-country markets.[54] In the Nigerian groundnut trade the "Syrian" Saul Raccah was the epitome of this layer of capital. In the early 1950s he was UAC's largest single contractor. "In 1954 UAC decided to end its contract with him because he had been using the £1.25m. advanced to him to buy in competition with its other buyers."[55] This must refer to Raccah buying a substantial part of the Kano groundnut crop on his own account, using capital advanced by Unilever. Shenton tells us that throughout the 1930s Raccah had "made steadily increasing inroads into the European firms' groundnut tonnage."[56] When the Syrians attempted to "bypass the European firms altogether by trading directly to Europe," the latter tried to have the colonial state abolish the native produce market in which indigenous traders sold groundnuts to the Syrians.[57] The whole period from the Depression to the Second World War, Shenton tells us, was "dominated by the attack of the more or less united European firms on the Syrian and African middlemen." Indeed, the "tenacious existence of these middlemen necessitated the expensive expansion of the firms' outstations, and ensured that the United Africa Company... could not establish commercial hegemony."[58]

One is dealing here, in competition of this sort, with a process of *combined accumulation* where "lead firms" and contractors *shared* the surplus-value extracted from peasant households[59] because *both* contributed to the exploitation of the latter. It would be wrong to see the bigger brokers as merely passive agents of what Fieldhouse has called "large-scale foreign merchant capital."[60] In some ways this "sharing" resembles the joint-venture agreements that became a favorite medium for the expansion of foreign manufacturing firms into markets like Brazil and India after the Second World War. The difference, of course, is that substantial brokers were also actual competitors, so that the relationship was fraught with tension and contracts could be terminated and then restarted just as easily. What the ubiquity of the broker reflected both in China and in India was the entrenched position of indigenous merchant capitals that were often very substantial indeed. As one British firm explained, "in the early days we (Peirce Leslie & Co.) did business with large and wealthy dealers." "Those were the days of the big merchants *who had complete control of the market*."[61] Yang Feng, Jardine Matheson's Shaghai comprador in the 1850s, was "immensely wealthy."[62] So were the various Indian merchant communities that sustained Britain's imperial grip over India and helped finance British expansion in the country.[63]

Having said this, it's important to bear in mind that there were numerous markets dominated by a mass of smaller capitals. Thus, in Santos, a major wholesale market for Brazilian coffee, "some 150 local brokers handled coffee, which strengthened their hold on trade."[64] In Lebanon, a mass of middlemen acted as brokers for the Beirut export houses, themselves as numerous as seventy-three in the years between 1904 and 1910. Lebanese brokers obtained credit from the banks in Beirut which they recycled into loans and advance payments, working as independent intermediaries between households engaged in cocoon production and the spinning mills and trading houses.[65] And in Egypt, where Greek middlemen likewise borrowed from the urban banks to re-lend to cotton growers at much higher rates, the Greek consul in Alexandria could describe them in 1913 as a "numerous and prospering class of Greeks... in the interior of Egypt," who made forward contracts for cotton to be able to "sell it to the large export houses with branches in the interior or in Alexandria after it had been ginned."[66]

"CHAINS" IN THE PRODUCE TRADES

H. J. R. Rawlings, the manager in charge of Holts' produce trade in Liverpool, described the advance system as "financing the marketing of the crop in the hope of getting a substantial proportion of tied customers and being able to buy at a rather lower price than they (the exporting houses) would have to pay" if all the produce were free produce.[67] Fieldhouse calls the system "one of the many devices used by UAC and virtually all the other foreign trading companies *as an essential means of maximizing their purchases of export produce.*"[68] Competition in most areas was fierce and all firms were anxious to keep up their purchases to retain market share. As one managing director responsible for the produce side of UAC's business wrote, "we must at all costs maintain our turnover."[69] Advances were thus integral to the way big commercial firms managed their investments to ward off competitors. As early as 1670 the English Factory in Surat, hard pressed for cash, had borrowed very large sums of money because of "the largeness of the Investments in all places *which must of necessity be supplied with cash to keep the weavers from falling off to other merchants.*"[70]

Marx encountered the advance system in its simplest form when he allowed for the theoretical possibility that the advances disbursed by the Bengal Opium Department to the growers of poppy it signed contracts with embodied a circulation of *capital.*[71] The theory of commercial capitalism developed in this book depends to some degree on extending this conception to the numerous trades and businesses where advances were used on a regular basis. The case Marx referred to (in passing, of course) was fairly simple in the sense that essentially it involved only three parties, (1) the government, (2) the cultivators, and (3) the opium merchants and dealers at the "sales" in Calcutta. The cultivators mostly came from peasant castes traditionally associated with labor-intensive cash crops like tobacco and opium along a vast tract in present-day eastern Uttar Pradesh and Bihar,[72] and were described as cultivating opium "at a great loss to themselves"[73] and "only for the sake of the advance."[74] In most markets, however, capital circulated through more complex chains that bound a whole battery of mercantile interests at very different levels of the commercial system. None of these chains or "trading machines" was like any other, as the following rapid survey of examples shows. It would be easiest to arrange them by moving consistently east, starting with the Atlantic seaboard of the US, the states of Mississippi and Louisiana which had well over one hundred thousand slaves in the early nineteenth century.

The articulated or chain-like structure of circulation under commercial capitalism can be viewed in at least two ways, first, in terms of the *internal complexity* of the "trading machines," how compressed or distended the chains were and their financial arrangements, and then also as vast *conglomerations of commercial interests* which, on a global scale, is essentially what commercial capital had come to signify by the nineteenth century. Thus in the cotton economy of the US South, "[c]ontemporary estimates were that the shippers, insurers, bankers, and merchants of New York received forty cents of every dollar spent in the cotton market."[75] New York's highly capitalized banks were able to offer "longer credit on better terms to those interested in buying cotton."[76] In the winter months, "[a]s the crop came to market in New Orleans, cotton merchants—who were often agents of merchant banks based in New York or Liverpool (Brown Brothers, Barings, N. M. Rothschild and Sons) ... provided advances against its eventual sale. In return for lending the factors (and thus the planters) money ... these cotton merchants and their merchant-banker backers received the right to sell (the crop) on a consignment basis." "The credit they offered generally took the form of a sight draft typically payable in New York or Liverpool sixty days after presentation." "In order to limit their risk, merchant bankers generally tried to limit the amount they advanced to three-quarters or so" of the expected value of the cotton.[77] American importers were able to buy sterling debt to pay for European imports once the sterling bills of exchange were sold into the interregional or international money market,[78] and so on, to illustrate the point about diverse commercial interests being "conglomerated" in the movement of circulation. And of course, *all* of these commercial interests were bound up with the desired perpetuation of slave labor.[79]

Samuel Smith, a Liverpool merchant whose firm would later become the biggest of the city's cotton brokers, has left a concise description of the cotton chain as it operated during the boom in Western India in the early 1860s. In letters published as *The Cotton Trade of India*, he mapped out four very different levels of a trading hierarchy ("the machinery of the cotton trade," as he called it) that extended from the villages in the cotton districts to large towns in the interior and from there to Bombay. They were (1) the petty village dealers or "small capitalists" who made advances to the growers at the time of sowing, (2) the "wealthier dealers in the large interior towns," wholesale dealers, who financed a major share of those advances and also, "very frequently," "simply acted as agents" for the Bombay merchants, (3) the "wealthy native merchants of Bombay" with whom those large dealers in turn signed contracts that gave them advances ranging from 25 to 50 percent of anticipated value, and finally, (4) the export firms or "shippers to England" with whom "the native merchants of Bombay have been in the habit of making large contracts," "though in this latter case it is not the custom to give advances."[80] The forward contracts between the Indian merchant and the foreign houses agreed on deliveries "at such a price as to reimburse him for his risk in advancing, pay the cost of transport, and leave him a fair profit."[81] Quality was a major problem in cotton but Smith was skeptical about arguments for the "introduction of European agency into the interior," that is, for export firms integrating vertically, and strongly underscored the lower transaction costs of dealing with "native dealers." "This is a business which can never suit a European house in Bombay," since it would have to "make separate agreements with some thousands of cultivators, and be willing to lie out of £50,000 or so, at present prices, for several months."[82] All the same, in the decades that followed European exporters did find solutions to these problems and had even driven the bigger Indian merchants out of the top end of the trade by 1875.[83]

Elsewhere in India, the capital invested in indigo was largely borrowed capital,[84] and it has been possible to argue that indigo planters simply "acted as middlemen between the cultivators and the agency and business houses in Calcutta."[85] The planters were essentially "up-country merchants supported by advances from the Calcutta agency houses."[86] In Farrukhabad in the North-Western Provinces where by 1860 some fifty different indigo concerns ran *ca*.150 factories, each supplied by twenty-five to thirty villages,[87] it was said that "indigo is made at factories from the plant purchased from landlords, who contract with the ryots."[88] In Lower Bengal the regime was more direct, in the sense that households grew indigo under contract to the factory against advances that usually amounted to two rupees for every third of an acre. Benoy Chowdhury suggested that planters preferred this system (called *ryoti*) because it was more profitable than using hired labor, since it essentially "involved an unpaid labour process."[89] As one planter put it, "the natives will not value the labor of themselves and families at anything while working for themselves."[90] Peasant family labor was the productive base of most of the produce trades, and its *subsumption into commercial capital* through the channels of circulation described here involved the appropriation of vast amounts of unpaid family labor. Cultivators had to sign a "properly stamped contract" at the time of the indigo advances, balances deliberately were never settled (doing so "would be tantamount to closing the factory," as one planter told an official enquiry)[91] and supervision was so intense it was described as "harassing and vexatious." "They say that they are required again and again to plough, to crush the clods, to remove stalks, to smooth the ground, to sow at the precise moment which the planter may dictate, until neither their time nor their labour can be called their own."[92] *Macaulay looked upon the indigo contracts as "of the same kind as one between a capitalist and a worker."*[93] The dye went through a succession of boom/slump cycles in the course of the nineteenth century, but in the 1870s when there was spectacular growth, one estimate put the repatriation of funds from north Bihar "at one million pounds sterling per annum."[94]

Jute was completely different, an "intensely competitive" market with a "profusion of intermediaries."[95] The Bengal jute industry was almost completely dominated by British capital.[96] On the commercial side, the biggest merchants in wholesale centers such as Narayangunj and Dhaka were European or Armenian, and both trade and manufacture had a plethora of trade associations of which some overtly excluded non-Europeans.[97] Jute was a highly organized industry, but also a perfect illustration of the integration of petty commodity producers into circulation chains where the coercion of the market had less to do with the debt devices typical of opium, cotton, and indigo and more with the more general state of dispossession of India's small peasantry. Jute was grown on minuscule holdings; by the 1930s more than three-quarters of rural families in the jute belt possessed less than two acres of land.[98] Krishna Bharadwaj calculated that jute was "particularly favoured by the very small farms of under 1.25 acres," since it absorbed a large amount of labor per acre and yielded a higher gross revenue per acre as well.[99] As if to reflect this fragmentation, circulation up the chain started with a mass of petty traders called *farias* or *paikars* who, in eastern Bengal, went about in small boats collecting small batches of raw jute which were then centralized at one of the bigger villages where the *bepari's* or merchant's boat was anchored.[100] "This smaller man (the *faria* or *paikar*) supplies the bigger *bepari* who collects in larger quantities and takes it to bigger centres," G. Morgan told the Royal Commission on Agriculture in the mid-1920s.[101] Morgan was proprietor of Morgan, Walker & Co., a firm of Calcutta jute brokers, and had been active in the trade for over forty years.[102] His oral testimony that the petty trader "buys the stuff outright" suggests that no advances were involved in jute.[103] The bigger traders (*beparis*) who collected from the *farias* then passed the raw jute either to up-country balers or to the big wholesale brokers/commission agents called *aratdars*, depending on whose capital financed their purchases.[104] (In the wholesale or "secondary" markets and in Calcutta "virtually all *aratdars* were Marwaris.")[105] The pricing of the jute was done by the big jute brokers in the import sheds of the balers before it was weighed, sorted into grades, baled, and shipped to Calcutta.[106] Up-country balers would sell their share of the half-pressed jute to the mills in Calcutta either through brokers such as Morgan, Walker & Co. (there were "about twenty" European jute brokers in the 1920s)[107] or directly through their own offices.[108] Of the 5.5 million bales of jute consumed by the mills, a little over half (three million bales) were sold directly by the "big European balers" such as Steels and Ralli Brothers, and the rest sold through the broking firms gathered in the Calcutta Jute Dealers' Association.[109] At the factory gate the mark-up on unit cost (what the cultivator received) was generally around 25 percent.[110] Despite this, it was generally thought that the way jute was traded "kept raw jute cheap."[111] The key to profitability both in Calcutta and Dundee "was to buy raw jute at as low a price as possible."[112] The sharp reduction in gross money income from rice and jute in the main jute-growing districts during the crash of the early 1930s triggered massive transfers of land through much of Bengal, leaving a land-poor peasantry in an even worse state of dispossession.[113]

Finally, briefly, in Cochinchina where the production of rice expanded from forty thousand tons in the late 1870s to 3,360,000 tons in the late 1920s,[114] the rice trade is a good example of the dense conglomeration of commercial interests that characterized the produce trades of the late nineteenth and early twentieth centuries. A powerful syndicate of paddy merchants at Cholon,[115] which had eighty members in 1930,[116] exerted a virtual monopoly over a massive wholesale trade, acting as the sole middlemen between the paddy growers and the milling and exporting firms. They employed agents who went from village to village in their boats, "gathering in sacks of rice and draining the harvest to the town." "Except for its actual growing, the collecting, husking, and exportation of rice is in Chinese hands," wrote a young American scholar in the 1930s.[117] Chinese merchants dominated every aspect of the rice trade.[118] In particular, the French were simply "unable to gain a foothold in the wholesaling of rice."[119] The rice millers, also Chinese, unlike in Burma where Europeans dominated the milling industry and financed the wholesale trade,[120] were a distinct layer of capital from the Cholon paddy merchants and were largely financed by the exporters through forward contracts.[121] The biggest mills could process five hundred to one thousand tons a day but competition was intense.[122] Finally, there were the Saigon-based export firms, both French and Chinese, who in turn were supported by the powerful French banking interests that financed the colony's export trade, the giant Banque de l'Indochine not the least of those. (There was a saying in Cochinchina—"Cholon belongs to the Banque de l'Indochine through the intermediary of the Chinese.")[123] In 1930, "some forty Chinese trading houses and eleven French concerns controlled more than 80 percent of exports."[124] Saigon itself, one of the world's biggest harbors for rice exports, was the only Indochinese port accessible to modern ships.

VELOCITIES OF CIRCULATION

The velocity of circulation of capital was a major determinant of the profitability of commercial capitals. Maxine Berg has even argued, "profits in the pre-industrial economy were determined by the velocity of circulating capital. Capital was accumulated by reducing the duration that stocks of goods were tied up between stages of the production process and marketing."[125] Or again, "Just as circulating capital dominated capital formation, so the greatest gains in productivity were to be had by cutting down the time of circulation, or, in other words, increasing the velocity of circulating capital."[126] Thus velocity was already an imperative when Turgot wrote his *Reflections* in the middle of the eighteenth century. He says there, "the Entrepreneur has the greatest possible interest in getting his capital returned to him very quickly."[127] And almost a century earlier, in 1681, William Freeman, a London merchant involved in sugar and slave trading, would aver, "a quick return is the life of trade."[128]

In the Baltic grain trade, which was dominated by the Amsterdam grain merchants, "money could be used three or even four times in one season,"[129] but this was certainly exceptional. Most velocities in international trade were much longer. Michel Balard has calculated the average turnover in the trade between Genoese capital and Byzantine markets at 12.3 months.[130] The Venetian *mude* (voyages) to Syria to fetch bulk bales of cotton involved a round trip of six months and "represented the fastest available return on merchant capital," according to Braudel.[131] The *mude*, which initially meant the periods prescribed for loading, were organized to encourage a more efficient use of ships. The Senate fixed terminal loading dates to force merchants to end their haggling and keep the ships moving. "Quicker turnaround meant not only more efficient use of shipping, but also more efficient use of merchants' capital. The shipper benefitted not only from cheaper freight rates but from quicker turnover of his mercantile investment."[132] In the East India trade, advances for cotton piece goods could begin nine or ten months before the cloth would be received by the Company's servants,[133] while the actual investment orders that also fixed weavers' wages preceded delivery by some two years.[134] Of course, these temporalities of capital were revolutionized in the third quarter of the nineteenth century with the expansion of railways, steam shipping, and new communication technologies, but the more efficient organization of the big firms would in any case have entailed a tendency to compress turnover times. Thus, the wealthy merchant houses that dominated Glasgow's tobacco trade in the eighteenth century were keen "to achieve rapid turnover of capital,"[135] and did so as well, at both ends of the circuit of their commercial capitals. By using the store system to "acquire as much tobacco in advance as was necessary," they could cut down the turnaround time of incoming vessels and save on freight costs, thus freighting ships in the shortest possible time,[136] *and* "[b]ecause the Glasgow firms actually owned the cargoes they imported they could dispose of it in huge sales to the French buyers in Scotland," again "turning over capital quickly by selling tobacco rapidly in bulk to European customers."[137] Probably reflecting both sorts of influences (speed of transport and size of firm), the average duration of the UAC's advances to its middlemen in West Africa "ranged from a minimum of ten days for Gold Coast cocoa to twenty-eight days for Nigerian palm kernels." "In 1947/8," Fieldhouse writes, "the largest amount advanced to Africans was £1.5m., which in fact *turned round several times* during the course of a single season."[138] This practice goes back to the nineteenth century, one British merchant telling parliament, "The moment the produce comes to hand we make them a remittance, so that they turn it over as often as possible in the course of a year."[139]

Velocities of circulation were affected by both transport and communication technologies. The Russian economist Lyashchenko described banks and railways as "instruments of capitalist trade turnover" and argued that "more rapid turnover by capitalist commercial methods" such as the discounting of invoices for goods in transit had allowed a mass of smaller capitals to enter the Russian grain trade in a big way.[140] "The colossal expansion of means of communication—ocean-going steamships, railways, electric telegraphs, the Suez canal—has genuinely established the world market for the first time," wrote Engels (with some exaggeration!) in a note to volume three of *Capital*.[141] Or again, "The main means of cutting circulation time has been improved communications," he writes in another of his addenda to volume three; "... the whole earth has been girded by telegraph cables. It was the Suez canal that really opened the Far East and Australia to the steamer"; "The turnover time of world trade as a whole has been reduced to the same extent (from months to weeks, JB), and the efficacy of the capital involved in it has been increased two or three times and more."[142] The "turnover time of world trade" was of course a reference to the velocity of circulation of commercial capitals. Marx was perfectly aware of these "material" influences, of the way use-value as such could acquire economic significance. In the *Grundrisse*, of the two examples he gives of this "form-determining" role of use-value, one relates to the durability of machines, since this purely physical aspect affects the turnover time of the total capital; the other, interestingly, concerns the remoteness of markets which, given the conditions of transport, involve a slower turnover, "as e.g. capitals working in England for the East India market return more slowly than those working for nearer foreign markets or for the domestic market."[143] Elsewhere he writes about "[c]ircumstances that shorten the average turnover of commercial capital, such as the development of the means of transport."[144] Moreover, with the expansion of the market under capitalism, he suggested, "not only does the mass of commercial capital grow, but so too does that of all the *capital invested in circulation*, e.g. in shipping, railways, telegraphs, etc."[145]

Banking was the other great lubricator of velocity. The link was clearly seen by Marx when he implied that the "development of the credit system" helped sustain a more rapid turnover of commercial capital.[146] The discounting of bills of exchange played a major role here because it financed both larger volumes of trade and a greater fluidity of circulation.[147] The speculation in bills of exchange that was rampant in the 1840s was at least partly fueled by the decision of the Bank of England's banking department to enter the discount market in a big way. Thus, "Bank discounts rose from £2 million to £12 million between the autumn of 1844 and the spring of 1846."[148] J. W. Gilbart's *The History and Principles of Banking* (1834) had already forewarned the dangers here. "Trade and speculation are in some cases so nearly allied," Gilbart wrote, "that it is impossible to say at what precise point trade ends and speculation begins ... Wherever there are banks, capital is more readily obtained, and at a cheaper rate. The cheapness of capital gives facilities to speculation...."[149] A secret committee of the House of Lords that sat to investigate the causes of the commercial crisis of 1847 laid a major part of the blame for the crisis on "over-trading" in the East India trade. The mechanism involved here was described in some detail by the committee, and a report in the *Manchester Guardian* quoted by Marx in *Capital* was clearly privy to this finding years before the report was officially published. About the big firms in the India trade the news report said:

> Houses in India, who had credit to pass their bills, were purchasers of sugar, indigo, silk, or cotton—not because the prices advised from London by the last overland mail promised a profit on the prices current in India, but because former drafts upon the London house would soon fall due, and must be provided for. What way so simple as to purchase a cargo of sugar, pay for it in bills upon the London house at ten months' date, transmit the shipping documents by the overland mail; and, in less than two months, the goods on the high seas, or perhaps not yet passed the mouth of the Hoogly, were pawned in Lombard Street—putting the London house in funds eight months before the drafts against those goods fell due. And all this went on without interruption or difficulty, as long as bill-brokers had abundance of money "at call," to advance on bills of lading and dock warrants, and to discount, without limit, the bills of India houses drawn upon the eminent firms in Mincing Lane.[130]

Advances against bills of lading became common practice in the Atlantic and East India trades by the 1840s, and Engels himself thought that the kind of "speculation" they allowed for actually continued until the opening of the Suez Canal and the expansion of telegraph networks enabled information to travel *substantially* faster than goods and made the abuse of credit involved in the use of long-dated bills impossible. As bills of lading became tradeable items, "cargoes themselves might pass 'virtually' through many hands between their departure," say, from New Orleans and their arrival at a Lancashire mill.[151] With steamships and telegraph connections, "[t]he process of buying and selling could be repeated many more times in a year."[152] The new commercial methods that came into vogue during the 1860s revolved essentially around a more rapid velocity of circulation. "Ralli & Co," writes Milne, "spent around £1,000 a year on telegraph messages to the East in the mid-1860s" and also "devised a code for use by all its branches and agencies, so that the problem of corrupted messages could be overcome."[153]

In his autobiography Dimitrios Vikelas described the dramatic changes that the new commercial methods of the late nineteenth century brought about in the fortunes of the Greek trading community. Explaining the decline of most of the major Greek merchant houses of London by the end of the nineteenth century, he wrote, "the most important reason [for] the disappearance of those merchant houses was the *change that occurred in trading itself.* Half a century before[,] the electric telegraph and the telephone [had not brought] the most distant countries in direct communication through instant understanding. The goods were loaded on sail vessels and months went by until they arrived [at] the port of consumption. In the meantime, the owners of the cargoes had enough time to speculate, by observing the fluctuation of the market. *At that time the merchants depended on their own capital* and on the credits of their correspondents; therefore, their transactions were very limited, but the dangers were also fewer than today, and moreover the merchants were more conservative. Today the growth of global trade has brought an increase of the number of banks; *the banks concentrate maximum capital, which has to be invested* (wherever it can be) ... That way the turnover of dealings increased immensely." "Today one could say that commerce aims mainly to the gain of a *small profit from big and rapid enterprises, which are continually repeated*. The few merchants who succeeded in applying the new system are still trading in a profitable way. The old Greek trade does not exist anymore and those old merchant houses, where new generations of merchants found work in succession, are now dissolving, causing national damage."[154]

FINAL REFLECTIONS

The "longue durée" of wholesale trade can easily be constructed as a chain of competitive struggles that ranged over much of the

Mediterranean and, later, of the entire globe—Venice against Genoa, Portugal against Venice, Holland against Portugal, England and France against Holland, and so on, and to some degree that history has been written in this way in one chapter of this book. But embedded within these *global* conflicts were smaller-scale confrontations or battles and numerous other sorts of capitalist competition. Of particular note, not highlighted here, was a vibrant pan-Asian trading system that began as early as the ninth century and survived down to the end of the sixteenth century and later. The Dutch were "astounded by their Gujarati rivals' capacity for competition" and admitted defeat in the Persian market.[155] The European companies were often alarmed by the sheer volume of indigo exports by Asian merchants to West Asian markets. Gujarati, Armenian, and Persian merchants dominated this trade.[156] Private British shipping at Calcutta faced "formidable competition" from Asian shipowners in the trade between Bengal and Surat.[157] Turkish merchants were the main buyers of Yemen's coffee, and at Mocha itself European merchants were not the most numerous or active traders in the eighteenth century.[158] And Aden had been the hub of a vast international trade *ca*.1400, going by the fact that its customs duties alone, on imports, ran consistently close to or above one million dinars in the final years of the fourteenth century and very early fifteenth![159] None of this has been mapped here, but the fact that it hasn't shouldn't obscure our vision of an international trading system that reached well beyond Europe.

What about China? Roy Bin Wong has argued, challengingly, that in contrast to Europe the Chinese state had no incentive to promote any sort of capitalism. "[The] opposition to what might have become a kind of commercial capitalism, had the government needed the merchants more and thus been supportive of them, does not mean that officials opposed markets and commerce more generally."[160] He also argues that "[i]ndustrial capitalism is not the necessary and obvious development out of commercial capitalism unless certain necessary technological changes occur."[161] For Europe itself he lists the possible ways in which commercial capitalism "mattered to the formation of industrial capitalism," mentioning among these the fact that the decision to shift to factory production of textiles was a decision made by commercial capitalists, and that commercial capitalism "developed ways of mobilizing capital" whose actual "concentration" was only achieved under industrial capitalism.[162] Finally, it was possible for rural industry to persist for centuries without generating the sort of "proto-industrialization dynamic" that saw whole industrial regions emerge in northern Europe.[163]

I read all this to mean that there is nothing inevitable about capitalism and that its emergence depends, crucially, not just on markets but on the state or at least a particular kind of state that sets out to encourage and bolster commercial expansion. Marx himself was quite clear that in the later middle ages both Venice and Genoa were ruled by powerful merchant interests. He referred to their merchants as "the most prominent people in those states" and described them as "subordinating the state more securely to themselves."[164] In other words, these were *medieval* states directly ruled by capitalist interests. The first modern territorial states, and, with them, the modern monarchies, emerged in the later fifteenth century,[165] and Engels in the "Supplement" describes Europe's trading companies as now having "greater nations" standing behind them. "Even Holland and Portugal, the smallest, were at least as big and powerful as Venice, the largest and strongest trading nation of the previous period."[166] Mehring (rather unlike Marx) described merchant capital as the "revolutionary force of the fourteenth, fifteenth and sixteenth centuries," and said, remarkably, "[r]evolutionary merchant capital *not only created modern absolutism* but also transformed the medieval classes of society."[167]

"Commercially organized capitalism" was characterized by the "sheer diversity and flexibility of its forms of production"[168] and by extreme versatility. Pearl fisheries,[169] hydraulic silk mills,[170] plantations,[171] shipping, real estate, textiles, tax farming[172]—there was practically no sector or type of investment that it did not invade, exploit, or monopolize. And as the example of Dubrovnik shows, merchants gravitated to the richest markets, hastening their development even further.[173] They were in the forefront of economic innovations, embodying a modernity which is best described as *purely capitalist*. Apart from bills of exchange and the other financial devices and modern ways of organizing business that were innovated in the later middle ages, the chief expression of this mercantile modernism was a minute knowledge of international markets. Branch organization was typical of the big Italian trading families, and a massive volume of commercial information was transmitted across those networks, going by the literally thousands or tens of thousands of letters that survive in various merchant archives.[174] The Greek merchant houses of the nineteenth century were, likewise, tight-knit family trading networks with high levels of vertical integration and branches throughout the Mediterranean and in England. What is striking in their case is the kind of tight integration between trade and shipping that was orchestrated by shipowners such as the Vaglianos and Embiricos.[175] In Odessa the Greek houses had agents living in the large centers where grain was collected, whereas Western merchants preferred to buy grain from middlemen (brokers) after its arrival in the port.[176] In the Bombay Presidency, Ralli Brothers began establishing purchasing agencies in the up-country cotton markets as early as the 1860s.[177] In Sind, where next to Volkart Brothers they were the biggest exporters of wheat, they had subagencies at the principal centers like Sukkur, Shikarpur, and Larkana.[178] In short, in its own way, Greek merchant capital belatedly captured a major share of both Ottoman and British trade thanks to business methods that were as efficient as any, in their own way.

Finally, patterns of economic domination bound up with the expansion of commercial capital were considerably wider than those of imperial control or straightforward colonialism. In fact, imperialism in the modern sense, that is, the division of the world in Hobsbawm's Age of Empire (1880–1914), marked a sharp *break* in the pattern defined by Britain's centrality in financial, trading, and shipping services. It reflected not the "anarchism of the bourgeoisie," as Hobsbawm called the liberalism of the nineteenth century[179] and the liberal-cosmopolitan order that British commerce had held in place, but the rapid emergence of "national economies" driven more by large-scale industry and "big business" than by trade per se.[180] "Imperialism" "was a novel term devised to describe a novel phenomenon."[181] This, if you like, is the point at which trade seriously began to be driven by industry in the sense in which Marx defined this dynamic, that is, as the "subordination of commercial to industrial capital." If the size of the world's merchant marine almost doubled between 1890 and 1914, whereas it had only risen from 10 to 16 million tons in 1840–1870,[182] during the apogee of British commercial expansion, the expansion of shipping now reflected the humongous demands of the new industrial capitals (American, German, and French as much, or more, than British).

As Engels drew closer to the end of his life in the 1890s (he died in 1895), oil, steel, and chemicals, not textiles, became the typical face of large-scale industry. In his addenda to volume three of *Capital*, Engels's sense of this new capitalist modernity was reflected in belated references to the surge of competition between "a whole series of competing industrial countries"[183] and to "gigantic" concentrations of capital in "cartels" and "trusts."[184] All this was new, anticipated but never witnessed by Marx. But the sense of capitalist novelty was of course also reflected in admiring references to the way submarine telegraph cables, steamers, and the completion of the Suez Canal had all dramatically compressed or accelerated the turnover of world trade. Between the writing of *Capital* and Engels's additions to the text a completely new world had emerged, defined by a much sharper sense of nationality, greater aggression in world politics, and a sense of living at new velocities.

The concentration of manufacturing capital had major implications for merchants. It allowed for the setting up of company sales offices and company-operated sales networks, and in the US by 1900 "the manufacturer was ascendant, the independent merchant in decline."[185] It also brought about new forms of retail capital in the shape of huge department stores that emerged in metropolises like Paris from the 1870s. Again, velocity of circulation was the driving imperative, with sales volumes running into many millions of francs or dollars and turned over more rapidly thanks to the lower margins that giant retailers were willing to accept.[186] In the "Convolutes" Walter Benjamin describes the department stores (*magasins de nouveautés*) as "temples consecrated to the religious intoxication of great cities," borrowing part of this striking expression from Baudelaire.[187] Advertising was common and extensive by the 1870s,[188] and increasingly linked to revolutionary new forms of energy such as electricity[189] which lighted up the shopping arcades and department stores. In the spheres where they survived in a substantial way, speed became an ever more essential part of the way commercial capitals had to operate. Thus in Zola's novel *Au Bonheur des Dames (The Ladies' Delight)* the central character Octave Mouret, owner of a vast department store of that name, explained to the banker Baron Hartmann that "the system of modern large-scale trading" and its "hugely increased power of accumulation" were based on a "continuous and rapid renewal of capital, which had to be converted into goods *as often as possible in a single year.*"[190]

The other thing Marx never lived to see was the expansion of French capitalism in Indochina, the *massive* concentration of French economic interests in rice, rubber, banking, and minerals that culminated in the stranglehold of a handful of banking groups by the 1920s.[191] To take an obvious example of this, from 1876 to 1914 the Banque de l'Indochine, "the financial arm of French imperialism in Asia," as its historian Marc Meuleau described it,[192] declared cumulative *net* profits of 107,311,000 gold francs on a paid-up capital of 12 million.[193] No British firm in India could have matched that scale and level of profitability, let alone the sheer concentration of capital implied in it. What was emerging in the late nineteenth century was an entirely new sort of capitalism, driven by modern industry but also bound up with more aggressive forms of expansion and

unprecedented degrees of vertical integration in industries like tobacco,[194] rubber, and oil, which dramatically reduced the dependence
of manufacturers on merchant capital.

The pattern of French domination in Indochina was more advanced than anything to be found in Britain's mercantile capitalism
in the late-Victorian decades. There was no British counterpart to
the French finance capital that dominated entire sectors of Indochina's economy. British capital's dependence on invisible earnings,
which was the hallmark of the largely commercial nature of British
capitalism, was also its crucial source of vulnerability once war disrupted the economic integration of the capitalist world and the worst
crisis capitalism had seen till then deepened the economic fragmentation and sense of chaos. The years from 1913 to 1937 saw a severe
decline in Britain's invisible income in real terms.[195] At the height of
the depression "[t]he classical Treasury model of the economy came
tumbling down in 1931," as the gold standard and free trade were
abandoned and City cosmopolitanism lay in ruins in the 1930s.[196]

APPENDIX: ISLAM AND CAPITALISM

The title of this essay is borrowed from the title of a famous book that the French Arabist Maxime Rodinson published in France in 1966. When Rodinson wrote *Islam and Capitalism*, the traumatic defeat of Nasser and the Arab states at the hands of Israel was still roughly a year away. But, as we know, that defeat was a major watershed both politically, precipitating the demise of Arab nationalism and the discrediting of the "secular" leaderships that touted it, and in a wider cultural sense because "the defeat" (as it came to be called) led to decades of bitter introspection and to the sustained if gradual expansion of a new political force throughout the Muslim world. What I shall do in this essay is start from the problematic that Rodinson grappled with in his seminal book, namely, whether, or, more correctly, in what sense, we can speak of capitalism in the Islamic world, and then expand the notion of capitalism to include the culture of modernity that Marx saw as central to what (to him in the *Communist Manifesto* at least) was still a new and revolutionary mode of production. The essay is thus divided into two rather distinct parts, the link between them being established by what I shall call "the indigenous form of capitalism" that characterized much of the Middle East at least till the economic revolution that swept through the Gulf in the 2000s.

Rodinson belonged to a generation when the largely formalist debates that dominated Marxism from the seventies had obviously made no special impact. Historians like Subhi Labib,[1] Halil Inalcik,[2] 'Abd al-'Aziz Duri,[3] Robert Mantran,[4] and Braudel[5] spoke of capitalism and capitalists in the Islamic world, since these seemed like the best way of characterizing the activity and economic structures connected with large-scale merchants and banking groups who were not discernibly different from their counterparts in medieval Italy. But

125

those of them who were familiar with the Arabic sources also knew that a notion of "capital" was frequently discussed both in the various schools of Islamic law and by writers like Ibn Khaldūn. *Al-māl* could of course have the generic meanings of "wealth," "property," "possessions," and so on but in the juristic discussions and numerous passages elsewhere it had the more correct meaning of a commodity or mass of commodities. By the tenth century the term *māliyya*, derived from it, came to mean "commercial exchange value," while the term *māl mutaqawwim* was a commodity whose exchange value was guaranteed by the law "against destruction, damage, or unauthorized appropriation. . . ."[6] Though *māl* by itself was often shorthand for capital (that is, for a sum of value earmarked for investment), *rās māl* was the proper term for "capital" and was frequently used in the plural to mean several distinct capitals (individual capital in Marx's sense), as when al-Wāqidī reports that the Qurayshi merchant Safwān b. Umayya complained that as long as Muhammad enforced his blockade of the coastal road to Gaza and forced the summer caravans to stay put in Mecca, "We are simply eating up our capitals (*na'kulu ru'ūs amwālna*)."[7] *Sāhib al-māl* usually meant "owner of capital," and *mutamawwil* was later the standard term for a capitalist. (In Ibn Khaldūn Rosenthal translates *mutamawwal* as "capital accumulation.") In a study published shortly before Rodinson's book appeared Labib could thus suggest that "The concept of 'capital' *is* used in medieval Islamic economic history. Ibn Khaldun has a detailed discussion of it," and he went on to say, "We shouldn't look for the first signs of the origins of capitalism in Europe or Egypt or among any specific group of merchants such as the Italians or the Karimi merchants. A mercantile estate (*eine Kaufmannschaft*) existed everywhere and consequently so did economic enterprises and profits."[8]

The question that Rodinson started with was to know if Islam conceived as a body of doctrine laid out in the Qur'an and the prophetic tradition (the *hadīth*) contained anything that either discouraged or militated against capitalist economic activity, and his answer was an emphatic "no." Rodinson saw the economic history of

Muslim-majority countries as characterized by what he called "the development of commercial capital in a clearly capitalistic direction" and argued, "Not only did the Muslim world know a capitalistic sector, but this sector was apparently the most extensive and highly developed in history before the sixteenth century."[9] In both sugar and textiles, for example, private capitalists could be found who employed wage-workers, often under supervision by the state.[10] I'm not aware of any detailed study of the textile industry comparable to Mohamed Ouerfelli's remarkable book on the medieval sugar industry,[11] but from this it is clear that Rodinson was less interested in pursuing any of these arguments in a more concrete, historical way, and was, as he himself noted, producing work of a "theoretical character."[12] The reason I make this point here is that he made no attempt to ask who the "private capitalists" were who invested in, say, the sugar refineries and textile factories of the Mamluk period (they were, in fact, overwhelmingly merchants, apart from the sultan, members of his family and the Mamluk amirs who were the quintessential power-élite),[13] and his one-line statement, "There was also a fairly extensive capitalist domestic industry," saw no further elaboration, although it was a crucial and interesting claim to advance.[14]

Elsewhere Rodinson wrote, "It is clear that the Koran in no way set out to modify the economic rules operating in the society in which it surfaced." "The Koran contains very few purely economic injunctions."[15] He went to great lengths to show that the sole exception to this, namely, the ban on usury, was widely circumvented both in the actual schools of law through the use of so-called "devices" and of course in practice. For example, interest-bearing loans were considered normal practice in the Ottoman Empire, and *fatwas* could always be obtained to give sanction to interest-bearing savings accounts. In the eleventh century, the legal scholar al-Tartūšī was alarmed that credit played such a major role in the commercial transactions in Alexandria.[16] But Rodinson went further and implied that the rationalism of the Qur'an and the "very special importance" ascribed by Muhammad to the individual[17] were both features that made Islam especially receptive to the pursuit and needs of business. It is striking that contracts of commercial exchange were the sole area of Islamic law where the hierarchies of sex, age, religion, and legal status gave way before an overriding equality grounded in "the capacity to reason soundly." Baber Johansen quotes Sarakhsī as saying, "In these contracts (that is, contracts of commercial exchange) all are equal."

Tijāra (trading activity) was essentially a means of valorizing capital. Sarakhsī was a leading exponent of the Hanafī school which was by far the most pragmatic and flexible in its approach to issues of business. For example, the Islamic equivalent of the *commenda* contract, called *mudāraba*, was justified by him in terms of its actual economic function. "Because people have a need for this contract," he writes. "For the owner of capital may not find his way to profitable trading activity, and the person who can find his way to such activity may not have the capital. And profit cannot be obtained except by means of both of these, that is, capital and trading activity."[18] The agent in such contracts had nearly unrestricted flexibility in Hanafī law, possibly reflecting commercial practices in Iraq where Abu Hanīfa, the founding jurist of this school, had been a cloth merchant. Since, as Zubaida says, "the trading middle classes of the Muslim [world] were also the major bearers of Islamic religious learning [and] it was from their ranks that the ulema and Qadis were recruited," it was always possible for the law to be shaped to accommodate the needs of merchants. Zubaida goes so far as to claim that "in the scriptures and traditions of Islam trade is conceived of as a desirable and virtuous activity," and there are certainly enough proof-texts in the Qur'an to support this view.[19] Commerce was one of four forms of "earning" (*al-kasb*), hence covered by the verse (2:267) Sarakhsī cited in connection with it, "Spend [give in charity] out of the good things you have earned" (*anfiqū min tayyibāti mā kasabtum*). Shaybānī, another jurist of the Hanafī school, starts his treatise *Kitāb al-Kasb* with the assertion: "seeking to earn is an obligation for every Muslim, just as seeking knowledge is an obligation."[20] The expression "pious

bourgeoisie" which Zubaida uses to characterize this urban milieu
with its close links between the merchants and the religious scholars
captures an important aspect of the way an early form of capitalism
was legitimized in the wider reaches of Islam's civil society.

The political economy that frames much of this history can be
described as a symbiosis between tributary Muslim states and commercial capital. Ibn Khaldūn saw this very clearly when in the
Muqaddimah he wrote: "wealth as a rule comes from their business
and commercial activities," referring to political regimes throughout the history of Islam down to his time. The kind of commerce he
had in mind was substantial, large-scale, capitalist trade. He says in
the *Muqaddimah*, "Commerce means the attempt to earn a living by
expanding your capital (*bi tanmīyat al-mal*) and the extent by which
capital is increased is called profit." Labor, he wrote, "is the essential basis of all profit and accumulation of capital." Taking both ideas together it followed that the most prosperous or developed states
were those with abundant supplies of labor available to those who
could make commercial use of it. "A large civilization yields large
profits because of the large amount of (available) labor, which is
the cause of (profit)."[21] Lacoste is therefore not far off the mark in
regarding Ibn Khaldūn as a forerunner of historical materialism.[22]
Indeed, he saw himself choosing a "remarkable and original method" in writing his work and described history as "information about
human social organization."[23] To him the most developed states (in
Europe, the Far East, and Islam) were those where capital had access to large reserves of labor and which, crucially, did not treat the
owners of capital unjustly. When they did, they triggered a dynamic
that usually led to their own downfall. Ibn Khaldūn notes in passing
that state officials and rulers were usually jealous of the capitalists
(*al-mutamawwil*),[24] implying that there was always a strong tempta-
tion to overtax the commercial sector or even move in and monopolize some leading sector, as the Mamluk Sultan Barsbay did with the
Egyptian sugar industry.[25]

Within the countries of Islam, large-scale commerce was driven by the concentration of demand in major metropolitan markets that also happened to be the seat of government and the base of some major ruling dynasty. In the Abbāsid period Baghdad epitomized a market of this sort and was unrivaled anywhere in the world for the sheer concentration of wealth and commercial activity. The estimate of one contemporary, Hilāl al-Sābi, that Baghdad in the later ninth century had an upper class (al-khassa) of some fifty thousand individuals is a rough measure of the scale of domestic demand.[26] The fragmentation of the caliphate that came with the decline of the Abbāsids served, if anything, to sustain the vibrancy of metropolitan markets by dispersing political power across a wider swathe of the Islamic world, so that capitals like Córdoba, Fez, Tunis, Kairouan, Cairo, and so on replicated the pattern of substantial concentrations of market demand on a less outsized but still important scale. Fez and Tunis both had more than 100,000 inhabitants, Cairo was considerably bigger (200,000 to 250,000 in 1348 when Paris and London were 80,000 and 60,000 respectively),[27] and Istanbul with 700,000 inhabitants in the sixteenth century was on Braudel's description "by far the largest European city" at the time.[28] Ibn Khaldūn who traveled extensively between most of these major centers saw them driving the business life of the Islamic world. But the great geographies that were written between the ninth and early thirteenth centuries show that the true heart of the system lay at a lower level, in smaller, commercially active centers like Basra, Nishapur, Bahnasā, Mahdia, Sfax, Palermo, and Almería and the vibrant networks they formed. They were the true backbone of the economy. Both state and private capital invested majorly in the commercial infrastructures known as *funduqs* (more correctly, *fanādiq*), *khans*, *qaysariyyas*, or *wikālas*, solid stone buildings that were square or oblong and opened on to the street "by means of a single, often monumental gate"[29] or (in the case of *qaysariyyas*) as many as six to eight gates. Cities like Cairo in the sixteenth century were dense concentrations of commercial capital,[30] and the *wikālas* and *khans* were where the bulk of wholesale trade took place, commercial establishments that Labib could even describe as "virtual stock exchanges."[31] According to Evliya Çelebi, Bulaq, the city's port area, had over seventy khans ca.1672.[32] One of the more substantial establishments of this sort in Basra was a reconverted seventh-century palace built by Zubayr b. al-'Awwam, one of the Companions of the Prophet. When al-Mas'ūdī visited Basra in 943, this structure teemed with merchants, bankers (arbāb al-amwāl), and maritime businesses.[33] In the Safarnama, written a century later, Nasir Khusraw claims that merchants residing temporarily in Basra would use only bankers' bills (khatt siraf).[34] In Nishapur, a major textile center, Ibn Hauqal states that the traders with "large masses of commodities and substantial capitals" (ahl al-badā'i' al-kibār wa al-amwāl al-ghizār) dominated the bigger funduqs and khans, leaving the more modest ones to a smaller scale of business. Here, in the less opulent commercial complexes there was no separation between trade and production, since he refers to "shops crammed with artisans."[35] In Bahnasā in Middle Egypt, another major textile town, al-Idrīsī tells us that no woolen or cotton fabrics were manufactured without printing the name of the factory (tiraz) on them.[36] Mahdia, in the Sahel, manufactured finely worked textiles that said "Made in Mahdia" which were widely exported since the workmanship was of such a high standard.[37] The port itself attracted merchant shipping from all parts of the Mediterranean. In Almería, according to al-Idrīsī, when the Almoravids still controlled those parts of Spain, a high-quality silk industry contained eight hundred looms (turuz, a term that is habitually mistranslated as "workshops" when it refers to silk)[38] and it's worth comparing that figure with the twelve hundred to two thousand silk looms that Venice was known to have at the end of the fifteenth century and in the early sixteenth.[39] Examples and descriptions of this sort could be multiplied almost indefinitely if one consulted a wider range of sources than I have, but they seem quite enough to me to suggest that the Islamic world had its own forms of commercial capitalism throughout the centuries that saw the emergence and expansion of capitalism in Venice, Genoa, and Florence.

So why did this largely commercial, pre-modern or medieval form of capitalism that formed such a large part of the structure of the traditional economy throughout the Middle East down to the final years of the Ottoman Empire (and in Iran, even later) not evolve into a modern capitalist economy? Assuming it makes sense to frame historical questions in this teleological way, of the various explanations advanced, two seem particularly appealing. Malise Ruthven has argued that the absence of the Roman-law concept of "legal personality," itself bound up with "the uncompromising individualism of the Shari'a," prevented any wider corporate solidarity from emerging in the merchant classes. "Islamic law did not recognize cities as such, nor did it admit corporate bodies." By contrast, "in the West the Church, the 'mystical body' of Christ which alone guaranteed salvation, became the archetype in law of a whole raft of secular corporations that succeeded it during the early modern period. The mystic qualities of fictional personhood originating in the Body of Christ were eventually devolved to joint stock companies and public corporations with tradable shares."[40] Translating this into my terms, the non-development of capitalism was less about a failure to emerge than about the failure to acquire a more collective, corporate form that could express and contribute to the solidarity of a class. Capitalists certainly existed in the Muslim world, but they failed to form the kind of collective solidarity implied in the notion of a "class." In volume three of *Capital* Marx had described Venice and Genoa as urban republics where the merchants "subordinated the state more securely to themselves," and implicit in some combination of Ruthven's argument with my own is the further crucial thesis that this singularly failed to happen anywhere in the Islamic world. This ties in with a second, and, to my mind, even more self-evident, explanation, which is the one Mielants proposes in his book, namely, that the failure of commercial capitalism in the Islamic world was essentially a failure of mercantilism.[41] It is a striking fact that there was never any Islamic counterpart of the West's violent mercantilist expansion. Again, the decisive factor here is the very different ways in which commercial capital and the state were bound to each other. The powerful state backing that English merchants received from the monarchy, what Brenner calls the "Crown-company partnership,"[42] had absolutely no equivalent among the numerous dynasties that, like the Ottomans, were willing to encourage trade but unwilling (or incapable) of the kind of aggressive expansion that the Portuguese monarchy unleashed in the opening years of the sixteenth century. Of course, once the European powers embarked on their expansion into Asian markets, Islamic commercial networks were a prime target across the whole region. The violence with which the Portuguese attacked and dismantled those networks was lucidly documented by the Kerala historian Zainuddin in a late-sixteenth century history called *Tuhfat al-Mujāhidīn*.

If, as Braudel claims, "Capitalism only triumphs when it becomes identified with the state, when it *is* the state,"[43] then the externality of the state to capital remained the chief limitation on Islamic capitalism and its transformative potential. Seen against the background of Europe's expansion and its own convulsive capitalist transformation, the sense of stagnation this began to generate was evident well before the Syrian journalist 'Abd al-Rahman al-Kawākibi wrote *The Nature of Despotism (Tabā'i' al-istibdād)* at the end of the nineteenth century, shortly before he was murdered by poisoning at the age of forty-seven. As early as 1867, Khayr al-Din al-Tunisi had published a tract called *Straightest Path to Know the Condition of States* in which he voiced strong opposition to the idea that "all acts and institutions of non-Muslims should be avoided."[44] Indeed, Kurzman has even claimed, "Support of capitalism was the dominant economic theme in the modernist Islamic movement. Khayr al-Din praised societies in which "the circulation of capital is expanded, profits increase accordingly, and wealth is put into the hands of the most proficient ... The modernist movement was bankrolled in part by industrialists and traders promoting international economic linkages."[45] But added to this entirely progressive sense of *having* to catch up with the West was the more profound sense of resentment that flowed from the forced marginalization of indigenous capital in those parts of the Ottoman world where, as in Egypt, "the commercial sector was wrested from indigenous hands"[46] by a combination of French and Syrian-Christian commercial interests, and French capital began to lobby for an invasion of Egypt toward the end of the eighteenth century. To say nothing of the deeper sense of degradation that was bound up with the colonization of the Arab Middle East, starting with France's invasion of Algeria and its large-scale dispossessions of tribal land, influx of settlers, banning of Arabic in government schools, and so on.

"The Islamic economic system should be such that he [the capitalist] is not permitted to accumulate wealth." So said Ali Shari'ati in a little known tract called *Islam's Class Bias*, published posthumously in 1980 and apparently his last work.[47] Shari'ati, of course, was seen by most sectors of the Iranian Left as the true ideologue of the revolution that toppled Muhammad Reza Shah in 1979, even though his own anti-clericalism conflicted sharply with the theocracy that Khomeini successfully instituted. But if Shari'ati's Alavi Shi'ism was an ideology radically opposed to capitalism, for all sectors of the religious Right in Islamic countries, from Mawdudi[48] to the Muslim Brotherhood[49] to Khomeini,[50] the defense of private property was an essential aspect of Qur'anic orthodoxy, so that the claims of social justice had to be reconciled with an economic order based on inequalities. This, in any case, was the heart of tradition, of the clergy's organic relationship with the propertied classes, in Gramsci's terms the *bloc* between the ulama and the devout bourgeoisie which to Shari'ati had destroyed Islam's class radicalism. Shari'ati's reading of Islam as riven by its duality between the "Islam of the caliphate, of the palace, and of the rulers" and the "Islam of the people, of the exploited, and of the poor"[51] was sharply contested by Khomeini's chief intellectual emissary among Iran's middle-class youth, Morteza Motahhari, who simply "reject[ed] the notion that early Islam belonged to the oppressed" and "[upheld] the Qur'anic principle that even the most depraved have the possibility of salvation." "To Mutahhari class harmony was vital... To his mind injustice came not from a wealthier class but from imperialism, secularism and Pahlavi oppression."[52] The gradient of the traditional form of capitalism that survived into the twentieth century was one that ran from merchant capital's entrenched economic position in Iran and the Gulf countries to its enforced colonial marginalization in Egypt and its non-existence or near-extinction in French-controlled Algeria. In Iran the *bazaaris* were a decisive part of the social and financial base of the Revolution, and the post-Revolution economy has even been characterized by writers like Ali Ansari as a "mercantile bourgeois republic."[53] Abrahamian has shown how profoundly concerned Khomeini was to retain the support of the more affluent merchants even as he unrelentingly attacked the sectors of capital linked to the monarchy. In Ali Khameini's description, the *bazaar* was the "bastion supporting the Republic,"[54] so that in this sense these forms of capital played a politically decisive role. But if so, nothing was further removed from this than the pattern that evolved in the Gulf where, as Jill Crystal argued, "the merchants were bought off collectively by the state," that is, depoliticized or politically marginalized in exchange for "a sizable portion of oil revenues" through real estate speculation, agencies for foreign firms, government contracts, and so on. "Oil transformed political life by freeing the rulers from their historical dependence on the merchants."[55] In fact, it did much more than that, because the Gulf, as Adam Hanieh shows in his seminal study, was the only sector of the Arab world where the 2000s saw a major watershed, completely transforming the nature of capitalism in the Gulf countries both by integrating capital across the region to create what he calls "Khaleeji capital" and by allowing for its rapid global integration, so that by the end of 2007 the Gulf Cooperation Council (GCC) state and private capital between them owned an estimated $2.2 trillion or more in foreign assets, more than the total held by China's central bank in the same year! The scale of development has been "prodigious," and arguably the Gulf is the only part of the contemporary Islamic world where a modern bourgeoisie has emerged, structured around large domestic conglomerates and qualitatively distinct from the merchant elites that straddled the main part of the twentieth century.[56]

Yet this is where the paradox or seeming paradox lies. If advanced forms of capitalism happily coexist with political and religious authoritarianisms, what do we make of Marx's vision in the *Manifesto*, where capital both internationalizes and strips away all inherited traditional obsolete forms of life? If none of the states in the Middle East are religious in any strict sense (and this includes Iran), none of them (with the exception of Turkey) can be described as secular either.[57] For example, in Egypt a constitutional amendment of 1980 made *shari'a the* principal source of legislation, creating a duality in the country's legal system. Moreover, "secular" leaders have, almost without exception, manipulated Islam for their own purposes and even encouraged Islamist forces. In Algeria Chadli Bendjedid, the army man who succeeded Boumediène, "quietly encouraged the Islamists as a means of reducing the Left."[58] In Egypt Sadat "gave strong moral and material support to Islamists in the mid-1970s... At the height of the bloody confrontations between the Egyptian state and the active Islamist organizations, the state used the mass media to promote a steadily increasing diet of religious programs."[59] And of course in Pakistan and Sudan military rulers "tried to buttress their legitimacy... by declaring the application of the *shari'a* in their legal systems."[60] These have also all been repressive regimes with staggering levels of censorship even under socialist leaders like Nasser.[61]

In the final preface to *All That Is Solid Melts into Air* Berman refers to the "still unfolding history of radical authoritarianism," with a passing mention of Khomeini.[62] In 2004 the Lebanese journalist Samir Kassir argued that the endemic lack of democracy in the Arab world and the civic powerlessness bound up with it were the main reasons why religion could emerge "to channel people's frustrations and express their demands for change."[63] By "religion" he meant the upsurge of Islamism that dominated the last quarter of the twentieth century. Kassir himself was assassinated in June 2005, most likely at the hands of the Syrian security apparatus. Islamism is not faith

but the manipulation of faith through schematic doctrinal construc-
tions based on fictional continuities with the past, literalist readings
of scripture (what Abu Zayd calls the "authoritarianism of the text"),
an aggressive cultural xenophobia, and a puritanical social conserv-
atism that seeks to stave off the emancipation of women and youth.
It transforms Islam into a political ideology whose aim is to create
an ostensibly Islamic state by enforcing the *shari'a* and peddling the
illusion that a *shari'a*-based government will finally embody God's
sovereignty on earth. It presupposes and exploits a culture of mass
religiosity and, as Ali Rahnema has shown in a brilliant book, in
Iran, under Ahmadinejad and his close aide Ayatollah Mesbah Yaz-
di, was capable of calculatedly encouraging superstition as a means
of short-term political manipulation.[64]

But, and it is essential to conclude by saying this, the ubiquitous
presence of an Islamist political sector and its inroads into the public
sphere might engender the illusion that Arab/Muslim cultural modernity is a dead letter today. To me it seems that nothing is further
from the truth. As the late Syrian philosopher and Marxist Sadiq
Jalal al-Azm noted in a vibrant essay on the Rushdie affair, none of
Rushdie's Western defenders "came anywhere near regarding him as
a Muslim dissident" comparable, say, to dissident writers in the then
Soviet bloc. This, al-Azm suggests, is because their own orientalist
assumptions about the contemporary Middle East interiorized the
Islamists' views of their societies as bastions or backwaters of con-
servatism. In truth, however, "intellectual life and cultural activity
in the Muslim world. . . is not as Islamically conformist, religiously
unquestioning and spiritually stagnant as one is led to believe from
the countless accounts, interpretations and explanations given by
Western commentators, critics, journalists, specialists, politicians,
and the media in general *à propos* of the Rushdie affair." Moreover,
al-Azm tells us, "within the entire realm of Islam the Arab world
produced the strongest and most vocal defense of Rushdie on the part
of intellectuals."[65] This tradition of "subversive intellectualism," as
I'd like to call it, has for decades been the true backbone of Arab

cultural modernity. Reiterating al-Kawākibi's scathing critique of despotism in a more contemporary world, it preserved the legacy of the *nahda* as what it clearly saw as an unfinished agenda. The modern Arabic novel seethes with subversion. From this vibrant and complex tradition of fiction (saturated with critiques of authoritarianism) to Saadallah Wannous's essays in *Qadāyā wa Shahādāt*[66] to iconoclastic pleas for a sexually open and liberated Arab society such as Muhammad Kamal al-Labwani's *Love and Sex in Fundamentalism and Imperialism* (1994)[67] to the numerous religious modernists who have emerged both in the Arab world and in Iran,[68] it is ultimately the consolidation and further expansion of this critical, anti-authoritarian, politically subversive strand of Middle Eastern culture that will give the emerging struggles for democracy the intellectual weapons they need to combat what al-Labwani calls "the culture of old extinct classes dressed up in the garb of true and authentic Islam."

ACKNOWLEDGEMENTS

I am deeply grateful to the Department of Development Studies, SOAS, for renewing my association with them over a span of many years and enabling me to sustain access to the brilliant collection of libraries in London. Gilbert Achcar, Adam Hanieh, Jens Lerche, Alessandra Mezzadri, and Subir Sinha have been among my most intellectually invigorating friends. The same is true, to at least as great a degree, of Henry Bernstein and Barbara Harriss-White, whom I've had the extreme good fortune of knowing for the most productive decades of my life. I absolutely must thank the kind and efficient librarians of the British Library, SOAS, LSE, Senate House, and UCL. Shaku, as always, has been generous, loving and supportive during the years I researched this book. And last but not least, I'd like to thank the team at Haymarket (Nisha Bolsey, Maya Marshall, and Duncan Thomas) for the patient and careful way in which they helped to get it ready, and to Jamie Kerry for the wonderful cover design.

NOTES

Chapter One

1. Robert S. Lopez and Irving W. Raymond, *Medieval Trade in the Mediterranean World* (New York, 1955), 176–77.

2. *Lopez and Raymond, Medieval Trade*, 38–41.

3. Victor Brants, *Esquisse des théories économiques des xiiie et xive siècles* (Louvain, 1895), 134, note 1, citing a passage where money (*pecunia*) is said to have "quandam seminalem rationem lucrosi, quem communiter capitale vocamus."

4. Cited Dale Kent, *The Rise of the Medici: Faction in Florence, 1426–1434* (Oxford, 1978), 142.

5. Vitorino Magalhães Godinho, *L'économie de l'Empire portugais aux XVe et XVIe siècles* (Paris, 1969), 645.

6. Fernand Braudel, *The Mediterranean and the Mediterranean World in the Age of Philip II*, 2 vols., trans. Siân Reynolds (London and New York, 1972), 465, which cites an "expert of the Banco di Rialto."

7. Irfan Habib, "Merchant Communities in Precolonial India," in *The Rise of Merchant Empires: State Power and World Trade, 1350–1750*, ed. James D. Tracy (Cambridge, 1990), 386–387.

8. Andreas Tietze, *Mustafa 'Ali's Counsel for Sultans of 1581*, 2 vols. (Vienna, 1982), vol. 2, 36, 38; Giancarlo Casale, *The Ottoman Age of Exploration* (Oxford, 2010), 184–185.

9. Gigliola Pagano de Divitiis, *English Merchants in Seventeenth-Century Italy*, trans. Stephen Parkin (Cambridge, 1997), 12, citing Leonardo Donà.

10. Lewis Roberts, *The Merchants Map of Commerce*, fourth edition (London, 1700), 295.

11. Anne-Robert-Jacques Turgot, "Reflections on the Formation and the Distribution of Wealth," in *Commerce, Culture, & Liberty: Readings on Capitalism Before Adam Smith*, ed. Henry C. Clark (Indianapolis, 2003), 518–563, at 538–539, T.'s description of the "use of capital advances in industrial enterprises."

12. P. J. Marshall, "Private British Trade in the Indian Ocean before 1800," in *India and the Indian Ocean, 1500–1800*, eds. Ashin Das Gupta and M. N. Pearson, (New Delhi, 1987), 291.

13. Ralph Davis, *The Rise of the English Shipping Industry* (London: Macmillan, 1962), 383–384.

14. Charles François Du Périer Dumouriez, *État Présent du Royaume de Portugal en l'Année MDCCLXVI* (Lausanne: Chez François Grasset & co., 1775), cited Stephen Fisher, "Lisbon as a Port Town in the Eighteenth Century,"

in *I porti come impresa economica*, ed. S. Cavaciocchi (Florence: Le Monnier, 1988), 723–24.

15. Karl Marx, *Grundrisse* (Pelican Books, 1973), 684–685, note.

16. Marx, *Grundrisse*, 460–461.

17. John Barber, *Soviet Historians in Crisis, 1928–1932* (London: Macmillan Press, 1981), 62. "Merchant capitalism" also figures in Rubin's lectures on the history of economic thought, where he argues that "a close alliance was formed (in Europe) between the state and the commercial bourgeoisie" during what he calls the "age of merchant capitalism"; see Isaac Ilyich Rubin, *A History of Economic Thought*, trans. Donald Filtzer (London, 1979), 25–26. The lectures were delivered in the late 1920s.

18. Maurice Dobb, *Studies in the Development of Capitalism* (London, 1963), 17–18, with the important footnote at 17.

19. Dobb, *Studies*, 151.

20. Dobb, *Studies*, 157.

21. Maurice Dobb, "A Reply," in *The Transition from Feudalism to Capitalism*, ed. Rodney Hilton (London, 1976), 62.

22. M. N. Pokrovsky, *Brief History of Russia*, 2 vols., trans. D. S. Mirsky (London, 1933), vol. 1, 282 (from the Appendix).

23. R. H. Tawney, "A History of Capitalism," *Economic History Review*, 2nd series, 2 (1950), 307–316, at 310–311; italics mine.

24. Barber, *Soviet Historians*, 57.

25. David Ormrod, *The Rise of Commercial Empires: England and the Netherlands in the Age of Mercantilism, 1650–1770* (Cambridge, 2003), 3.

26. R. H. Tawney, *Religion and the Rise of Capitalism* (Pelican Books, 1938), 194.

27. Tawney, *Religion*, 232–233.

28. Tawney, *Religion*, 141; italics mine.

29. Tawney, *Religion*, 180.

30. R. H. Tawney, *Business and Politics Under James I* (Cambridge, 1958), 77.

31. Eric Williams, *Capitalism and Slavery* (Chapel Hill and London, 1994; orig. 1944), 210.

32. Geoffrey Ingham, *Capitalism Divided? The City and Industry in British Social Development* (Macmillan, 1984).

33. John Brewer, *The Sinews of Power: War, Money and the English State, 1688–1783* (London, 1989).

34. P. J. Cain and A. G. Hopkins, *British Imperialism, 1688–2000*, 2nd edition (London and New York: Routledge, 2002).

35. Ingham, *Capitalism Divided?*, 97, 150–151.

36. Cain and Hopkins, *British Imperialism*, 281.

37. Cain and Hopkins, *British Imperialism*, 88.

38. P. Vilar, "Problems of the Formation of Capitalism," *Past and Present*, 10 (Nov., 1956), 15–38, at 26.

39. Braudel, *Mediterranean*, 443–444, 430ff.

40. Braudel, *Mediterranean*, 441.

41. Fernand Braudel, "La longue durée," in *Écrits sur l'histoire* (Paris, 1969), 53–54, 65.

42. Roland Mousnier, *Les XVIe et XVIIe siècles*, fifth edition (Paris, 1967; orig. 1953), 84–85, 98. It is significant that in her long discussion of Mousnier's work the Soviet historian Lublinskaya nowhere objected to the category itself, see A. D. Lublinskaya, *French Absolutism: The Crucial Phase 1620–1629*, trans. Brian Pearce (Cambridge, 1968), chapter 1, e.g., "Mousnier discusses in fair detail the economic situation in the sixteenth century, describing this primarily in terms of the tempestuous development of commercial capitalism" (p. 7).

43. Manuel Nunes Dias, *O capitalismo monárquico português (1415–1549)*, 2 volumes (Coimbra, 1963).

44. Charles Carrière, *Négociants marseillais au XVIIIe siècle*, 2 vols. (Marseilles, 1973); C. Carrière, M. Courdurié, M. Gutsatz, and R. Squarzoni, *Banque et capitalisme commercial. La lettre de change au XVIIIe siècle* (Marseilles, 1976).

45. Catharina Lis and Hugo Soly, *Poverty and Capitalism in Pre-Industrial Europe* (Atlantic Highlands, NJ, 1979).

46. Béatrice Veyssarat, *Négociants et fabricants dans l'industrie cotonnière suisse, 1760–1840* (Lausanne, 1982).

47. Peter Kriedte, *Peasants, Landlords and Merchant Capitalists: Europe and the World Economy, 1500–1800* (Leamington Spa, 1983), with a German original from 1980.

48. David Ormrod, *English Grain Exports and the Structure of Agrarian Capitalism, 1700–1760* (Hull, 1985).

49. Robert W. Shenton, *The Development of Capitalism in Northern Nigeria* (London, 1986).

50. Joseph C. Miller, *Way of Death: Merchant Capitalism and the Angolan Slave Trade, 1730–1830* (London, 1988).

51. Roy Bin Wong, *China Transformed: Historical Change and the Limits of European Experience* (Ithaca, 1997).

52. Leo Noordegraaf, "The New Draperies in the Northern Netherlands, 1500–1800," in *The New Draperies in the Low Countries and England, 1300–1800*, ed. N. B. Harte, (Oxford, 1997), 173–195.

53. Sergio Tognetti, *Un'industria di lusso al servizio del grande commercio* (Florence, 2002).

54. Scott P. Marler, *The Merchants' Capital: New Orleans and the Political Economy of the Nineteenth-Century South* (Cambridge, 2013).

55. Some examples of this: Hermann Kellenbenz, "Autour de 1600: le commerce du poivre des Fugger et le marché international du poivre," *Annales ESC*, 11 (1956), 1–28, "l'esprit du capitalisme commercial" (at p. 27); J. V. Polišenský, *The Thirty Years War*, trans. Robert Evans (London, 1971), 26, "the forces of commercial and financial capitalism"; T. H. Lloyd, *The English Wool Trade in the Middle Ages* (Cambridge, 1977), 251, "The London exporters (of wool) were dominated by a small group of merchant capitalists"; Barry Supple, "The Nature of Enterprise," in *The Economic Organization of Early Modern Europe*, eds. E. E. Rich and C. H. Wilson, *(CEHE, 5)* (Cambridge, 1977), 435, "In the generation of successful heavy industry, mercantile capital and

capitalists were of supreme significance"; "commercial capitalists"; Andre
Gunder Frank, *Capitalism and Underdevelopment in Latin America* (Pelican
Books, 1971), 59, "the spread and development of mercantile capitalism in
the world in general and in Chile and Latin America in particular"; Leroy
Vail and Landeg White, *Capitalism and Colonialism in Mozambique* (London,
1980), 2, "mercantile capitalism's most rapacious agents, the slave traders"; D.
A. Washbrook, "Law, State and Agrarian Society in Colonial India," *Modern
Asian Studies*, 15 (1981), 649–721, "the commercial capitalism encouraged by
the growth of the colonial export trades" (at 679), "urban-based mercantile
capitalists" (at 688–9); Jonathan I. Israel, *Dutch Primacy in World Trade,
1585–1740* (Oxford, 1989), 18, "Europe's great merchant capitalists"; Stanley
D. Chapman, *Merchant Enterprise in Britain from the Industrial Revolution to
World War I* (Cambridge, 1992), 13, "British mercantile capitalism"; Elena
Frangakis-Syrett, *The Commerce of Smyrna in the Eighteenth Century* (Athens,
1992), 8, "mercantile capitalism"; Rajnarayan Chandavarkar, *The Origins
of Industrial Capitalism in India* (Cambridge, 1994), 46, "Western India,
and in particular the Gujarat region, was the scene of an active mercantile
capitalism before the advent of colonial rule"; R. Étienne, Y. Makaroun, F.
Mayet, *Un grand complexe industriel à Tróia (Portugal)* (Paris, 1994), 166,
"tout permet de caractériser un capitalisme marchand, qui sous-tend aussi
l'industrie céramique" (about the salted fish industry of southern Portugal
in Roman times); Michel Balard, "Les hommes d'affaires occidentaux ont-
ils asphyxié l'économie byzantine?," in *Europa medievale e mondo bizantino*,
eds. G. Arnaldi and G. Cavallo (Rome, 1997), 255–265, "capitalisme commercial et financier du monde moderne" (about the fourteenth and fifteenth
centuries); Anthony Webster, *The Richest East India Merchant: The Life and
Business of John Palmer of Calcutta* (Woodbridge, 2007), 110, "the system of
mercantile capitalism which had operated since the 1780s"; John Darwin,
After Tamerlane: The Rise and Fall of Global Empires, 1400–2000 (New York,
2008), 149, "a distinctive type of mercantile capitalism" (about textiles in the
Coromandel).

56. Cited in E. H. Carr, *The Bolshevik Revolution 1917–1923, Volume 2* (Pelican
Books, 1966), 98.

57. Jean-Paul Sartre, *Critique de la raison dialectique* (Paris, 1960), 236 ("les
structures du capitalisme mercantile").

58. Jean-Paul Sartre, *Questions de méthode* (Paris, 1960), 60 ("le conflit sécu-
laire des capitalismes mercantiles").

59. Ormrod, *Rise of Commercial Empires*, 16.

60. Karl Marx, *Capital, Volume 3*, trans. David Fernbach (London, 1981),
379–380.

61. Marx, *Capital, Volume 3*, 442.

62. Marx, *Capital, Volume 3*, 445.

63. Marx, *Capital, Volume 3*, 446–447.

64. Karl Marx, *Capital, Volume 2*, trans. David Fernbach (London, 1978),
318–319.

65. Frederick Engels, "Supplement and Addendum to Volume 3 of *Capital*," in
Marx, *Capital, Volume 3*, 1027–47, at 1043.

66. Marx, *Capital, Volume 3*, 452.

67. Marx, *Capital, Volume 3*, 452; italics mine.

68. See Chapter 5 below.

69. Marx, *Capital, Volume 3*, 453.

70. Marx, *Capital, Volume 3*, 453–454; said here about the Italian luxury industries of the fifteenth century and taken from his notes on Adam Smith, cf. Marx, *Grundrisse*, 858.

71. Karl Marx, *Theories of Surplus-Value, Part III* (Moscow, 1971), 469–470; italics mine.

72. See David Ormrod, "R. H. Tawney and the Origins of Capitalism," *History Workshop Journal*, 18 (1984), 138–159.

73. Dobb, *Studies*, 145.

74. The crucial passage is at Dobb, *Studies*, 143.

75. Georges Lefebvre, "Some Observations," in *Transition*, ed. Sweezy et al., 122–127, at 125–126.

76. Sven Beckert, *Empire of Cotton: A New History of Global Capitalism* (Allen Lane, 2014), 138–148.

77. A. V. Chayanov, *The Theory of Peasant Economy*, edited by Daniel Thorner, Basile Kerblay, and R. E. F. Smith (Homewood, Illinois, 1966), 49.

78. Chayanov, *Theory of Peasant Economy*, 257; Chayanov's italics.

79. Chayanov, *Theory of Peasant Economy*, 257; I have altered "trading undertakings" to "commercial undertakings."

80. Chayanov, *Theory of Peasant Economy*, 257–258.

81. Chayanov, *Theory of Peasant Economy*, 261–262.

82. Chayanov, *Theory of Peasant Economy*, 262.

Chapter Two

1. Ray Turrell, *Scrap-Book 1809–1922* (Englefield Green, 1987), 183.

2. A. C. Wood, *A History of the Levant Company* (London, 1935), 235.

3. Zhu Yu cited John Chaffee, "Diasporic Identities in the Historical Development of the Maritime Muslim Communities of Song-Yuan China," *Journal of the Economic and Social History of the Orient*, 49 (2006), 395–420, at 404.

4. Al-Maqrizi, *Khitat*, i, 174 cited Subhi Y. Labib, *Handelsgeschichte Ägyptens im Spätmittelalter (1171-1517)* (Wiesbaden, 1965), 30.

5. J. von Ghistele, *Voyage en Égypte*, cited Mohamed Tahar Mansouri, "Les communautés marchandes occidentales dans l'espace mamlouk," in *Coloniser au Moyen Âge*, eds. Michel Balard and Alain Ducellier (Paris, 2000), 89–114, at 91.

6. Donald M. Nicol, *Byzantium and Venice: A Study in Diplomatic and Cultural Relations* (Cambridge, 1988), 96–99, who also notes that Alexios Komnenos's *chrysobull* of 1082 had "envisaged a permanent colony of resident Venetian traders on the Golden Horn in the heart of Constantinople" (p. 61). Michael Hendy, *Studies in the Byzantine Monetary Economy, ca.300–1450* (Cambridge, 1985), 593–594, estimates the number of those detained at three thousand, against the (unlikely) figure of "10,000" given in the *Historia Ducum Veneticorum*.

7.   Ennio Concina, *Fondaci* (Venice, 1997), 68–69.

8.   Reinhold C. Mueller, *The Venetian Money Market* (Baltimore and London, 1997), 314.

9.   Michel Balard, "Latins in the Aegean and the Balkans (1300–1400)," in *The Cambridge History of the Byzantine Empire, 500–1492*, ed. Jonathan Shepard (Cambridge, 2009), 834–851, at 842.

10. David Abulafia, *The Great Sea* (London, 2012), 325–326.

11. Concina, *Fondaci*, 82–83.

12. Henri Bresc, "Palermo in the Fourteenth–Fifteenth Century: Urban Economy and Trade," in *A Companion to Medieval Palermo*, ed. Annliese Nef (Leiden and Boston, 2013), 235–268, at 258; *The Travels of Ibn Jubayr*, trans. R. J. C. Broadhurst (London, 1952), 348.

13. Jean-Léon l'Africain, *Description de l'Afrique*, trans. A. Épaulard, 2 vols. (Paris, 1956), vol. 2, 382.

14. Paul Melon, *De Palerme à Tunis par Malte, Tripoli et la côte* (Paris, 1885), 175ff.

15. Méropi Anastassiadou, *Les Grecs d'Istanbul au XIXe siècle* (Leiden and Boston, 2012), 154, 367.

16. Braudel, *Mediterranean*, vol. 2, 809, 817 (Botero's figure of "160,000" lacks all credibility).

17. Roberts, *Map*, 268.

18. Wood, *History*, 239.

19. Cited Léon Kontente, *Smyrne et l'Occident* (Montigny, 2005), 347–348.

20. Philip Mansel, *Levant: Splendour and Catastrophe on the Mediterranean* (London, 2010), 24.

21. G. Doria, "Conoscenza del mercato e sistema informativo: il know-how dei mercanti-finanzieri genovesi nei secoli XVI e XVII," in *La repubblica internazionale del denaro tra XV e XVII secolo*, eds. Aldo De Maddalena and Hermann Kellenbenz (Bologna, 1986), 57–121, at 103–4.

22. Fisher, "Lisbon as a Port Town," 722ff.

23. Vassilis Kardasis, *Diaspora Merchants in the Black Sea: The Greeks in Southern Russia, 1775–1861* (Lexington Books, 2001), 87.

24. Kardasis, *Diaspora Merchants*, 86 (quoting a local official); Gelina Harlaftis, *A History of Greek-Owned Shipping* (London, 1996), 42.

25. J. C. Wilkinson, "Suhar (Sohar) in the Early Islamic Period: The Written Evidence," in *South Asian Archaeology 1977* (Naples, 1979), 887–907, at 889.

26. Wilkinson, "Suhar," 892.

27. Jean Aubin, "La ruine de Sîrâf et les routes du Golfe Persique aux XIe et XIIe siècles," *Cahiers de civilisation médiévale*, 2 (1959), 295–301, at 295.

28. Wilkinson, "Suhar," 899.

29. Wilkinson, "Suhar," 894.

30. Niebuhr, *Travels through Arabia and Other Countries of the East*, cited Calvin H. Allen Jr., "The Indian Merchant Community of Masqat," *Bulletin of the School of Oriental and African Studies*, 44 (1981), 39–53, at 41.

31. Allen, "Masqat," 43–45.

32. Allen, "Masqat," 48.

33. A 1393 letter shows the city's biggest foreign merchants writing to the Rasulid sultan Ashraf II seeking the ruler's permission to invoke his name in their *khutbah*, see Sebastian R. Prange, *Monsoon Islam: Trade and Faith on the Medieval Malabar Coast* (Cambridge, 2018), 263–265.

34. João de Barros, *Da Asia*, cited M. N. Pearson, "Brokers in Western Indian Port Cities," *Modern Asian Studies*, 22 (1988), 455–472, at 464.

35. Mansel Longworth Dames (trans.), *The Book of Duarte Barbosa*, 2 vols. (New Delhi, 1989), vol. 2, 75–77.

36. Armando Cortesão (trans.), *The Suma Oriental of Tomé Pires*, 2 vols. (Haklyut Society, 1944), vol. 1, 78.

37. Albert Gray (trans.), *The Voyage of François Pyrard de Laval*, vol. 1 (London, 1887), 404.

38. Dames, *The Book of Duarte Barbosa*, vol. 2, 175.

39. Luis Filipe F. R. Thomaz, "Malaka et ses communautés marchandes au tournant du 16e siècle," in *Marchands et hommes d'affaires asiatiques dans l'Océan Indien et la Mer de Chine 13e–20e siècles*, eds. Denys Lombard and Jean Aubin (Paris, 1988), 31–48, at 33.

40. Paul Wheatley, *The Golden Khersonese* (Kuala Lumpur, 1961), 312.

41. Thomaz, "Malaka," 36–37.

42. Thomaz, "Malaka," 42–43.

43. [Sebastião Manrique], *Travels of Fray Sebastien Manrique, 1629–43*, trans. C. E. Luard, vol. 2 (Oxford, 1927), 355.

44. Manrique, *Travels*, vol. 2, 360–361.

45. Niccolao Manucci, *Storia do Mogor, or Mogul India 1653–1708*, trans. William Irvine, vol. 2 (London, 1907), 186.

46. Husam Muhammad Abdul Mu'ti, "The Fez Merchants in Eighteenth-Century Cairo," in *Society and Economy in Egypt and the Eastern Mediterranean, 1600–1900*, eds. Nelly Hanna and Raouf Abbas (Cairo, 2005).

47. R. H. Hewsen (trans.), *The Geography of Ananias of Širak (Ašxarhac'oyc')* (Wiesbaden, 1992), 74A*.

48. Ibn Hauqal, *Configuration de la terre (Kitab surat al-'ard)*, trans. J. H. Kramers and G. Wiet, 2 vols. (Beirut, 1964), vol. 2, 331.

49. Al-Muqaddasi, *The Best Divisions for Knowledge of the Regions*, trans. Basil Collins (Reading, 2001), 171 ("the finest quality flax is grown in Busir").

50. Ibn Hauqal, *Configuration*, vol. 2, 436 (basing this on merchants' testimony).

51. Idrisi, *La première géographie de l'Occident*, trans. Jaubert and Annliese Nef (Paris, 1999), 192–193.

52. Al-Muqaddasi, *Best Divisions*, 198.

53. Tenth century: E. Levi Provençal, " La 'Description de l'Espagne' d'Ahmad al-Razi," *Al-Andalus*, 18 (1953), 51–108, at 93; fourteenth century: Michel Balard, *La Romanie Génoise (XIIe-debut du XVe siècle)*, 2 vols. (Rome, 1978), 846, "le grand port d'exportation de l'huile d'olive."

54. Idrisi, *La première géographie*, 248–249.

55. Idrisi, *La première géographie*, 192.

56. Doria, "Conoscenza del mercato," 81–82.

57. Damien Coulon, *Barcelone et le grand commerce d'Orient au Moyen Âge* (Madrid, 2004), 380.

58. Labib, *Handelsgeschichte*, 316.

59. A. L. Udovitch, "International Trade and the Medieval Egyptian Countryside," in *Agriculture in Egypt from Pharaonic to Modern Times*, eds. Alan K. Bowman and Eugene Rogan (The British Academy, 1999), 267–285, at 270–271.

60. Abulafia, *Great Sea*, 264, based on Genizah sources.

61. Mueller, *Venetian Money Market*, 304 (which says, "perhaps").

62. Mueller, *Venetian Money Market*, 354.

63. Maureen F. Mazzaoui, *The Italian Cotton Industry in the Later Middle Ages, 1100–1600* (Cambridge, 1981), 46.

64. Magalhães Godinho, *L'économie de l'Empire portugais*, 722.

65. Richard Ehrenberg, *Capital and Finance in the Age of the Renaissance*, trans. H. M. Lucas (London, 1928), 280.

66. Braudel, *Mediterranean*, 197.

67. Pagano de Divitiis, *English Merchants*, 124–125.

68. Patrick Boulanger, *Marseille, marché international de l'huile d'olive* ([Marseilles], 1996), 57.

69. C. H. Kauffman, *The Dictionary of Merchandiɀe*, fourth edition (London, 1815), 244.

70. Kauffman, *Dictionary*, 245.

71. Boulanger, *Marseille*, 56.

72. Wood, *History*, 164.

73. Alexander Hamilton, *A New Account of the East Indies*, ed. Sir William Foster, 2 vols. (London, 1930), vol. 1, 31–2.

74. Nancy Um, *The Merchant Houses of Mocha: Trade and Architecture in an Indian Ocean Port* (Seattle, 2009), 43.

75. Patricia Risso, *Oman and Muscat: An Early Modern History* (London, 1986), 77; Um, *Merchant Houses*, 43–44.

76. Um, *Merchant Houses*, 45.

77. André Raymond, "Une famille de grands négociants en café au Caire dans la première moitié du XVIIIe siècle: les Sharaybi," in *Le commerce du café avant l'ère des plantations colonials*, ed. M. Tuchscherer (Cairo, 2001), 111–124, at 111.

78. Raymond, "Sharaybi," 116.

79. Muʿti, "Fez merchants," 133–135.

80. E. M. Herzig, "The Rise of the Julfa Merchants in the Late Sixteenth Century," in *Safavid Persia*, ed. Charles Melville (London, 1996), 305–322, at 315–318.

81. H. W. Van Santen, *De Verenigde Ooost-Indische Compagnie in Gujarat en Hindustan, 1620–1660* (Leiden University PhD, 1982), 211.

82. Ghulam A. Nadri, *The Political Economy of Indigo in India, 1580–1930* (Leiden, 2016), 67, 94.

83. P. J. Marshall, *East Indian Fortunes: The British in Bengal in the Eighteenth Century* (Oxford, 1976), 221.

84. C. A. Bayly, *Rulers, Townsmen and Bazaars: North Indian Society in the Age of British Expansion, 1770–1870* (Cambridge, 1983), 229.

85. Bayly, *Rulers*, 234.

86. Kauffman, *Dictionary of Merchandize*, 251.

87. Kauffman, *Dictionary of Merchandize*, 363.

88. T. M. Devine, *The Tobacco Lords: A Study of the Tobacco Merchants of Glasgow and their Trading Activities, ca.1740–1790* (Edinburgh, 1975), 64ff.

89. Trevor Burnard, *Planters, Merchants, and Slaves: Plantation Societies in British America, 1650–1820* (Chicago, 2015), 203.

90. Miller, *Way of Death*, 177.

91. Burnard, *Planters*, 205. Burnard estimates that "[p]erhaps £200,000 per annum passed through the hands of Kingston merchants" (p. 203).

92. G. S. P. Freeman-Grenville, *The French at Kilwa Island* (Oxford, 1965), 92–93.

93. Marler, *Merchants' Capital*, 16, 22, 36.

94. Marler, *Merchants' Capital*, 16.

95. Walter Johnson, *River of Dark Dreams: Slavery and Empire in the Cotton Kingdom* (Cambridge, MA, 2013), 84.

96. David Kynaston, *The City of London, Volume 1: A World of Its Own, 1815–1890* (London, 1994), 167.

97. Martin Lynn, *Commerce and Economic Change in West Africa: The Palm Oil Trade in the Nineteenth Century* (Cambridge, 1997), 84.

98. Graeme J. Milne, *Trade and Traders in Mid-Victorian Liverpool: Mercantile Business and the Making of a World Port* (Liverpool, 2000), 50.

99. Evridiki Sifneos, "'Cosmopolitanism' as a Feature of the Greek Commercial Diaspora," *History and Anthropology*, 16 (2005), 97–111, at 105–6.

100. Kardasis, *Diaspora Merchants*, 28, where he says that in the 1850s "Jewish merchants comprised 53 percent of the total commercial community in Odessa."

101. Patricia Herlihy, *Odessa: A History, 1794–1914* (Cambridge, MA, 1986), 93.

102. Claude Malon, *Le Havre colonial de 1880 à 1960* (Le Havre, 2006), 66, 109, 113ff.

103. Malon, *Le Havre colonial*, 65, quoting René Godez.

104. James R. Scobie, *Revolution on the Pampas: A Social History of Argentine Wheat, 1860–1910* (Austin, 1964), 102.

105. Scobie, *Revolution on the Pampas*, 93, 103.

106. Yen-p'ing Hao, *The Commercial Revolution in Nineteenth-Century China: The Rise of Sino-Western Mercantile Capitalism* (Berkeley, 1986), 144; italics mine.

107. Hao, *Commercial Revolution*, 145.

108. Hao, *Commercial Revolution*, 154.

109. H. E. W. Braund, *Calling to Mind* (Oxford, 1975), 39.

110. Indu Banga, "Karachi and Its Hinterland under Colonial Rule," in *Ports and Their Hinterlands in India, 1700–1950*, ed. Indu Banga (New Delhi, 1992), 337–358, at 342–343.

111. Robert Ilbert, *Alexandrie 1830–1930. Histoire d'une communauté citadine*, 2 vols. (Cairo, 1996).

112. Kais Firro, "Silk and Agrarian Changes in Lebanon, 1860–1914," *International Journal of Middle East Studies*, 22 (1990), 151–169.

113. Marx, *Capital, Volume 3*, 673.

114. Marx, *Capital, Volume 3*, 655–656.

115. Cf. Rudolf Hilferding, *Finance Capital: A Study of the Latest Phase of Capitalist Development*, trans. Morris Watnick and Sam Gordon (London, 1981), 210: "The greater part of commercial capital consists of credit."

116. Mueller, *Venetian Money Market*, chapter 8.

117. Mueller, *Venetian Money Market*, 314–317.

118. Kate Fleet, *European and Islamic Trade in the Early Ottoman State* (Cambridge, 1999), 19, note 36.

119. Mueller, *Venetian Money Market*, 316.

120. Ehrenberg, *Capital and Finance*, 322.

121. Mueller, *Venetian Money Market*, 313, cf. "assets kept in constant circulation" (at 312).

122. Braudel, *Mediterranean*, 507–508.

123. Marx, *Capital, Volume 3*, 653.

124. Sevket Pamuk, *A Monetary History of the Ottoman Empire* (Cambridge, 1999), 84.

125. Lakshmi Subramanian, *Indigenous Capital and Imperial Expansion: Bombay, Surat and the West Coast* (Delhi, 1996), 55–56.

126. Violet Barbour, *Capitalism in Amsterdam in the Seventeenth Century* (Ann Arbor, 1950), 53.

127. Carrière, *Banque et capitalisme commercial*, 71.

128. Carrière, *Banque et capitalisme commercial*, 180.

129. Carrière, *Banque et capitalisme commercial*, 193.

130. R. C. Nash, "The Organization of Trade and Finance in the British Atlantic Economy, 1600–1800," in *The Atlantic Economy during the Seventeenth and Eighteenth Centuries*, ed. Peter A. Coclanis, (Charleston, SC, 2005), 95–151, at 98.

131. Nash, "Organization of Trade," 99; cf. R. B. Sheridan, "The Commercial and Financial Organization of the British Slave Trade, 1750–1807," *Economic History Review*, 2nd ser., 11 (1958), 249–63, who notes that by the late eighteenth century "slave remittances generally took the form of bills of exchange" (p.253), so that "London was as deeply involved in the slave trade as the much maligned Liverpool" (p.263).

132. Nash, "Organization of Trade," 101–2.

133. P. Machado, *Ocean of Trade: South Asian Merchants, Africa and the Indian Ocean, ca.1750–1850* (Cambridge, 2014), 66.

134. Subramanian, *Indigenous Capital*, 147–148.

135. Marshall, *East Indian Fortunes*, 222.

136. Marshall, *East Indian Fortunes*, 223–224.

137. Nicholas Mayhew, *Sterling: The Rise and Fall of a Currency* (Allen Lane, 1999), 108.

138. Kynaston, *City of London, Volume 1*, 331.

139. See Hamish McRae and Frances Cairncross, *Capital City: London as a Financial Centre* (Methuen, 1985), 6–7; David Kynaston, *The City of London, Volume 2: Golden Years, 1890–1914* (London, 1995), 8–10; Paul Ferris, *The City* (London, 1960), 60; Ingham, *Capitalism Divided?*, 43–45.

140. G. A. Fletcher, *The Discount Houses in London* (London, 1976), 12.

141. Kynaston, *City of London, Volume 1*, 87.

142. Mayhew, *Sterling*, 180, citing Lord Overstone (Samuel Jones Loyd).

143. Nash, "Organization of Trade," 129–130, 133.

Chapter Three

1. Braudel, *Mediterranean*, 348.

2. Paul Magdalino, "Medieval Constantinople," in *The Economic History of Byzantium from the Seventh through the Fifteenth Century*, ed. Angeliki E. Laiou, 3 vols. (Washington, 2002), vol.2, 529–537, at 536.

3. Paul Magdalino, *The Empire of Manuel I Komnenos, 1143–1180* (Cambridge, 1993), 120.

4. Marie-France Auzépy, "State of Emergency (700–850)," in *Cambridge History of the Byzantine Empire*, ed. Shepard, 251–291, at 259.

5. Cf. Angeliki E. Laiou, "The Byzantine City: Parasitic or Productive?" in *Economic Thought and Economic Life in Byzantium*, eds. Cécile Morrisson and Rowan Dorin (Aldershot, 2013), no.12, 10, "the internal market expanded tremendously in the period from the ninth through the twelfth century."

6. Paul Magdalino, "The Maritime Neighborhoods of Constantinople: Commercial and Residential Functions, Sixth to Twelfth Centuries," *Dumbarton Oaks Papers*, 54 (2000), 209–226, at 218–219, where he notes: "The Golden Horn is not flushed out by currents or waves."

7. Paul Magdalino, *Constantinople médiévale. Études sur l'évolution des structures urbaines* (Paris, 1996), 25.

8. Magdalino, "Maritime Neighborhoods," 212–214.

9. Magdalino, "Maritime Neighborhoods," 219–221.

10. Magdalino, "Medieval Constantinople," 534.

11. Magdalino, "Medieval Constantinople," 534 (fires).

12. Speros Vryonis Jr., "Byzantine *demokratia* and the Guilds in the Eleventh Century," *Dumbarton Oaks Papers*, 17 (1963), 289–314, at 291–292, note 9.

13. A. P. Kazhdan and Ann Wharton Epstein, *Change in Byzantine Culture in the Eleventh and Twelfth Centuries* (Los Angeles, 1985), 176.

14. Benjamin of Tudela, Komroff's translation of the passage, cited Louise Buenger Robbert, "Rialto Businessmen and Constantinople, 1204–61," *Dumbarton Oaks Papers*, 49 (1995), 43–58, at 44, note 5. The standard translation of this passage implies that this was the annual intake, which would make it impossibly low.

15. So described by Gino Luzzatto, *Storia economica di Venezia dall'XI al XVI secolo* (Venice, 1961), 21.

16. Nicolas Oikonomidès, *Hommes d'affaires grecs et latins à Constaninople (XIIIe-XVe siècles)* (Montreal, 1979), 24.

17. Angeliki E. Laiou, "Byzantine Trade with Christians and Muslims and the Crusades," in *The Crusades from the Perspective of Byzantium and the Muslim World*, eds. Angeliki E. Laiou and Roy Parviz Mottahedeh (Washington, 2001), 157–192, at 159.

18. Nicolas Oikonomidès, "The Economic Region of Constantinople," in *Social and Economic Life in Byzantium*, ed. Elizabeth Zachariadou (Aldershot, 2004), no. 13, 235.

19. Charles Diehl, *Byzantium: Greatness and Decline*, trans. Naomi Walford (New Brunswick, N.J., 1957), 191–2; also in Diehl, "The Economic Decay of Byzantium," in *The Economic Decline of Empires*, ed. Carlo M. Cipolla (London, 1970), 94–95.

20. Peter Charanis, "Social Structure and Economic Policies in the Byzantine Empire," in *The Decline of Empires*, ed. S. N. Eisenstadt (Englewood Cliffs, NJ, 1967), 93.

21. Charanis, "Social Structure," 93.

22. E. Malamut, "Byzance colonisée: politique et commerce sous le règne d'Andronic II (1282–1328)," in *Les échanges en Méditerranée médiévale*, eds. E. Malamut and Mohamed Ouerfelli (Aix-en-Provence, 2012), 121–152, at 123–126.

23. Angeliki E. Laiou, "The Byzantine Economy in the Medieval Trade System," *Dumbarton Oaks Papers*, 34-35 (1980-81), 177–222, at 210, "the Byzantines rarely were able to gain access to the Western and Italian markets"; Angeliki E. Laiou, "The Palaiologoi and the World Around Them (1261–1400)," in *Cambridge History of the Byzantine Empire*, ed. Shepard, 803–833, at 821, "The markets of Italy were almost closed to them."

24. Oikonomidès, *Hommes d'affaires*, 85.

25. Laiou, "Palaiologoi," 820–821, "What the Byzantine merchants could not do was to engage in long-distance trade."

26. Oikonomidès, *Hommes d'affaires*, 24–35 places considerable emphasis on this.

27. Oikonomidès, *Hommes d'affaires*, 31.

28. Oikonomidès, *Hommes d'affaires*, 31–32, contrasting Italian attitudes with those displayed later by the Turks.

29. Niketas Choniates cited Diehl, *Byzantium*, 192; Diehl, "Economic Decay," 96. Cf. *O City of Byzantium, Annals of Niketas Choniates*, trans. Harry J. Magoulias (Detroit, 1984), 97, where the translation reads, "They amassed great wealth and became so arrogant and impudent that not only did they behave belligerently to the Romans but they also ignored imperial threats and commands."

30. Nicolas Svoronos, "Société et organisation intérieure dans l'empire byzantin au XIe siècle," in *Études sur l'organisation intérieure, la société et l'économie de l'Empire Byzantin*, ed. Nicolas Svoronos, (London, 1973), no. 9, at 8–10 (essential remarks); Paul Lemerle, *Cinq Études sur le XIe siècle byzantin* (Paris, 1977), esp. 287ff.

31. Lemerle, *Cinq Études*, 285–286.

32. Nicolas Oikonomides, "Entrepreneurs," in *The Byzantines*, ed. Guglielmo Cavallo (Chicago, 1997), 144–171, at 163.

33. Lemerle, *Cinq Études*, 307, "véritable capitulation économique."

34. Venetians did much of their business through Greek wholesalers. We know this because the latter were exempted from the 10 percent duty or *kommerkion* only in 1126 *after* the Venetians protested and John II forbade officials from exacting any duty on those transactions, cf. Marco Pozza and Giorgio Ravegnani, *I trattati con Bisanzio, 992–1198* (Venice, 1993), 51ff., at 54–5.

35. See Robbert, "Rialto businessmen."

36. Fleet, *European and Islamic Trade in the Early Ottoman State*.

37. Balard, *La Romanie génoise*, t.2, 869.

38. Georges Pachymérès, *Relations historiques, t.2, livres IV-VI*, ed. Albert Failler, trans. Vitalien Laurent (Paris, 1984), 534. The translation is from Lopez and Raymond, *Medieval Trade in the Mediterranean World*, 127–28. They mistakenly suggest that "narrow waters" refers to the Black Sea, but access to the latter was tightly controlled at this time and of little interest to the Venetians till much later, see Michel Balard, "Il Mar Nero, Venezia e l'Occidente intorno al 1200," in *Venedig und die Weltwirtschaft um 1200*, ed. Wolfgang von Stromer (Stuttgart, 1999), 191–201. The round brackets are my insertions.

39. Silvano Borsari, *Venezia e Bisanzio nel XII secolo. I rapporti economici* (Venice, 1988), 99 refers to the "massive presence of the Venetian aristocracy in the trade with Byzantium" in the early twelfth century. Gerhard Rösch, *Der venezianische Adel bis zur Schließung des Großen Rats* (Sigmaringen, 1989) is the best study on the Venetian side. By the thirteenth century a circle of twenty-four families dominated the political and commercial life of Venice, controlling close to half the membership of the Maggior Consiglio and all the leading offices in the city's newfound colonial empire. The most important of these, that of the *podestà* of Constantinople, was filled from their ranks sixteen out of the seventeen times known to us (p.135).

40. Balard, *La Romanie génoise*, t.2, 524.

41. Elisabeth Malamut, *Les îles de l'empire byzantin VIIIe-XIIe siècles*, 2 vols. (Paris, 1988), t.2, 441.

42. Hendy, *Studies*, 593–596.

43. Balard, *La Romanie génoise*, t.2, 876–877.

44. David Jacoby, "The Venetian Quarter of Constantinople from 1082 to 1261," in David Jacoby, *Commercial Exchange Across the Mediterranean* (Aldershot, 2005), no. 3, 163.

45. Jacoby, "Venetian Quarter," 154.

46. Balard, *La Romanie génoise*, t.1, 118.

47. Balard, *La Romanie génoise*, t.2, 682.

48. Balard, "Latins in the Aegean," 834, who refers to both "colonial wars" and "carve-up."

49. Oikonomidès, *Hommes d'affaires*, 35; Oikonomidès, "Entrepreneurs," 166–167.

50. Oikonomidès, "Entrepreneurs," 167.

51. Laiou, "Palaiologoi," 821.

52. See John W. Barker, "Late Byzantine Thessalonike: A Second City's Challenges and Responses," *Dumbarton Oaks Papers*, 57 (2003), 5–33, at 18.

53. Laiou, "Palaiologoi," 823.

54. Oikonomidès, *Hommes d'affaires*, 121–22.

55. Nicolas Oikonomides, "Byzantium between East and West (XIII-XV cent.)," *Byzantinische Forschungen*, 13 (1988), 319–332, at 329.

56. Mario Del Treppo and Alfonso Leone, *Amalfi medioevale* (Naples, 1977), 121ff.

57. Michel Balard, "Amalfi et Byzance (Xe-XIIe siècles)," *Travaux et Memoires*, 6 (1976), 85–95.

58. Peter Schreiner, "Bilancio pubblico, agricoltura e commercio a Bisanzio nella seconda metà del XII secolo," in von Stromer, *Venedig und die Weltwirtschaft*, 177–189, at 184. The contrast is with Asia Minor and the Balkans.

59. David Jacoby, "Silk in Western Byzantium before the Fourth Crusade," *Byzantinische Zeitschrift*, 84, nos. 1-2 (1991-1992), 452–500, at 475ff.

60. M. Martin, "The Venetians in the Byzantine Empire before 1204," in *Byzantium and the West, c.850–c.1200*, ed. J. D. Howard-Johnston (Amsterdam, 1988), 201–214, at 212.

61. Michel Balard, "Latin Sources and Byzantine Prosopography: Genoa, Venice, Pisa and Barcelona," in *Byzantines and Crusaders in Non-Greek Sources, 1025–1204*, ed. Mary Whitby (Oxford, 2007), 39–58, at 45; Nicol, *Byzantium and Venice*, 105.

62. Fleet, *European and Islamic Trade*, 102.

63. Fleet, *European and Islamic Trade*, 97.

64. Balard, *La Romanie génoise*, t.2, 738ff.

65. Al-Jazari's *Chronicle of Damascus* cited Mansouri, "Communautés marchandes occidentales," 100.

66. "Rapid growth, etc." from Prange, *Monsoon Islam*, 108.

67. Mazzaoui, *Italian Cotton Industry*, 46, 51.

68. Mohamed Ouerfelli, *Le sucre. Production, commercialisation et usages dans le Méditerranée médiévale* (Leiden, 2008), 46.

69. Gino Luzzatto, *Studi di storia economica veneziana* (Padua, 1954), 118ff.; Ouerfelli, *Sucre*, 115ff.

70. *Travels of Ibn Jubayr*, 61.

71. Abulafia, *Great Sea*, 297.

72. See Chapter 2, n.4.

73. David Jacoby, "The Economic Function of the Crusader States of the Levant," in David Jacoby, *Medieval Trade in the Eastern Mediterranean and Beyond* (Routledge, 2018), no. 4, 119.

74. Ouerfelli, *Sucre*, 355.

75. Angeliki E. Laiou, "Un notaire vénitien à Constantinople: Antonio Bresciano et le commerce international en 1350," in *Les Italiens à Byzance,* eds. Michel Balard, Angeliki E. Laiou and Catherine Otten-Froux (Paris, 1987), 79–151, at 79 ("l'importation massive des étoffes de l'Italie et de la Flandre").

76. Coulon, *Barcelone et le grand commerce d'Orient*, 304–305, citing Ashtor's data.

77. Braudel, *Mediterranean*, 387.

78. John Day, "The Levant Trade in the Middle Ages," in *Economic History of Byzantium*, vol. 2, ed. Laiou, 807–814, at 811 (ten merchant galleys).

79. Day, "Levant Trade," 808.

80. Prange, *Monsoon Islam*, 50.

81. Geneviève Bouchon, "Les musulmans du Kerala à l'époque de la découverte portugaise," *Mare Luso-Indicum*, 2 (1973), 3–59, at 26–27.

82. Mark Horton, *Shanga: The Archaeology of a Muslim Trading Community on the Coast of East Africa* (London, 1996), 419.

83. Michael Pearson, *The Indian Ocean* (London, 2003), 78.

84. Pearson, *Indian Ocean*, 76.

85. Prange, *Monsoon Islam*, 264–265.

86. Dames, *The Book of Duarte Barbosa*, vol.2, 76.

87. Prange, *Monsoon Islam*, 193–194.

88. Luís Filipe Thomaz, "Le Portugal et l'Afrique au XVe siècle: les debuts de l'expansion," *Arquivos do Centro Cultural Português*, 26 (1989), 161–256.

89. Thomaz, "Portugal et l'Afrique," 225, 187.

90. Thomaz, "Portugal et l'Afrique," 169–70.

91. Charles Verlinden, *Les origines de la civilisation atlantique de la Renaissance à l'Âge des Lumières* (Neuchatel, 1966), 12.

92. Luís Filipe Thomaz, "Portuguese Sources on Sixteenth Century Indian Economic History," in *Indo-Portuguese History: Sources and Problems*, ed. John Correia-Afonso (Bombay, 1981), 99–113, at 104.

93. T. F. Earle and John Villiers, eds., *Albuquerque Caesar of the East* (Warminster, 1990), 6.

94. Earle and Villiers, *Albuquerque*, 81.

95. Earle and Villiers, *Albuquerque*, 83.

96. The expression is from J. H. Parry, *The Age of Reconnaissance* (New York, 1964), 264.

97. *The Itinerary of Ludovico di Varthema of Bologna from 1502 to 1508*, trans. John Winter Jones (London, 1928), 71.

98. Magalhães Godinho, *L'économie de l'Empire portugais*, 652.

99. Earle and Villiers, *Albuquerque*, 113 (letter dated April 1, 1511).

100. Pius Malekandathil, *Portuguese Cochin and the Maritime Trade of India, 1500–1663* (New Delhi, 2001), 48.

101. Malekandathil, *Portuguese Cochin*, 152–153.

102. Malekandathil, *Portuguese Cochin*, 152.

103. Cf. Nunes Dias, *O capitalismo monárquico português*.

104. Sanjay Subrahmanyam, *The Portuguese Empire in Asia, 1500–1700* (London, 1992), 275, "a curious combination of mercantilism and messianism."

105. Malekandathil, *Portuguese Cochin*, 121.

106. *Tohfat-ul-Mujahideen: An Historical Work in the Arabic Language*, trans. M. J. Rowlandson (London, 1833), 111–2.

107. *Tohfat-ul-Mujahideen*, 152.

108. *Tohfat-ul-Mujahideen*, 152–153.

109. Prange, *Monsoon Islam*, 146.

110. Magalhães Godinho, *L'économie de l'Empire portugais*, 630.

111. Jan Kieniewicz, "Pepper Gardens and Market in Precolonial Malabar," *Moyen Orient & Océan Indien*, 3 (1986), 1–36, at 7 (Costa's estimate); Malekandathil, *Portuguese Cochin*, 114 (1520s).

112. Malekandathil, *Portuguese Cochin*, 202.

113. Thomaz, "Portuguese Sources," 101.

114. Kieniewicz, "Pepper Gardens," 11.

115. Malekandathil, *Portuguese Cochin*, 49.

116. Malekandathil, *Portuguese Cochin*, 154.

117. Kieniewicz, "Pepper Gardens," 21–23.

118. Magalhães Godinho, *L'économie de l'Empire portugais*, 638–39; Malekandathil, *Portuguese Cochin*, 201.

119. Braudel, *Mediterranean*, 543–570.

120. Sanjay Subrahmanyam and Luís Filipe F. R. Thomaz, "Evolution of Empire: the Portuguese in the Indian Ocean during the Sixteenth Century," in *The Political Economy of Merchant Empires*, ed. James D. Tracy (Cambridge, 1991), 298–331, at 303.

121. Richard A. Goldthwaite, *The Economy of Renaissance Florence* (Baltimore, 2009), 159.

122. Goldthwaite, *Economy*, 45.

123. Goldthwaite, *Economy*, 46.

124. Malekandathil, *Portuguese Cochin*, 217.

125. Malekandathil, *Portuguese Cochin*, 207.

126. Malekandathil, *Portuguese Cochin*, 132. James C. Boyajian, *Portuguese Trade in Asia under the Habsburgs, 1580–1640* (Baltimore, 1993) upscales the extent of private capital involvement in the Portuguese trade with Asia and argues that toward the end of the sixteenth century a substantial part of the investment in both trade sectors (carriera and "country trade") came from wealthy New Christian merchant families whose networks straddled Lisbon, Goa, Cochin, etc., as well as the entire region from Bengal to Macao. "[F]rom the 1580s return cargo worth 5 million cruzados and more reached Lisbon annually" (168).

127. Malekandathil, *Portuguese Cochin*, 203–206, 256.

128. Prange, *Monsoon Islam*, 223.

129. Casale, *Ottoman Age*, 115.

130. Casale, *Ottoman Age*, 115–6; all italics mine.

131. So too Casale, *Ottoman Age*, 116.

132. Magalhães Godinho, *L'économie de l'Empire portugais*, 729–730.

133. Magalhães Godinho, *L'économie de l'Empire portugais*, 728–729, referring to a "deep commercial depression."

134. Magalhães Godinho, *L'économie de l'Empire portugais*, 727, 729.

135. Fernand Braudel, *Out of Italy, 1450–1650*, trans. Siân Reynolds (Paris, 1991), 117.

136. Braudel, *Mediterranean*, 552.

137. Hermann Kellenbenz, "Le commerce du poivre des Fugger et le marché international du poivre," *Annales ESC*, first ser., 11 (1956), 1–28, at 5.

138. Luca Molà, *The Silk Industry of Renaissance Venice* (Baltimore, 2000), 62.

139. Pagano de Divitiis, *English Merchants*, 22.

140. H. R. Trevor-Roper, "The Reformation and Economic Change," in *Capitalism and the Reformation*, ed. M. J. Kitch (London, 1967), 24–36, at 32.

141. Israel, *Dutch Primacy in World Trade*, 70–71.

142. Geoffrey Parker, *Spain and the Netherlands, 1559–1659* (Fontana/Collins, 1979), 192.

143. Israel, *Dutch Primacy*, 42.

144. Israel, *Dutch Primacy*, Chapter 6.

145. Israel, *Dutch Primacy*, 68.

146. Wood, *History*, 106.

147. Israel, *Dutch Primacy*, 346ff.

148. Israel, *Dutch Primacy*, 335.

149. The best characterization can be found in Louis Dermigny, "Le fonctionnement des compagnies des Indes I: L'organisation et le rôle des compagnies," in *Sociétés et compagnies de commerce en Orient et dans l'Océan indien*, ed. M. Mollat (Paris, 1970), 443–451.

150. David Hume, *Essays*, edited by E. F. Miller, revised edition (Indianapolis, 1987), 88, from the essay "Of Civil Liberty," 87ff.

151. See Istvan Hont, *Jealousy of Trade: International Competition and the Nation-State in Historical Perspective* (Cambridge, MA, 2005).

152. Hont, *Jealousy of Trade*, 54, citing Adam Smith, *Wealth of Nations*, IV.iii.2.13; italics mine.

153. Hume, *Essays*, 327–328.

154. Gustav von Schmoller, *The Mercantile System and Its Historical Significance* (New York, 1896), 64.

155. K. N. Chaudhuri, *The Trading World of Asia and the English East India Company, 1660–1760* (Cambridge, 1978), 5.

156. Sir William Temple, *Observations Upon the United Provinces of the Netherlands*, edited by Sir George Clark (Oxford, 1972).

157. Israel, *Dutch Primacy*, 16; italics mine.

158. Israel, *Dutch Primacy*, 71–72.

159. Israel, *Dutch Primacy*, 160.

160. Webster, *Richest East India Merchant*, 24.

161. Israel, *Dutch Primacy*, 77, with Savary des Bruslons's estimate.

162. Israel, *Dutch Primacy*, 260ff.

163. Israel, *Dutch Primacy*, 356ff.

164. Israel, *Dutch Primacy*, 256 ("In the scale of their inter-Asian trade, the Dutch had no rivals").

165. Israel, *Dutch Primacy*, 186–187 ("The Dutch Company connected the various trade zones of Asia in ways that the English Company could not do and never did").

166. Israel, *Dutch Primacy*, 176–178.

167. Israel, *Dutch Primacy*, 16.

168. Israel, *Dutch Primacy*, 67.

169. Israel, *Dutch Primacy*, 175.

170. Ralph Davis, *English Merchant Shipping and Anglo-Dutch Rivalry in the Seventeenth Century* (London, 1975), 10.

171. Chaudhuri, *Trading World*, 215.

172. Om Prakash, *The Dutch East India Company and the Economy of Bengal, 1630–1720* (Princeton, 1985), 12.

173. Chaudhuri, *Trading World*, 94.

174. Israel, *Dutch Primacy*, 124–25.

175. Israel, *Dutch Primacy*, 130.

176. Richard von Glahn, *Fount of Fortune: Money and Monetary Policy in China, 1000–1700* (Oakland, CA, 1996), 226–227.

177. Glahn, *Fount of Fortune*, 226, 228.

178. Meilink-Roelofz cited Prakash, *Dutch East India Company*, 15, note 21.

179. Prakash, *Dutch East India Company*, 118; italics mine.

180. Israel, *Dutch Primacy*, 176–77.

181. Prakash, *Dutch East India Company*, 16.

182. Israel, *Dutch Primacy*, 247.

183. Israel, *Dutch Primacy*, 257.

184. Temple, *Observations*, 117.

185. Israel, *Dutch Primacy*, 203, 260–261.

186. Israel, *Dutch Primacy*, 204.

187. Davis, *English Merchant Shipping*, 31.

188. Davis, *English Merchant Shipping*, 32.

189. David Ormrod, "The Demise of Regulated Trading in England," in *Merchants and Industrialists within the Orbit of the Dutch Staple Market*, eds. Leo Noordegraaf and C. Lesger (The Hague, 1995), 253–268, at 255.

190. Israel, *Dutch Primacy*, 296, 285.

191. Israel, *Dutch Primacy*, 311.

192. Kontente, *Smyrne*, 294.

193. Israel, *Dutch Primacy*, 203.

194. Kontente, *Smyrne*, 328.

195. Israel, *Dutch Primacy*, 382.

196. Nicolas Mesnager's *mémoire* to the Council of Commerce (December 1700), cited C. W. Cole, *French Mercantilism, 1683–1700* (New York, 1971; orig. 1943), 238.

197. Israel, *Dutch Primacy*, 383.

198. Israel, *Dutch Primacy*, 384–389.

199. Israel, *Dutch Primacy*, 390–391.

200. Israel, *Dutch Primacy*, 379.

201. Christopher Hill, *The Century of Revolution, 1603–1714* (Edinburgh, 1961), 141.

202. Robert Brenner, *Merchants and Revolution* (Cambridge, 1993), 4ff.

203. Brenner, *Merchants and Revolution*, 16ff.

204. Brenner, *Merchants and Revolution*, 21.

205. Brenner, *Merchants and Revolution*, 22.

206. Brenner, *Merchants and Revolution*, 30; italics mine.

207. Brenner, *Merchants and Revolution*, 41.

208. Pagano de Divitiis, *English Merchants*, 177.

209. Ralph Davis, "English Foreign Trade, 1660–1700," *Economic History Review*, 2nd ser., 7 (1954), 150–66, at 150; B. Dietz, "Overseas Trade and Metropolitan Growth," in *London 1500–1700: The Making of the Metropolis*, eds. A. L. Beier and Roger Finlay (London, 1986), 130.

210. Hill, *Century of Revolution*, 186.

211. Davis, *Rise of the English Shipping Industry*, 15 (tonnage expands from 115,000 to 340,000 in 1629–1686); Davis, *English Merchant Shipping*, 1-2 (shipping industry nearly doubles in size in 1660–1689).

212. K. G. Davies, *The Royal African Company* (London, 1957), 57.

213. Nuala Zahedieh, *The Capital and the Colonies: London and the Atlantic Colonies, 1660–1700* (Cambridge, 2010), 138.

214. Dietz, "Overseas Trade," 123.

215. Zahedieh, *Capital and the Colonies*, 57.

216. Zahedieh, *Capital and the Colonies*, 58, table 3.2.

217. Zahedieh, *Capital and the Colonies*, 64.

218. Zahedieh, *Capital and the Colonies*, 7.

219. Davis, "English Foreign Trade," 153, who refers to the "new mass markets" created by the "cheapness of the supply" drawn from the English settlements and trading centers outside Europe.

220. Dunn, *Sugar and Slaves*, 48.

221. Zahedieh, *Capital and the Colonies*, 62.

222. Brenner, *Merchants and Revolution*, 65, 71–72.

223. Brenner, *Merchants and Revolution*, 73.

224. Brenner, *Merchants and Revolution*, 78.

225. Brenner, *Merchants and Revolution*, 79ff.

226. "Middling stratum": Brenner, *Merchants and Revolution*, 160.

227. Brenner, *Merchants and Revolution*, 75, with table 2.1 at 76.

228. Wood, *History of the Levant Company*, 42ff.

229. Wood, *History of the Levant Company*, 64.

230. Pagano de Divitiis, *English Merchants*, 122.

231. Pagano de Divitiis, *English Merchants*, 118.

232. Pagano de Divitiis, *English Merchants*, 123.

233. Thomas Mun, *A Discourse of Trade from England unto the East-Indies* (1621), cited Wood, *History*, 43.

234. Wood, *History of the Levant Company*, 43.

235. Cited Brenner, *Merchants and Revolution*, 68.

236. Pagano de Divitiis, *English Merchants*, 70, referring to "a remarkable increase in the chartering of English ships in the Mediterranean as a whole and in Italy in particular," from the 1670s onward.

237. Pagano de Divitiis, *English Merchants*, 129–32.

238. Wood, *History of the Levant Company*, 21.

239. Wood, *History of the Levant Company*, 215–216.

240. Wood, *History of the Levant Company*, 125.

241. Wood, *History of the Levant Company*, 127.

242. Wood, *History of the Levant Company*, 102ff., 105.

243. Wood, *History of the Levant Company*, 106ff., 119, 120.

244. Wood, *History of the Levant Company*, 140ff. on the Company's decline.

245. Wood, *History of the Levant Company*, 128.

246. Cited Wood, *History of the Levant Company*, 127.

247. Wood, *History of the Levant Company*, 152.

248. Wood, *History of the Levant Company*, 151.

249. Wood, *History of the Levant Company*, 155–56.

250. Roger Owen, *The Middle East in the World Economy, 1800–1914* (London, 1993), 83. The French dominated the western trade with Istanbul in the eighteenth century, and Galata had the largest French community in the Levant by 1769, cf. Fariba Zarinebaf, *Mediterranean Encounters: Trade and Pluralism in Early Modern Galata* (Oakland, CA, 2018), 194, "By the mid-eighteenth century, French trade in Istanbul was two-thirds of all Western trade with the capital."

251. Ormrod, *Rise of Commercial Empires*, 41.

252. Nash, "Organization of Trade," 123.

253. S. D. Smith, *Slavery, Family, and Gentry Capitalism in the British Atlantic: The World of the Lascelles, 1648–1834* (Cambridge, 2006), 141.

254. Smith, *Gentry Capitalism*, 182.

255. Smith, *Gentry Capitalism*, 156–57.

256. Nash, "Organization of Trade," 124.

257. James Oakes, *Slavery and Freedom: An Interpretation of the Old South* (New York, 1990), 55.

258. Nash, "Organization of Trade," 95.

259. Webster, *Richest East India Merchant*, 7.

260. Brewer, *Sinews of Power*, xv.

261. Hill, *Century of Revolution*, 188; cf. K. N. Chaudhuri, *The English East India Company* (London, 1965), 30, "the promoters of the Company included some of the richest and most powerful City merchants who had a hand in practically every branch of English overseas trade," and his further assertion "managerial control of the Company's affairs remained firmly in the hands of the City merchants" (p.21).

262. Chaudhuri, *Trading World of Asia*, 61.

263. Cain and Hopkins, *British Imperialism*, 90.

264. Chaudhuri, *Trading World of Asia*, 165, 170ff.

265. Chaudhuri, *Trading World of Asia*, 45.

266. Chaudhuri, *Trading World of Asia*, 131ff.

267. Chaudhuri, *Trading World of Asia*, 282.

268. Chaudhuri, *Trading World of Asia*, 258; italics mine.

269. Chaudhuri, *Trading World of Asia*, 71.

270. For example, Chaudhuri, *Trading World of Asia*, 253.

271. Cited Chaudhuri, *Trading World of Asia*, 148.

272. Chaudhuri, *Trading World of Asia*, 143.

273. Chaudhuri, *Trading World of Asia*, 145, citing John Deane's statement to the Bengal Public Consultations of July 1731.

274. Chaudhuri, *Trading World of Asia*, 307.

275. Chaudhuri, *Trading World of Asia*, 308.

276. See Hameeda Hossain, *The Company Weavers of Bengal: The East India Company and the Organization of Textile Production in Bengal, 1750–1813* (New Delhi, 1988).

277. Hossain, *Company Weavers of Bengal*, 165, 175.

278. Kanakalatha Mukund, *The Trading World of the Tamil Merchant: Evolution of Merchant Capitalism in the Coromandel* (Chennai, 1999), 72.

279. Chaudhuri, *Trading World of Asia*, 66.

280. Wolfgang von Stromer, "Une clé du succès des maisons de commerce d'Allemagne du Sud: le grand commerce associé au Verlagssystem," *Revue Historique*, 285 (1991), 29–49.

281. For a case study, see Mukund, *Trading World of the Tamil Merchant*.

282. Chaudhuri, *Trading World of Asia*, 355–356.

283. Chaudhuri, *Trading World of Asia*, 357.

284. Marshall, "Private British Trade," 279.

285. Cosmopolitan and largely Muslim-dominated, see Arasaratnam's essay in Sinnapah Arasaratnam and Aniruddha Ray, *Masulipatnam and Cambay: A History of Two Port-Towns, 1500–1800* (New Delhi, 1994).

286. Chaudhuri, *Trading World of Asia*, 210.

287. Marshall, *East Indian Fortunes*, 78.

288. Marshall, *East Indian Fortunes*, 78 ("had been reduced to a trickle").

289. Marshall, *East Indian Fortunes*, 20.

290. Marshall, *East Indian Fortunes*, 152; Hossain, *Company Weavers of Bengal*, 75.

291. Marshall, *East Indian Fortunes*, 248.

292. Marshall, *East Indian Fortunes*, 255.

293. P. J. Marshall, "Economic and Political Expansion: The Case of Oudh," *Modern Asian Studies*, 9 (1975), 465–482, at 476–477.

294. Marshall, *East Indian Fortunes*, 24.

295. Davis, *Rise of the English Shipping Industry*, 15.

296. Webster, *Richest East India Merchant*, 27–28.

297. Marshall, *East Indian Fortunes*, 48.

Chapter Four

1. Paul Nizan, *Aden, Arabie*, trans. Joan Pinkham, foreword by Jean-Paul Sartre (Boston, 1970), 112.

2. Nizan, *Aden, Arabie*, 112–3.

3. Nizan, *Aden, Arabie*, 112; all italics mine.

4. Nizan, *Aden, Arabie*, 113.

5. Nizan, *Aden, Arabie*, 111.

6. Nizan, *Aden, Arabie*, 116.

7. Nizan, *Aden, Arabie*, 102.

8. Nizan, *Aden, Arabie*, 102.

9. Owen, *Middle East in the World Economy*, 156, table 27; the bulk of this in Mount Lebanon.

10. E. R. J. Owen, *Cotton and the Egyptian Economy, 1820–1914* (Oxford, 1969), 89.

11. Harlaftis, *History of Greek-Owned Shipping*, 67.

12. Harlaftis, *History*, 35, "wild competition."

13. Geoffrey Jones, *Merchants to Multinationals: British Trading Companies in the Nineteenth and Twentieth Centuries* (Oxford, 2000), 39.

14. Robert Blake, *Jardine Matheson: Traders of the Far East* (London, 1999), 248.

15. Owen, *Middle East in the World Economy*, 103.

16. Owen, *Middle East in the World Economy*, 126.

17. Royal Commission on Opium, *Minutes of Evidence Taken before the Royal Commission on Opium* (London, 1894), vol.2, 448 (from S. Laing's budget statement dated April 16, 1862).

18. Kynaston, *City of London, Volume 1*, 220.

19. Jones, *Merchants to Multinationals*, 40.

20. Kynaston, *City of London, Volume 1*, 239.

21. Webster, *Richest East India Merchant*, 40, 42.

22. Webster, *Richest East India Merchant*, 59.

23. Webster, *Richest East India Merchant*, 117.

24. Webster, *Richest East India Merchant*, 123, 130.

25. Webster, *Richest East India Merchant*, 112, citing John Crawfurd's analysis.

26. Benoy Chowdhury, *Growth of Commercial Agriculture in Bengal (1757–1900)* (Calcutta, 1964), 83; Michael Greenberg, *British Trade and the Opening of China, 1800–42* (New York, 1979; orig. 1951), 165.

27. Greenberg, *British Trade*, 34.

28. Webster, *Richest East India Merchant*, 121–22.

29. Webster, *Richest East India Merchant*, 110; italics mine.

30. Blake, *Jardine Matheson*, 59; most recently, Alain Le Pichon, *China Trade and Empire: Jardine, Matheson & Co. and the Origins of British Rule in Hong Kong, 1827–1843* (Oxford, 2006), with the description of Jardine Matheson & Co. as a "fully-fledged capitalist enterprise" by 1843 (at 35).

31. Greenberg, *British Trade*, 113. Forty thousand chests were equivalent to *ca.* 4.8 million pounds of opium (!), Le Pichon, *China Trade and Empire*, 20.

32. Blake, *Jardine Matheson*, 37ff.

33. Blake, *Jardine Matheson*, 60 (Company's conduct), 78 (Whigs), 106 (lobbying).

34. Greenberg, *British Trade*, 164; Le Pichon, *China Trade and Empire*, 33.

35. Blake, *Jardine Matheson*, 82.

36. Blake, *Jardine Matheson*, 90ff.

37. Blake, *Jardine Matheson*, 108.

38. J. Y. Wong, *Deadly Dreams: Opium, Imperialism, and the Arrow War (1856–1860)* (Cambridge, 1998), 210, 311.

39. Edward Le Fevour, *Western Enterprise in Late Chi'ing China: A Selective Survey of Jardine, Matheson and Company's Operations, 1842–1895* (Cambridge, MA, 1968), 19.

40. Le Fevour, *Western Enterprise*, 20.

41. Le Fevour, *Western Enterprise*, 25–26.

42. Le Fevour, *Western Enterprise*, 27–28.

43. Le Fevour, *Western Enterprise*, 28.

44. Le Fevour, *Western Enterprise*, 28–29.

45. Chapman, *Merchant Enterprise in Britain*, 237–239.

46. Chapman, *Merchant Enterprise in Britain*, 115, with note 18.

47. Amiya Kumar Bagchi, *Private Investment in India, 1900–1939* (Cambridge, 1972), 163.

48. Chapman, *Merchant Enterprise in Britain*, 291, table 10.1.

49. P. Pugh, *Great Enterprise: A History of Harrisons & Crosfield*, edited by G. Nickall (Harrisons & Crosfield, 1990), 76.

50. Hilferding, *Finance Capital*, 119.

51. Jones, *Merchants to Multinationals*, 289.

52. Chapman, *Merchant Enterprise in Britain*, 125; it is therefore puzzling that he also states (at 237) "Yules controlled assets in excess of £1.2m (in 1899), but their actual capital was evidently much less."

53. Michael Kidron, *Foreign Investments in India* (London, 1965), 6.

54. Kidron, *Foreign Investments*, 11.

55. Bagchi, *Private Investment in India*, 176.

56. Bagchi, *Private Investment in India*, 262–263.

57. Pugh, *Great Enterprise*, 38–42.

58. Nicholas J. White, *British Business in Post-Colonial Malaysia, 1957–70* (London and New York, 2004), 4.

59. Andrew Yule & Co., *Andrew Yule & Co. Ltd., 1863–1963* (printed for private circulation, 1963), 12.

60. Chapman, *Merchant Enterprise in Britain*, 212.

61. Chapman, *Merchant Enterprise in Britain*, 213.

62. Bagchi, *Private Investment in India*, 162.

63. Banga, "Karachi," 356.

64. Braund, *Calling to Mind*, 74.

65. Braund, *Calling to Mind*, 24.

66. Braund, *Calling to Mind*, 40–41.

67. Bagchi, *Private Investment in India*, 180.

68. Maria Misra, *Business, Race, and Politics in British India, c.1850–1960* (Oxford, 1999) is a lucid study of the culture of the British managing agency houses and their gradual decline after the First World War, thanks in part to their self-defeating isolation. Gradual—the British managing agencies still controlled the bulk of listed companies in 1947. However, from the 1940s a lot of the agencies were taken over by Indian capital.

69. Karl Marx and Frederick Engels, "Manifesto of the Communist Party," in Karl Marx, *The Revolutions of 1848*, trans. David Fernbach (Harmondsworth, 1973), 71.

70. S. D. Chapman, "The International Houses: the Continental Contribution to British Commerce, 1800–1860," *Journal of European Economic History*, 6 (1977), 5–48, at 19.

71. Chapman, "International Houses," 39.

72. Charles Issawi, "British Trade and the Rise of Beirut, 1830–1860," *International Journal of Middle East Studies*, 8 (1977), 91–101, at 96.

73. Issawi, "British Trade," 97.

74. Issawi, "British Trade," 98.

75. Chapman, "International Houses," 41; Chapman, *Merchant Enterprise in Britain*, 158.

76. Stanley Jackson, *The Sassoons* (London, 1968), 35.

77. Jackson, *The Sassoons*, 45.

78. Jackson, *The Sassoons*, 59.

79. Kardasis, *Diaspora Merchants*, 160.

80. Going by the table in Chapman, *Merchant Enterprise in Britain*, 291.

81. Cain and Hopkins, *British Imperialism*, 152, 154.

82. Kynaston, *City of London, Volume 1*, 167.

83. Chapman, "International Houses," 42 (table).

84. Chapman, "International Houses," 42–43.

85. Lynn, *Commerce*, 31.

86. Lynn, *Commerce*, 44.

87. Owen, *Cotton and the Egyptian Economy*, 161 (table 21), 198 (table 38).

88. John F. Richards, "The Opium Industry in British India," *The Indian Economic and Social History Review*, 3 (2002), 149–80, at 155, 163; Carl A. Trocki, *Opium, Empire and the Global Political Economy* (Routledge, 1999), 94, citing Crawfurd's estimate for *ca.*1836.

89. R. Graham, *Britain and the Onset of Modernization in Brazil, 1850–1914* (Cambridge, 1968), 25.

90. Anthony Webster, *Gentlemen Capitalists: British Imperialism in South East Asia, 1770–1890* (London, 1998), 213 (exports of Bombay Burmah Trading Corporation).

91. W. P. McGreevey, *An Economic History of Colombia, 1845–1930* (Cambridge, 1971), 196.

92. Charles Robequain, *The Economic Development of French Indo-China*, trans. Isabel A. Ward (London, 1944), 220, table 17.

93. Webster, *Gentlemen Capitalists*, 230.

94. G. B. Kay, *The Political Economy of Colonialism in Ghana: A Collection of Documents and Statistics, 1900–1960* (Cambridge, 1972), 334, table 21a.

95. Hubert Bonin, *CFAO (1887–2007). La réinvention permanente du commerce outre-mer* (Paris, 2007), 293.

96. H. A. Antrobus, *A History of the Assam Company 1839–1953* (Edinburgh, 1957), 95.

97. Bagchi, *Private Investment in India*, 268.

98. W. K. M. Langley, *Century in Malabar: The History of Peirce Leslie & Co. Ltd., 1862–1962* (Madras, 1962), 51.

99. Frederick Johnson Pedler, *The Lion and the Unicorn in Africa: A History of the Origins of the United Africa Company, 1787–1931* (London, 1974), 165.

100. Harlaftis, *History of Greek-Owned Shipping*, 24–25.

101. Cain and Hopkins, *British Imperialism*, 248.

102. Cain and Hopkins, *British Imperialism*, 289.

103. Banga, "Karachi," 340.

104. Graham, *Brazil*, 76.

105. R. H. Macaulay, *History of the Bombay Burmah Trading Corporation, Ltd. 1864–1910* (London, 1934), 26.

106. Wong, *Deadly Dreams*, 408–409 (including table 16.12).

107. Cain and Hopkins, *British Imperialism*, 157, 201.

108. Cain and Hopkins, *British Imperialism*, 165, table 5.8.

109. Cain and Hopkins, *British Imperialism*, 158ff.

110. See the seminal analysis in E. H. H. Green, "The Influence of the City over British Economic Policy *ca.* 1880–1960," in *Finance and Financiers in European History, 1880–1960*, ed. Youssef Cassis (Cambridge and Paris, 1992), 193–218, at 208–209.

111. Cain and Hopkins, *British Imperialism*, 383.

112. Wong, *Deadly Dreams*, 218ff., 310ff.

113. J. Y. Wong, "British Annexation of Sind in 1843: An Economic Perspective," *Modern Asian Studies*, 31 (1997), 225–244; Wong, *Deadly Dreams*, 419ff.

114. Webster, *Gentlemen Capitalists*, 227; Macaulay, *History of the Bombay Burmah Trading Corporation*, 14ff.

115. Webster, *Gentlemen Capitalists*, 225, 227.

116. W. S. Blunt, *Secret History of the English Occupation of Egypt* (London, 1922; orig. 1907), 139.

117. Blunt, *Secret History*, 98.

118. Kynaston, *City of London, Volume 1*, 339.

119. Mansel, *Levant*, 117.

120. Kynaston, *City of London, Volume 1*, 338.

121. Mansel, *Levant*, 122.

122. Roger Owen, "Egypt and Europe: from French Expedition to British Occupation," in *Studies in the Theory of Imperialism*, eds. Roger Owen and Bob Sutcliffe, 195–209, at 203, 205. The occupation had strong support in the expat upper classes, cf. Alexander Kitroeff, *The Greeks and the Making of*

Modern Egypt (Cairo and New York, 2019), 55, "Almost a year after the bombardment took place, 2,600 wealthy European inhabitants of Alexandria and other towns signed a petition asking that the occupation become permanent."

123. E. Frangakis-Syrett, *The Commerce of Smyrna in the Eighteenth Century (1700–1820)* (Athens, 1992), 85.

124. Owen, *Middle East in the World Economy*, 83.

125. Gelina Harlaftis, "The 'Eastern Invasion': Greeks in Mediterranean Trade and Shipping in the Eighteenth and Nineteenth Centuries," in *Trade and Cultural Exchange in the Early Modern Mediterranean: Braudel's Maritime Legacy*, eds. Maria Fusaro, Colin Heywood, Mohamed-Salah Omri (London, 2010), 223–252, at 244.

126. Harlaftis, "'Eastern Invasion,'" 244.

127. Harlaftis, "'Eastern Invasion,'" 245–246.

128. Frangakis-Syrett, *Commerce of Smyrna*, 109–11.

129. Kardasis, *Diaspora Merchants*, 84.

130. Kardasis, *Diaspora Merchants*, 151.

131. Kardasis, *Diaspora Merchants*, 149–50.

132. Kardasis, *Diaspora Merchants*, 145, note 82.

133. David S. Landes, *Bankers and Pashas: International Finance and Economic Imperialism in Egypt* (London, 1958), 26.

134. H. Holland, *Travels in the Ionian Isles, Albania, Thessaly, Macedonia, etc. during the Years 1812 and 1813*, cited Landes, *Bankers and Pashas*, 26.

135. Harlaftis, *History of Greek-Owned Shipping*, 50–1, cites a figure of "500"!

136. Roderick Beaton, *An Introduction to Modern Greek Literature* (Oxford, 1994), 338.

137. "Caractère des gens du pays, leur commerce," *ca*.1750, Paris, AN, Affaires Étrangères, cited Edhem Eldem, "Istanbul: From Imperial to Peripheralized Capital," in *The Ottoman City between East and West: Aleppo, Izmir, and Istanbul*, eds. Edhem Eldem, Daniel Goffman, and Bruce Masters (Cambridge, 1999), 159.

138. Anastassiadou, *Les Grecs d'Istanbul*, 158–60.

139. Harlaftis, *History*, 40ff.

140. Kardasis, *Diaspora Merchants*, 154, table 7.4.

141. Chapman, *Merchant Enterprise in Britain*, 158–159; italics mine.

142. Harlaftis, *History*, 41.

143. Anastassiadou, *Les Grecs d'Istanbul*, 168ff.; Mihail-Dimitri Sturdza, *Dictionnaire historique et généalogique des grandes familles de Grèce, d'Albanie et de Constantinople* (Paris, 1983), 224–225.

144. Sturdza, *Dictionnaire historique et généalogique des grandes familles de Grèce*, 152.

145. On Vikelas's account of the Greek business diaspora, see Ariadni Moutafidou, "Greek Merchant Families Perceiving the World: The Case of Demetrius Vikelas," *Mediterranean Historical Review*, 23 (2008), 143–64.

146. Mansel, *Levant*, 103.

147. Mansel, *Levant*, 192, citing a centenary booklet of C. Whittall & Co.

148. Henk Driessen, "Mediterranean Port Cities: Cosmopolitanism Reconsidered," *History and Anthropology*, 16 (2005), 129–41, at 133; Mansel, *Levant*, 170; both citing the Austrian consul-general Charles de Scherzer.

149. Mansel, *Levant*, 169.

150. Fawwaz Traboulsi, *A History of Modern Lebanon*, second edition (London, 2012), 116ff., with Issawi, "British Trade," 98.

151. Thomas Philipp, *Acre: The Rise and Fall of a Palestinian City, 1730–1831* (New York, 2001), 132.

152. Robert Ilbert, *Alexandrie 1830–1930. Histoire d'une communauté citadine*, 2 vols. (Cairo, 1996), 245.

153. Robert Mabro, "Alexandria 1860–1960: The Cosmopolitan Identity," in *Alexandria Real and Imagined*, eds. A. Hirst and M. S. Silk (Aldershot, 2004), 247–262, at 254ff., based on the census data.

154. Mabro, "Alexandria."

155. Elizabeth M. Holt, *Fictitious Capital: Silk, Cotton, and the Rise of the Arabic Novel* (New York, 2017), 41.

156. Mansel, *Levant*, 107.

157. Ilbert, *Alexandrie*, 129.

158. Beckert, *Empire of Cotton*, 233.

159. Mansel, *Levant*, 69–70.

160. Beckert, *Empire of Cotton*, 293.

161. Mansel, *Levant*, 137.

162. Michael Haag, *Alexandria: City of Memory* (New Haven, 2004), 10.

163. Owen, *Cotton and the Egyptian Economy*, 357.

164. Ilbert, *Alexandrie*, 257.

165. Alexander Kitroeff, *The Greeks in Egypt 1919–1937: Ethnicity and Class* (London, 1989), 80. Kitroeff, *The Greeks and the Making of Modern Egypt*, 102, notes that "Throughout the interwar period the two great Greek-owned firms, Choremi, Benachi Cotton Company and C.M.Salvago Company, remained the biggest exporters."

166. Haag, *Alexandria*, 71.

167. Kitroeff, *Greeks in Egypt*, 79.

168. Kitroeff, *Greeks in Egypt*, 80–81.

169. Ilbert, *Alexandrie*, 266–267.

170. Ilbert, *Alexandrie*, 270.

171. What follows is based on Katerina Trimi, "La famille Benakis: un paradigme de la bourgeoisie grec alexandrine," in *Figures anonymes, figures d'élite*, eds. M. Anastassiadou and B. Heyberger (Istanbul, 1999), 83–102.

172. Mansel, *Levant*, 139, "persuaded by his friend the charismatic Greek politician Emmanuel Venizelos."

173. Kitroeff, *Greeks in Egypt*, 80, followed by Haag, *Alexandria*, 72–73.

174. Sami Zubaida, "Cosmopolitanism and the Middle East," in *Cosmopolitanism, Identity and Authenticity in the Middle East*, ed. Roel Meijer (Richmond, 1999), 15–33, at 26; Mansel, *Levant*, 139.

175. Trimi, "La famille Benakis," 102.

176. Mansel, *Levant*, 138.

177. Robert Ilbert and Ilios Yannakakis, *Alexandrie, 1860–1960* (Paris, 1992), 29.

178. Mansel, *Levant*, 139.

179. Arnold Wright, *Twentieth Century Impressions of Egypt* (London, 1909), 429, also in Haag, *Alexandria*, 15. In *Justine* Durrell has Darley say, "Not to care about gain, that is what Alexandria recognizes as madness," Lawrence Durrell, *The Alexandria Quartet* (London: Faber & Faber, 1969), 30.

180. Haag, *Alexandria*, 64.

181. From "The City," in C. P. Cavafy, *Collected Poems*, trans. Edmund Keeley and Philip Sherrard (London, 1984), 22.

Chapter Five

1. Hilferding, *Finance Capital*, 208–209.

2. Marx, *Theories of Surplus-Value, Part III*, 527.

3. Duncan Bythell, *The Sweated Trades: Outwork in Nineteenth-century Britain* (London, 1978), 13.

4. Bythell, *Sweated Trades*, 35.

5. Bythell, *Sweated Trades*, 36.

6. Bythell, *Sweated Trades*, 66.

7. Bythell, *Sweated Trades*, 72.

8. Bythell, *Sweated Trades*, 146.

9. Carlo Poni, "Proto-industrialization, Rural and Urban," *Review (Fernand Braudel Center)*, 9 (1985), 305–314, at 306; italics mine.

10. So too Jürgen Schlumbohm, "Relations of Production–Productive Forces–Crises in Protoindustrialization," in *Industrialization Before Industrialization: Rural Industry in the Genesis of Capitalism*, eds. Peter Kriedte, Hans Medick, Jürgen Schlumbohm, trans. Beate Schempp (Cambridge, 1981), 94–125, at 104; "... capitalist production which began within the putting-out system."

11. Karl Marx, *Capital, Volume 1*, trans. Ben Fowkes (London, 1976), 358.

12. Marx, *Capital, Volume 1*, 425.

13. Tessie P. Liu, *The Weaver's Knot: The Contradictions of Class Struggle and Family Solidarity in Western France, 1750–1914* (Ithaca, 1994), 166, 171.

14. Lis and Soly, *Poverty and Capitalism*, 105.

15. Schlumbohm, "Relations of Production," 101. On proto-industry see the essays in *Industrialization Before Industrialization*, eds. Kriedte, Medick, and Schlumbohm.

16. Lis and Soly, *Poverty and Capitalism*, 150. The expression was used by Hans Medick in a seminal essay, "The Proto-Industrial Family Economy," *Social History* 1 (1976), 291–315, which pointed to the higher average household size among rural cottage workers (because of the low age at marriage and of children staying longer with their parents) and to the centrality of women's labor to the "proto-industrial" family.

17. Pierre Goubert, *Beauvais et le Beauvaisis de 1600 à 1730* (Paris, 1960).

18. Poni, "Proto-industrialization," 312–313.

19. Bruno Dini, "Lavoratori dell' Arte della Lana a Firenze nel XIV e XV secolo," in *Artigiani e salariati. Il mondo del lavoro nell'Italia dei secoli XII-XV* (Pistoia, 1984), 27–68, at 31.

20. Eleanora Carus-Wilson, "The Woollen Industry," in *Cambridge Economic History of Europe, Volume 2: Trade and Industry in the Middle Ages,* eds. M. Postan and E. E. Rich (Cambridge, 1952), 355–428, at 386.

21. Marx, *Grundrisse,* 510–511, where the term "manufacture" seems to include the activity of putters-out.

22. Bythell, *Sweated Trades,* 15.

23. Bythell, *Sweated Trades,* 15–16.

24. Bythell, *Sweated Trades,* 16.

25. Bythell, *Sweated Trades,* 46, 18, 67.

26. Bythell, *Sweated Trades,* 17.

27. Liu, *Weaver's Knot,* 66.

28. Liu, *Weaver's Knot,* 69.

29. Raymond de Roover, "Labour Conditions in Florence around 1400," in *Florentine Studies: Politics and Society in Renaissance Florence,* ed. Nicolai Rubinstein (London, 1968), 277–313, at 298.

30. Tognetti, *Un'industria di lusso al servizio del grande commercio,* 26–38.

31. Goldthwaite, *Economy,* 306.

32. Fernand Braudel, "European Expansion and Capitalism: 1450–1650," in *Chapters in Western Civilization, Volume 1,* third edition (New York, 1961), 245–288, at 265–266.

33. Goldthwaite, *Economy,* 339.

34. Goldthwaite, *Economy,* 303.

35. Tognetti, *Un'industria di lusso,* 85.

36. From the extract of the *Chronicle* translated in Lopez and Raymond, *Medieval Trade in the Mediterranean World,* 71–74, at 72.

37. Raymond de Roover, "A Florentine Firm of Cloth Manufacturers: Management and Organization of a Sixteenth-Century Business," in *Business, Banking and Economic Thought in Late Medieval and Early Modern Europe,* ed. Julius Kirshner (Chicago, 1974), 85–113, at 86–91; Goldthwaite, *Economy,* 299–300.

38. Tognetti, *Un'industria di lusso,* 26; also called "la classe mercantile-bancaria" at 23.

39. Alfred Doren, *Die Florentiner Wollentuchindustrie vom vierzehnten bis zum sechzehnten Jahrhundert. Ein Beitrag zur Geschichte des modernen Kapitalismus* (Stuttgart, 1901).

40. Gene A. Brucker, "The Ciompi Revolution," in *Florentine Studies,* ed. Rubinstein, 314–356, at 320, 322.

41. Brucker, "Ciompi Revolution," 319, 322.

42. Steven A. Epstein, *Wage Labor and Guilds in Medieval Europe* (Chapel Hill, 191), 252.

43. De Roover, "Labour Conditions," 300.

44. Frederick Antal, *Florentine Painting and its Social Background* (Cambridge, MA, 1986), 24, "the *ciompi*, the lowest group, consisting of some 9,000 wool workers."

45. About this extraordinary workers' revolt, usually called the "Ciompi revolution," Steven Epstein commented, "When the Ciompi had a guild for a couple of months, they stood the definition of a guild on its head. Far from revealing themselves to be in the thrall of cultural hegemony about guilds or incapable of formulating an ideological program of their own, the Ciompi brought the vision of corporate society to its logical conclusion—a guild for everyone, a short step away from the state" (Epstein, *Wage Labor and Guilds*, 253).

46. De Roover, "Florentine Firm," 96–97.

47. De Roover, "Florentine Firm," 98; De Roover, "Labour Conditions," 301.

48. Alessandro Stella, "'La bottega e i lavoranti': approche des conditions de travail des Ciompi," *Annales ESC*, 44 (1989), 529–551, calculates an average workshop size of forty-seven employees for the Strozzi woolen enterprise, of whom twenty-nine were workers (*lavoranti*) (p.543).

49. De Roover, "Labour Conditions," 301, "as far as we know, they did not play a conspicuous part in the Ciompi Revolt."

50. Gayot, *Les draps de Sedan*, cited William H. Sewell Jr., "The Empire of Fashion and the Rise of Capitalism in Eighteenth-Century France," *Past and Present*, no.206 (2010), 81–120, at 112–3.

51. This is argued by de Roover, "Florentine Firm," 93, 102.

52. Federigo Melis, *Aspetti della vita economica medievale (Studi nell'Archivio Datini di Prato)* (Siena, 1962), 511, a detail noted by Rudolf Holbach, *Frühformen von Verlag und Grossbetrieb in der gewerblichen Produktion (13.–16. Jahrhundert)* (Stuttgart, 1994), 149.

53. Goldthwaite, *Economy*, 301–302.

54. De Roover, "Labour Conditions," 297.

55. De Roover, "Labour Conditions," 300; italics mine.

56. Goldthwaite, *Economy*, 290–291.

57. Goldthwaite, *Economy*, 284.

58. Goldthwaite, *Economy*, 291–293; Pagano de Divitiis, *English Merchants*, 136–38, where it is called a "commercial strategy."

59. Pagano de Divitiis, *English Merchants*, 137.

60. Pagano de Divitiis, *English Merchants*, 138.

61. Pagano de Divitiis, *English Merchants*, 138–41.

62. Justin Godart, *L'ouvrier en soie. Monographie du tisseur Lyonnais* (Paris, 1899), 90–91.

63. Carlo Poni, "Fashion as Flexible Production: the Strategies of the Lyons Silk Merchants in the Eighteenth Century," in *World of Possibilities: Flexibility and Mass Production in Western Industrialization*, eds. Charles F. Sabel and Jonathan Zeitlin (Cambridge, 1977), 37–74, at 47–48.

64. Sewell, "Empire of Fashion," 94.

65. Sewell, "Empire of Fashion," 94–95.

66. Sewell, "Empire of Fashion," 97.

67. Sewell, "Empire of Fashion," 87–88; italics mine.
68. Sewell, "Empire of Fashion," 90.
69. Poni, "Lyons Silk Merchants," 49–50.
70. Poni, "Lyons Silk Merchants," 41.
71. Sewell, "Empire of Fashion," 93.
72. Sewell, "Empire of Fashion," 94.
73. Poni, "Lyons Silk Merchants," 64–65.
74. Sewell, "Empire of Fashion," 92.
75. Poni, "Lyons Silk Merchants," 42.
76. Sewell, "Empire of Fashion," 86.
77. Poni, "Lyons Silk Merchants," 67.
78. Bythell, *Sweated Trades*, 47.
79. Sewell, "Empire of Fashion," 100–101.
80. This and the two following paragraphs are based entirely on Wynn's remarkable history of the company, Antony Wynn, *Three Camels to Smyrna: The Story of the Oriental Carpet Manufacturers Company* (London, 2008). Wynn was the OCM buyer in Hamadan in 1972–76.
81. Wynn, *Smyrna*, 25–26.
82. Wynn, *Smyrna*, 24.
83. Wynn, *Smyrna*, 30.
84. "Levantine" is used here in the strict sense defined by Oliver Jens Schmitt, *Levantiner. Lebenswelten und Identitäten einer ethnokonfessionellen Gruppe im osmanischen Reich im "langen 19. Jahrhundert"* (Munich, 2005), that is, to mean Christians (mainly Catholics) of western European origin permanently resident in the main Ottoman urban centers who were distinct both from the other Christian minorities (Greeks, Armenians, etc.) as well as from more recent European immigrants. In the late nineteenth century, Levantine-controlled businesses held up better in Smyrna than they did in Istanbul (pp.239–40).
85. Wynn, *Smyrna*, 31.
86. Wynn, *Smyrna*, 48.
87. Wynn, *Smyrna*, 78.
88. Wynn, *Smyrna*, 39.
89. Wynn, *Smyrna*, 39.
90. Wynn, *Smyrna*, 39.
91. Wynn, *Smyrna*, 45.
92. Wynn, *Smyrna*, 212, citing Bryan Huffner's diary of his travels through Iran in the late 1940s.
93. Wynn, *Smyrna*, 49 (Tabrizi monopoly), 56 (Americans).
94. Wynn, *Smyrna*, 55.
95. Wynn, *Smyrna*, 61.
96. Wynn, *Smyrna*, 159 (A. C. Edwards to Jim Baker).
97. Wynn, *Smyrna*, 54.

98. In Kerman, where most of the carpet factories worked under contract to various European firms, a British consular report for the year 1913 notes that "the conditions of the trade are notoriously scandalous and highly injurious to the health and well-being of the workers, *who are largely children*," cited Wynn, *Smyrna*, 91–92; italics mine.

99. Wynn, *Smyrna*, 85 ("insistence on rigorous quality control at every level of production").

100. Wynn, *Smyrna*, 175.

101. Wynn, *Smyrna*, 255.

102. Wynn, *Smyrna*, 77.

103. Wynn, *Smyrna*, 173.

104. Wynn, *Smyrna*, 173.

105. Wynn, *Smyrna*, 232.

106. Wynn, *Smyrna*, 234.

107. International Trading Division of the Bowater Organisation, *History and Activities of the Ralli Trading Group*, [no page numbers] section on "Carpets"; all italics mine.

108. Wynn, *Smyrna*, 270–272.

Chapter Six

1. Bayly, *Rulers, Townsmen*, 293.

2. Chaudhuri, *Trading World*, 148.

3. The big German metal traders of the late nineteenth century are a good example, see Susan Becker, "The German Metal Traders before 1914," in *The Multinational Traders*, ed. Geoffrey G. Jones (London, 1998), 66–85.

4. Langley, *Century in Malabar*, 35.

5. Theodore K. Rabb, *Enterprise and Empire: Merchant and Gentry Investment in the Expansion of England, 1575–1630* (Cambridge, MA, 1967), 53, table 3.

6. Stefano Angeli, *Proprietari, commercianti e filandieri a Milano nel primo Ottocento. Il mercato delle sete* (Milan, 1982), 112–13.

7. Molà, *Silk Industry*, 303.

8. Pagano di Divitiis, *English Merchants*, 169ff.

9. Giorgio Cracco, *Società e stato nel Medioevo veneziano (secoli xii-xiv)* (Florence, 1967), 195.

10. Ibn Hajar al-'Asqalani cited Éric Vallet, *L'Arabie marchande. État et commerce sous les sultans rasûlides du Yémen* (Paris, 2010), 513–514.

11. Vallet, *L'Arabie marchande*, 527.

12. Doria, "Conoscenza del mercato," 73–74; Braudel, *Mediterranean*, 507, "about sixty bankers."

13. Nash, "Organization of Trade," 133.

14. K. G. Davies, "The Origins of the Commission System in the West India Trade," *Transactions of the Royal Historical Society*, fifth ser., 2 (1952), 89–107, at 104–5.

15. Gordon Jackson, *Hull in the Eighteenth Century* (Oxford, 1972), 96.

16. Patrick Chorley, *Oil, Silk and Enlightenment* (Naples, 1965), 39.

17. Greenberg, *British Trade*, 30.

18. Blake, *Jardine Matheson*, 143.

19. Lynn, *Commerce*, 101.

20. Robert Greenhill, "The Brazilian Coffee Trade," in *Business Imperialism, 1840–1930*, ed. D. C. M. Platt (Oxford, 1977), 198–230, at 207–8.

21. Owen, *Middle East in the World Economy*, 252.

22. Scobie, *Revolution on the Pampas*, 93, 106. The top two were Bunge y Born and Dreyfus.

23. Dorabjee B. Contractor, *A Handbook of Indian Cotton for Merchants, Shippers, Mills, Factory-Owners, and Others Interested in the Cotton Trade*, second edition (Bombay, 1928), 38–39.

24. D. K. Fieldhouse, *Merchant Capital and Economic Decolonization: The United Africa Company, 1929–1987* (Oxford, 1994), 9.

25. Catherine Boone, *Merchant Capital and the Roots of State Power in Senegal, 1930–1985* (Cambridge, 1992), 44.

26. Pierre Brocheux and Daniel Hémery, *Indochina: An Ambiguous Colonization, 1858–1954* (Berkeley, 2009), 169.

27. Braund, *Calling to Mind*, 41.

28. Shenton, *Development of Capitalism*, 97.

29. Shenton, *Development of Capitalism*, 16; italics mine.

30. Shenton, *Development of Capitalism*, 17.

31. Frederick Pedler, *The Lion and the Unicorn in Africa: The United Africa Company 1787–1931* (London, 1974), 183; Shenton, *Development of Capitalism*, 83.

32. Fieldhouse, *Merchant Capital*, 112.

33. Fieldhouse, *Merchant Capital*, 426.

34. Fieldhouse, *Merchant Capital*, 438.

35. Fieldhouse, *Merchant Capital*, 444.

36. Fieldhouse, *Merchant Capital*, 426.

37. Fieldhouse, *Merchant Capital*, 443–444; italics mine.

38. Fieldhouse, *Merchant Capital*, 119.

39. Fieldhouse, *Merchant Capital*, 121.

40. Fieldhouse, *Merchant Capital*, 148, summarizing Jan-Georg Deutsch, "Educating the Middlemen," (SOAS PhD 1990).

41. Bonin, *CFAO*, 297, note 65 (annual report dated May 30, 1938).

42. Cheng Siok-Hwa, *The Rice Industry of Burma, 1852–1940* (Kuala Lumpur and Singapore, 1968), 64–68.

43. Laurence Marfaing, *Evolution du commerce au Sénégal, 1820–1930* (Paris, 1991), 218–222.

44. Marfaing, *Commerce au Sénégal*, 234.

45. Marfaing, *Commerce au Sénégal*, 211.

46. Braudel, *Mediterranean*, 548.

47. *Itinerary of Ludovico di Varthema*, 67.

48. Chaudhuri, *Trading World*, 308.

49. Chaudhuri, *Trading World*, 147.

50. Lynn, *Commerce*, 67.

51. Lynn, *Commerce*, 71.

52. Lynn, *Commerce*, 80.

53. Ralli Brothers, *Calcutta Handbook* (1888), cited Chapman, *Merchant Enterprise in Britain*, 128.

54. Christof Dejung, *Die Fäden des globalen Marktes. Eine Sozial- und Kulturgeschichte des Welthandels am Beispiel der Handelsfirma Gebrüder Volkart, 1851–1999* (Cologne, 2013), 105–112.

55. Fieldhouse, *Merchant Capital*, 444, note 92.

56. Shenton, *Development of Capitalism*, 88–89.

57. Shenton, *Development of Capitalism*, 87–88.

58. Shenton, *Development of Capitalism*, 94.

59. Cf. Shenton, *Development of Capitalism*, 15: "These African merchants performed a useful service to capital but they also appropriated a share of surplus value and profit."

60. Fieldhouse, *Merchant Capital*, 111.

61. Langley, *Century in Malabar*, 45–46; italics mine. Volkart managers described the Indian broker as the "central figure" around whom business was transacted, the "connecting link between the European firm and the dealers", cf. Dejung, *Gebrüder Volkart*, 108. The best description of Indian commercial organization in the early twentieth century is Rajat Kanta Ray's paper in *The Indian Economic and Social History Review*, 25 (1988), 263–318.

62. Blake, *Jardine Matheson*, 136.

63. Subramanian, *Indigenous Capital and Imperial Expansion*; Prasannan Parthasarathi, "Merchants and the Rise of Colonialism," in *Institutions and Economic Change in South Asia*, eds. Burton Stein and Sanjay Subrahmanyam (Delhi, 1996), 85–104.

64. Greenhill, "Brazilian Coffee," 213.

65. Firro, "Silk and Agrarian Changes," 160–161.

66. Kitroeff, *Greeks in Egypt*, 85.

67. Fieldhouse, *Merchant Capital*, 120.

68. Fieldhouse, *Merchant Capital*, 121; italics mine.

69. Fieldhouse, *Merchant Capital*, 115–116.

70. Chaudhuri, *Trading World*, 257; italics mine.

71. Karl Marx, *Zur Kritik der politischen Oekonomie*, in *Marx-Engels Gesamtausgabe*, *II/2* (Berlin, 1980), 201, note 1; Karl Marx, *A Contribution to the Critique of Political Economy* (Moscow, 1970), 140, "Of course capital, too, is advanced in the form of money and it is possible that the money advanced is capital advanced."

72. J. F. Richards, "The Indian Empire and Peasant Production of Opium in the Nineteenth Century," *Modern Asian Studies*, 15 (1981), 59–82, at 72–73.

73. Royal Commission on Opium, *Minutes of Evidence Taken before the Royal Commission on Opium* (London, 1894), vol.3, 27 (from the evidence of Revd Prem Chand).

74. Royal Commission on Opium, *Minutes of Evidence Taken before the Royal Commission* (London, 1894), vol.3, 138 (evidence of Syed Kalk Husein).

75. Johnson, *River of Dark Dreams*, 257.

76. Johnson, *River of Dark Dreams*, 257–258.

77. Johnson, *River of Dark Dreams*, 259.

78. Johnson, *River of Dark Dreams*, 260.

79. Philip S. Foner, *Business & Slavery: The New York Merchants & the Irrepressible Conflict* (Chapel Hill, 1941).

80. Samuel Smith, *The Cotton Trade of India* (London, 1863), 20–22.

81. Smith, *Cotton Trade*, 22.

82. Smith, *Cotton Trade*, 34.

83. Marika Vicziany, "Bombay Merchants and Structural Changes in the Export Community, 1850 to 1880," in *Economy and Society: Essays in Indian Economic and Social History*, eds. K. N. Chaudhuri and Clive J. Dewey (Delhi, 1979), 163–96.

84. Chowdhury, *Growth of Commercial Agriculture in Bengal*, 122.

85. Colin M. Fisher, "Planters and Peasants: The Ecological Context of Agrarian Unrest on the Indigo Plantations of North Bihar, 1820–1920," in *The Imperial Impact*, eds. Dewey and Hopkins, 114–131, at 114.

86. Asiya Siddiqi, *Agrarian Change in a Northern Indian State: Uttar Pradesh 1819–1833* (Oxford, 1973), 145.

87. Elizabeth Whitcombe, *Agrarian Conditions in Northern India, Volume 1: The United Provinces under British Rule, 1860–1900* (New Delhi, 1971), 171–72.

88. John Phipps, *A Series of Treatises on the Principal Products of Bengal, No.1 Indigo*, cited Siddiqi, *Agrarian Change*, 147.

89. Binay Bhushan Chaudhuri, "Growth of Commercial Agriculture in Bengal—1859–1885," *Indian Economic and Social History Review*, 7 (1970), 211–251, at 219, contrasting the systems known respectively as *ryoti* or *assamiwar* and *zerat*.

90. Chowdhury, *Growth of Commercial Agriculture*, 130.

91. Indigo Commission Bengal, *Report of the Indigo Commission Appointed under Act XI of 1860* (Calcutta, 1860), 37 (evidence of J. Cockburn).

92. Indigo Commission Bengal, *Report*, 16, where it is said, "The planters all urge that strict supervision over each successive agricultural operation is… necessary."

93. Cited Chowdhury, *Growth of Commercial Agriculture*, 162; italics mine.

94. Fisher, "Planters and Peasants," 119 (growth), 130 (capital repatriation).

95. Omkar Goswami, *Industry, Trade, and Peasant Society: The Jute Economy of Eastern India, 1900–1947* (Delhi, 1991), 41–51.

96. Bagchi, *Private Investment in India*, 262–263.

97. Bagchi, *Private Investment in India*, 264–266.

98. Saugata Mukherji, "Agrarian Class Formation in Modern Bengal, 1931–51," *Economic and Political Weekly*, 21/4 (January 25) (1986), PE-11–27, at 12.

99. Krishna Bharadwaj, *Production Conditions in Indian Agriculture: A Study Based on Farm Management Surveys* (Cambridge, 1974), 69.

100. Royal Commission on Agriculture in India, *Volume IV: Evidence Taken in the Bengal Presidency* (London, HMSO, 1927), 291 (§ 21753) (from the oral evidence of G. Morgan).

101. Royal Commission, *Evidence in Bengal*, 276 (§ 21482).

102. Thirty-seven of those in Bengal—Royal Commission, *Evidence Taken in Bengal*, 279 (§ 21527).

103. Royal Commission, *Evidence in Bengal*, 276 (§ 21484).

104. Royal Commission, *Evidence in Bengal*, 276–277 (§§ 21485–21488), 283 (§ 21626).

105. Goswami, *Jute Economy*, 50.

106. Royal Commission, *Evidence in Bengal*, 284 (§ 21633), "I should say the jute broker is the man who prices the jute in the import sheds of the balers."

107. Royal Commission, *Evidence in Bengal*, 280 (§ 21549).

108. Royal Commission, *Evidence in Bengal*, 284 (§ 21631, through the broker), (§21638, "through their own offices").

109. Royal Commission, *Evidence in Bengal*, 284 (§§ 21636–21637).

110. Royal Commission, *Evidence in Bengal*, 282 (§§ 21594–21596).

111. Gordon T. Stewart, *Jute and Empire: the Calcutta Jute Wallahs and the Landscapes of Empire* (Manchester, 1998), 43–44.

112. Stewart, *Jute and Empire*, 44.

113. See Mukherji, "Agrarian Class Formation in Modern Bengal."

114. The figures are from Yves Pégourier, *Le marché du riz d'Indochine* (Paris, 1937), 3.

115. Pégourier, *Marché du riz*, 52.

116. Brocheux and Hémery, *Indochina*, 122.

117. Virginia Thompson, *French Indo-China* (London, 1937), 169.

118. Martin J. Murray, *The Development of Capitalism in Colonial Indochina (1870–1940)* (Berkeley, 1980), 449–451.

119. Pierre Brocheux, *The Mekong Delta: Ecology, Economy, and Revolution, 1860–1960* (Madison, 1995), 69.

120. Cheng, *Rice Industry of Burma*.

121. Pégourier, *Marché du riz*, 54.

122. Pégourier, *Marché du riz*, 63.

123. Brocheux and Hémery, *Indochina*, 122; Banque de l'Indochine financed over half of Saigon's rice exports (p.147).

124. Brocheux and Hémery, *Indochina*, 122.

125. Maxine Berg, Pat Hudson, and Michael Sonenscher, "Manufacture in Town and Country before the Factory," in *Manufacture in Town and Country before the Factory*, eds. Maxine Berg, Pat Hudson, and Michael Sonenscher (Cambridge, 1983), 1–32, at 8.

126. Berg, Hudson, and Sonenscher, "Manufacture," 12.

127. Turgot, "Reflections," 542.

128. Cited Zahedieh, *Capital and the Colonies*, 72.

129. Milja van Tielhof, *The "Mother of All Trades": The Baltic Grain Trade in Amsterdam from the Late Sixteenth to the Early Nineteenth Century* (Leiden, etc., 2002), 119.

130. Balard, *La Romanie génoise*, t.2, 871.

131. Braudel, *Out of Italy*, 37.

132. Frederic C. Lane, "Fleets and Fairs: the Functions of the Venetian *muda*," in *Studi in onore di Armando Sapori*, 2 vols. (Milan, 1957), vol. 1, 649–663, at 656.

133. Marshall, *East Indian Fortunes*, 36.

134. Hossain, *Company Weavers*, 51.

135. Devine, *Tobacco Lords*, 68.

136. Devine, *Tobacco Lords*, 58 (turnaround time).

137. Devine, *Tobacco Lords*, 58 (bulk sales), 64 (French buyers).

138. Fieldhouse, *Merchant Capital*, 121.

139. J. Aspinall Tobin cited C. W. Newbury, "Credit in Early Nineteenth Century West African Trade," *Journal of African History*, 13 (1972), 81–95, at 91.

140. See the excerpts from P. I. Lyashchenko translated in *Commercialization and Agriculture in Late Imperial Russia*, ed. Hari Vasudevan (Calcutta, 1998), esp. 63, 86–91.

141. Engels in Marx, *Capital, Volume 3*, 620, note 8.

142. Engels in Marx, *Capital, Volume 3*, 164. Velocities could increase dramatically: the Secretary to the Chief Commissioner of the Central Provinces claimed that "Merchandise, instead of taking two months in transit between Nagpur and Bombay, is now conveyed in three to four days," Charles Grant, *The Gazetteer of the Central Provinces of India*, 2nd edn. (Nagpur, 1870), 338. The reference here was to railway expansion in the 1860s.

143. Marx, *Grundrisse*, 685.

144. Marx, *Capital, Volume 3*, 425.

145. Marx, *Capital, Volume 3*, 426.

146. Marx, *Capital, Volume 3*, 418, "... as the turnover of commercial capital accelerates (and this is also where the function of money as means of payment predominates, with the development of the credit system)."

147. Nash, "Organization of Trade," 128–131.

148. Mayhew, *Sterling*, 164.

149. Cited Marx, *Capital, Volume 3*, 532.

150. *Manchester Guardian*, November 24, 1847, cited Marx, *Capital, Volume 3*, 536–537; clearly based on British Parliamentary Papers, *Second Report from the Secret Committee of Commercial Distress; with the Minutes of Evidence*, August 8, 1848, 118, § 7823: "Is not this the practice of houses in good credit, that they purchase goods, and pay for them by their own drafts: they sell their bills upon London, and, by the sale of their bills upon London, *drawing upon their houses in London at ten months' date*, are in a condition to purchase goods with the produce of those bills: those goods are immediately shipped from Calcutta; and the bills of lading are transmitted overland by the same mail by which their own drafts upon their houses in London are sent: the bills of lading are in the possession of the house here; and from the time of accepting the bills, the bills have probably eight months to run after their

arrival here; they have then the bills of lading in their possession; and *they have not to pay the bills representing the produce for eight months after that period*; are you aware that that has been the system carried on to a great extent, and that *those bills of lading have been immediately handed over to produce brokers, and that bills of exchange have been drawn against those bills of lading, and that those bills of exchange have been discounted in Lombard-street, and thereby an enormous amount of capital has been raised*; and that merchants connected with India, and carrying on trade by means of those long-dated bills, could go on for a great number of years, furnishing themselves with an enormous amount of capital to transact business, when they had, in fact, no real capital, provided they had only credit in Calcutta"; italics mine.

151. Milne, *Trade and Traders*, 114.

152. Milne, *Trade and Traders*, 129.

153. Milne, *Trade and Traders*, 130.

154. Vikelas, *My Life* (in Greek), pt.2 (written over 1901–7), cited Moutafidou, "Demetrius Vikelas," 149–150; italics mine.

155. H. W. van Santen, "Trade between Mughal India and the Middle East, and Mughal Monetary Policy, ca.1600–1660," in *Asian Trade Routes*, ed. Karl Reinhold Haellquist (London, 1991), 87–95, at 88–89.

156. Nadri, *Political Economy of Indigo*, 93.

157. Marshall, *East Indian Fortunes*, 78.

158. Um, *Merchant Houses of Mocha*, 44–45.

159. Paul Lunde, "Arabic Sources for the Ming Voyages," in *Natural Resources and Cultural Connections of the Red Sea*, eds. J. Starkey, P. Starkey, and T. Wilkinson (Oxford, 2007), 229–246, at 234, citing al-Khazraji's history of the Rasulids.

160. Wong, *China Transformed*, 146–147.

161. Wong, *China Transformed*, 53.

162. Wong, *China Transformed*, 57–58.

163. Wong, *China Transformed*, 39–40.

164. Marx, *Capital, Volume 3*, 736–737.

165. Braudel, *Out of Italy*, 37–38.

166. Engels in Marx, *Capital, Volume 3*, 1040–1041.

167. Franz Mehring, *Absolutism and Revolution in Germany, 1525–1848* (London, 1975), 1, 3; italics mine.

168. Sewell, "Empire of Fashion," 116.

169. Ronald Latham, trans., *The Travels of Marco Polo* (Penguin Books, 1958), 260–261; Jill Crystal, *Oil and Politics in the Gulf: Rulers and Merchants in Kuwait and Qatar* (Cambridge, 1990), 37–38.

170. Carlo Poni, "All'origine del sistema di fabbrica. Tecnologia e organizzazione produttiva dei mulini da seta nell'Italia settentrionale (sec.xvii–xviii)," *Rivista Storica Italiana*, 88 (1976), 444–497.

171. K. M. Stahl, *The Metropolitan Organization of British Colonial Trade* (London, 1951), chapter 4 (plantation interests of British merchant houses in the Malayan rubber industry—four hundred sterling companies controlling estates managed by the leading agency houses).

172. Fleet, *European and Islamic Trade*, 136–139; Sturdza, *Dictionnaire historique et généalogique*, 224–225 (Baltazzi).

173. Zdenko Zlatar, *Dubrovnik's Merchants and Capital in the Ottoman Empire (1520–1620)* (Istanbul, 2010), 21–24 (massive concentration on Belgrade).

174. Doria, "Conoscenza del mercato," 76–78.

175. Harlaftis, *History of Greek-Owned Shipping*, 89–102; Gelina Harlaftis, *Greek Shipowners and the State, 1945–1975* (London, 1993); and Gelina Harlaftis, "From Diaspora Traders to Shipping Tycoons: The Vagliano Bros," *Business History Review*, 81 (2007), 237–68, esp. 251–66.

176. Kardasis, *Diaspora Merchants*, 82.

177. Vicziany, "Bombay Merchants," 185.

178. Royal Commission on Agriculture in India, *Volume 4: Evidence Taken in Sind* (London, HMSO, 1927), 148.

179. Eric Hobsbawm, *The Age of Empire, 1875–1914* (New York, 1989), 40.

180. Hobsbawm, *Age of Empire*, 39–42.

181. Hobsbawm, *Age of Empire*, 60.

182. Hobsbawm, *Age of Empire*, 50, 62.

183. Engels in Marx, *Capital, Volume 3*, 620, note 8.

184. Engels in Marx, *Capital, Volume 3*, 1046–1047.

185. G. Porter and H. C. Livesay, *Merchants and Manufacturers: Studies in the Changing Structure of Nineteenth-Century Marketing* (Baltimore, 1971), 137–144, 147.

186. Michael B. Miller, *The Bon Marché: Bourgeois Culture and the Department Store, 1869–1920* (London, 1981), 26–29.

187. Walter Benjamin, *The Arcades Project*, trans. Howard Eiland and Kevin McLaughlin (Harvard University Press, 2002), 61.

188. Miller, *Bon Marché*, 26.

189. Oil and electricity are so described by Hobsbawm, *Age of Empire*, 44.

190. Émile Zola, *Au Bonheur des Dames (The Ladies' Delight)*, trans. Robin Buss (Penguin Books, 2001), 73–75. The novel depicts the capitalism of the *grands magasins* of the Second Empire with great exuberance, doubtless because Zola based his writing of it on "extensive research on the department stores themselves and information supplied by expert witnesses" (p.xxi, translator's introduction).

191. The best description of these is Patrick Morlat, "Les réseaux patronaux français en Indochine (1918–1928)," in *L'esprit économique impérial (1830–1970)*, eds. H. Bonin, C. Hodeir, and J. F. Klein (Paris, 2008), 615–629.

192. Marc Meuleau, *Des pionniers en Extrême-Orient. Histoire de la Banque de l'Indochine (1875–1975)* (Paris, 1990), 155.

193. Brocheux and Hémery, *Indochina*, 171; based on the calculations of Yasuo Gonjo, cf. appendix 9, 397–98.

194. Howard Cox, *The Global Cigarette: Origins and Evolution of British American Tobacco, 1880–1945* (Oxford, 2000), 57.

195. Cain and Hopkins, *British Imperialism*, 435.

196. Green, "Influence of the City," 210; Cain and Hopkins, *British Imperialism*, 460–463. Michael B. Miller, *Europe and the Maritime World: A Twentieth-Century History* (Cambridge, 2012) points out that "British shipping never fully recovered from abandoned networks and markets during the war" (p.249). "As a seafaring nation, Britain never recovered from this wartime experience" (237). On the other hand, the war had an even more devastating effect on German merchant shipping, with half of Germany's merchant marine disappearing. German (and Dutch and other Continental) trading firms figure prominently in Miller's fascinating account of the way ports, and shipping and trading companies, built *networks* that were essentially "Eurocentric in their construction but joined in every sea with indigenous shipping and trading circles" (209). Crucially, the war "could not eradicate all the cosmopolitan connections established over preceding decades" (235), and "globalization, viewed from a maritime perspective, *remained deeply entrenched throughout the (twentieth) century*" (11; italics mine).

Appendix

1. Subhi Labib, "Capitalism in Medieval Islam," *Journal of the Economic and Social History of the Orient*, 29 (1969), 79–96.

2. Hilal Inalcik, "Capital Formation in the Ottoman Empire," *Journal of Economic History*, 29 (1969), 97–140.

3. Abdelaziz Duri, *Arabische Wirtschaftsgeschichte*, trans. J. Jacobi (Zurich, 1979).

4. Robert Mantran, *Istanbul dans la seconde moitié du XVII siècle: essai d'histoire institutionelle, économique et sociale* (Paris, 1962), 428, "les éléments capitalistes susceptibles de procéder à des achats en grandes quantités," on wholesalers in wheat and livestock products.

5. E.g., Fernand Braudel, *The Mediterranean and the Mediterranean World in the Age of Philip II*, 2 vols. (London, 1975), vol. 1, 548–549.

6. Baber Johansen, "Commercial Exchange and Social Order in Hanafite Law," in *Law and the Islamic World: Past and Present*, eds. Christopher Toll and Jakob Skovgaard-Petersen (Copenhagen, 1995), 81–95, at 90.

7. *The Kitāb al-Maghāzī of al-Wāqidī*, ed. Marsden Jones, vol. 1 (London, 1966), 197.

8. Subhi Labib, *Handelsgeschichte Ägyptens im Spatmittelalter (1171–1517)* (Wiesbaden, 1965), 120.

9. Maxime Rodinson, *Islam and Capitalism*, trans. Brian Pearce (Penguin Books, 1977), 34, 56.

10. Rodinson, *Islam and Capitalism*, 51–52.

11. Mohamed Ouerfelli, *Le sucre. Production, commercialisation et usages dans le Méditerrannée médiévale* (Leiden, 2008). Throughout this monograph Ouerfelli refers to "entrepreneurs," "businessmen" (*hommes d'affaires*), "industrial enterprises," "substantial sums of capital" (*importants capitaux*), and "capital investments" but avoids the term "capitalism" and omits any discussion of the theoretical issue raised by Rodinson's book.

12. Rodinson, *Islam and Capitalism*, x, "My book is, then, of a theoretical character."

13. Ouerfelli, *Sucre*, 56, 73–74, 79, 84, 89ff., 98.

14. Rodinson, *Islam and Capitalism*, 53.

15. Maxime Rodinson, *Marxism and the Muslim World*, trans. Michael Pallis (New York, 1981), 151.

16. Labib, *Handelsgeschichte Ägyptens*, 280.

17. Maxime Rodinson, *Muhammad*, trans. Anne Carter (London, 2002), 98, 146 ("a recognition of the value of the individual personality").

18. Al-Sarakhsī, *Kitāb al-Mabsūt*, vol. 22, p.19; Abraham L. Udovitch, *Partnership and Profit in Medieval Islam* (Princeton, 1970), 175.

19. Sami Zubaida, "Economic and Political Activism in Islam," *Economy and Society*, 1 (1972), 308–338, at 322.

20. See Michael Bonner, "The *Kitāb al-kasb* attributed to al-Shaybānī," *Journal of the Oriental American Society*, 121 (2001), 410–427, at 415.

21. Ibn Khaldūn, *The Muqaddimah: An Introduction to History*, trans. Franz Rosenthal, 3 vols. (Princeton, 1958), vol. 2, 291, 297 (translation modified), 274 (trans. modified), 246.

22. Yves Lacoste, *Ibn Khaldun: The Birth of History and the Past of the Third World* (London, 1984), 153.

23. Ibn Khaldūn, *Muqaddimah*, vol. 1, 11, 71.

24. Ibn Khaldūn, *Muqaddimah*, vol. 2, 249.

25. Ouerfelli, *Sucre*, 100.

26. Hilāl al-Sābi," *Rusūm Dār al-Khilāfah (The Rules and Regulations of the 'Abbāsid Court)*, trans. E. A. Salem (Beirut, 1977), 23.

27. André Raymond, *Arab Cities in the Ottoman Period: Cairo, Syria and the Maghreb* (Aldershot, 2002), no. ix, 144, with the estimates for Paris and London taken from J. C. Russell.

28. Fernand Braudel, "European Expansion and Capitalism, 1450–1650," in *Chapters in Western Civilization*, third edition (New York, 1961), vol. 1, 255.

29. André Raymond, "The Economy of the Traditional City," in *The City in the Islamic World*, eds. Salma Khadra Jayyusi et al., 2 vols. (Leiden, 2008), vol. 1, 737–757, at 738.

30. "When Thenaud came to Cairo (1512), he was told that more than two hundred merchants in the city possessed fortunes of over one million gold pieces," Nelly Hanna, *An Urban History of Būlāq in the Mamluk and Ottoman Periods* (Cairo, 1983), 20.

31. Labib, "Capitalism in Medieval Islam," 85. On *wikālas*, *fanādiq*, and similar establishments, see Labib, *Handelsgeschichte Ägyptens*, 290ff. (Cairo); Éric Vallet, *L'Arabie marchande. État et commerce sous les sultans rasūlides du Yémen* (Paris, 2010), 134–135 (Aden); and the general surveys in A. Raymond and G. Wiet, *Les marchés du Caire* (Cairo, 1979), 2–22; Ennio Concina, *Fondaci. Architettura, arte, e mercatura tra Levante, Venezia, e Alemagna* (Venice, 1997); and Olivia Remie Constable, *Housing the Stranger in the Mediterranean World* (Cambridge, 2009).

32. Erich Prokosch, *Kairo in der zweiten Hälfte des 17. Jahrhunderts beschreiben von Evliya Çelebi* (Istanbul, 2000), 221.

33. Al-Mas'ūdī, *Murūj al-dhahab wa-ma'ādin al-jawhar* (Baghdad, 1938), vol. 2, 222; *Les Prairies d'Or*, trans. Barbier de Meynard et Pavet de Courteille, revised and edited by C. Pellat (Paris, 1971), vol. 3, 616 (§1579).

34. Nāsir-i Khosrau, *Sefer Nameh*, trans. Charles Schefer (Paris, 1881), 236.

35. Ibn Hauqal, *Kitāb sūrat al-'ard*, ed., J. H. Kramers (Leiden, 1938–1939), 432, lines 10ff.; *Configuration de la terre*, trans. J. H. Kramers and G. Wiet, 2 vols. (Paris, 1964), vol. 2, 418.

36. Al-Idrīsī, *Opus Geographicum*, eds. A. Bombaci et al. (Naples and Rome, 1971), fasc. 2, 130; *La première géographie de l'Occident*, trans. Jaubert, new ed., Henri Bresc and Annliese Nef (Paris, 1999), 123.

37. Al-Idrīsī, *Opus Geographicum* (Naples, 1972), fasc. 3, 281–282; *Première géographie*, 183–184.

38. Al-Idrīsī, *Opus Geographicum* (Naples, 1975), fasc. 5, 562; *Première géographie*, 281–282. Labib, "Capitalism in Medieval Islam," 88 rightly translates *turuz al-harir* as "looms."

39. Luca Molà, *The Silk Industry of Renaissance Venice* (Baltimore, 2000), 17.

40. Malise Ruthven, *Islam in the World*, third edition (New York, 2006), 167–169.

41. Eric H. Mielants, *The Origins of Capitalism and the Rise of the West* (Philadelphia, PA, 2007), 150–152.

42. Robert Brenner, *Merchants and Revolution* (Cambridge, 1993), 65.

43. Fernand Braudel, *Afterthoughts on Material Civilization and Capitalism* (Baltimore and London, 1977), 64.

44. Cited Mohamed Elhachmi Hamdi, *The Politicisation of Islam: A Case Study of Tunisia* (Boulder, CO, 1998), 121.

45. Charles Kurzman, ed., *Modernist Islam, 1840–1940: A Sourcebook* (New York, 2002), 18–19.

46. Peter Gran, *Islamic Roots of Capitalism: Egypt, 1760–1840* (Austin, 1979), 10–11.

47. Ervand Abrahamian, *A History of Modern Iran* (Cambridge, 2008), 145–146.

48. Seyyed Vali Reza Nasr, *Mawdudi and the Making of Islamic Revivalism* (Oxford, 1996), 105: "Throughout his career Mawdudi remained a staunch defender of private property... He objected to land reform in the Punjab throughout the 1950s."

49. "They [Egypt's Muslim Brothers] have maintained vague notions of social justice, but have not used the vocabulary of socialism, or shown any hostility to private property... More recently, persons and organisations associated with the Brotherhood have been very active in business and finance, especially with the rise of the Islamic banks and investment companies," Sami Zubaida, *Islam, the People and the State* (London, 1993), 49–50. And of course, even more recently, the Brotherhood's first nominee for president in the 2012 elections was Khayrat al-Shatir, a "multimillionaire businessman," Carrie Rosefsky Wickham, *The Muslim Brotherhood: Evolution of an Islamist Movement* (Princeton, 2013), 254–255.

50. Ervand Abrahamian, *Khomeinism: Essays on the Islamic Republic* (Berkeley, 1993), Chapter 2.

51. Shari'ati, *Islamshenasi*, cited Ervand Abrahamian, *Iran Between Two Revolutions* (Princeton,1982), 470.

52. Vanessa Martin, *Creating an Islamic State: Khomeini and the Making of a New Iran* (London, 2000), 85.

53. Ali M. Ansari, *Iran, Islam and Democracy* (London, 2006); in Ali M. Ansari, *Modern Iran: The Pahlavis and After*, second edition (London, 2007), he refers to "an alliance of interests between the 'mercantile bourgeoisie'... and the patrimonial presidency of Rafsanjani," adding, "Rafsanjani would govern with the interests of the merchant classes in mind, interests which coincided with his own commercial background, while the *bazaar* would help finance the presidency" (pp. 302–3).

54. Cited Abrahamian, *History of Modern Iran*, 179.

55. Jill Crystal, *Oil and Politics in the Gulf: Rulers and Merchants in Kuwait and Qatar* (Cambridge, 1990).

56. Adam Hanieh, *Capitalism and Class in the Gulf Arab States* (Basingstoke, 2011).

57. Hugh Roberts has made the point for Algeria, see Roberts, "The Algerian Bureaucracy," in *Sociology of "Developing Societies": The Middle East*, eds. Talal Asad and Roger Owen (London, 1983), 95–114, at 101–2: "Algeria is not a religious state, even if we cannot describe it as a secular one."

58. Hugh Roberts, *The Battlefield Algeria 1988–2002* (London, 2003), 20.

59. Fouad Zakariyya, *Myth and Reality in the Contemporary Islamist Movement* (London, 2005), 20.

60. Sami Zubaida, *Law and Power in the Islamic World* (London, 2003), 158.

61. Censorship under Nasser is documented in detail by Marina Stagh, *The Limits of Freedom of Speech: Prose Literature and Prose Writers in Egypt under Nasser and Sadat* (Stockholm, 1993).

62. Marshall Berman, *All That Is Solid Melts into Air: The Experience of Modernity* (Penguin Books, 1988), 10–11.

63. Samir Kassir, *Being Arab* (London, 2006), 28.

64. Ali Rahnema, *Superstition as Ideology in Iranian Politics: From Majlesi to Ahmadinejad* (Cambridge, 2011).

65. Sadik J. al-Azm, "The Importance of Being Earnest about Salman Rushdie," *Die Welt des Islams*, 31 (1991), 1–49, at 2, 30, 35.

66. Elizabeth Suzanne Kassab, *Contemporary Arab Thought: Cultural Critique in Comparative Perspective* (New York, 2010), 58–65.

67. See the discussion in Joseph Massad, *Desiring Arabs* (Chicago, 2007), 239ff.

68. Mahmud Muhammad Taha was probably among the most important of these. He was hanged by the Sudanese dictator Nimeiri in 1985. See Edward Thomas, *Islam's Perfect Stranger: The Life of Mahmud Muhammad Taha, Muslim Reformer of Sudan* (London, 2009). More recent examples of this philosophically grounded, often radically modernist, "immanent" critique of *salafi* or traditionalist Islam can be seen in Andreas Christmann, ed., *The Qur'an, Morality and Critical Reason: The Essential Muhammad Shahrur* (Leiden, etc., 2009), and Mahmoud Sadri and Ahmad Sadri, eds., *Reason, Freedom and Democracy in Islam: Essential Writings of Abdolkarim Soroush* (New York, 2000).

SELECT BIBLIOGRAPHY

The bibliography shortlists books and papers that seem especially apt for the way trade, commercial organization, and merchant's capital are discussed, and for the light they shed on the purely commercial side of the history of capitalism. No attempt is made to group the literature by periods, regions, or subject matter, much less to be comprehensive about any of these. And by and large, where an item has been cited repeatedly in my notes, it is unlikely to be listed here as well.

Banaji, Jairus. "Merchant Capitalism, Peasant Households, and Industrial Accumulation: Integration of a Model." *Journal of Agrarian Change* 16, no. 3 (2016): 410–431.

Beckert, Sven. *Empire of Cotton: A New History of Global Capitalism.* London: Allen Lane, 2014.

Bernstein, Henry. "Notes on Capital and Peasantry." *Review of African Political Economy* 4, no. 10 (1977): 60–73.

Bonin, Hubert. *CFAO (1887–2007). La réinvention permanente du commerce outre-mer.* Paris, 2007.

Brandon, Pepijn. *War, Capital, and the Dutch State (1588–1795).* Leiden: Brill, 2015.

Braudel, Fernand. *The Mediterranean and the Mediterranean World in the Age of Philip II.* 2 vols. Translated by Siân Reynolds. London: Collins, 1972.

———. *The Wheels of Commerce: Civilization and Capitalism, Fifteenth–Eighteenth Century, Volume 2.* London: Phoenix Press, 1972.

Brenner, Robert. *Merchants and Revolution: Commercial Change, Political Conflict, and London's Overseas Traders, 1550–1653.* Cambridge: Cambridge University Press, 1993.

Bythell, Duncan. *The Sweated Trades: Outwork in Nineteenth-Century Britain.* London: Batsford, 1978.

Cain, P. J., and A. G. Hopkins. *British Imperialism, 1688–2000.* Second edition. London: Longman, 2002.

Chapman, Stanley D. *Merchant Enterprise in Britain from the Industrial Revolution to World War I.* Cambridge: Cambridge University Press, 1992.

Chorley, Patrick. *Oil, Silk and Enlightenment: Economic Problems in XVIIIth Century Naples*. Naples: Istituto Italiano per gli Studi, 1965.

Devine, T. M. *The Tobacco Lords: A Study of the Tobacco Merchants of Glasgow and Their Trading Activities, ca.1740–1790*. Edinburgh: Edinburgh University Press, 1975.

Fieldhouse, D. K. *Merchant Capital and Economic Decolonization: The United Africa Company, 1929–1987*. Oxford: Clarendon Press, 1994.

Frangakis-Syrett, Elena. *Trade and Money: The Ottoman Economy in the Eighteenth and Early Nineteenth Centuries*. Istanbul: Isis Press, 2007.

Green, E. H. H. "The Influence of the City over British Economic Policy ca.1880–1960." In *Finance and Financiers in European History 1880–1960*, edited by Youssef Cassis, 193–218. Cambridge: Editions de la Maison des Sciences de l'Homme, 1992.

Harlaftis, Gelina. *A History of Greek-Owned Shipping*. London: Routledge, 1996.

Harriss-White, Barbara. *Rural Commercial Capital: Agricultural Markets in West Bengal*. New Delhi: Oxford University Press, 2008.

Harvey, Charles and Jon Press. "The City and International Mining, 1870–1914." *Business History* 32, no.3 (1990): 98–119.

Ho, Chuimei. "The Ceramic Boom in Minnan during Song and Yuan Times." In *The Emporium of the World: Maritime Quanzhou, 1000–1400*, edited by Angela Schottenhammer, 237–281. Leiden: Brill, 2001.

Hobsbawm, Eric. *The Age of Empire, 1875–1914*. New York: Vintage Books, 1989.

Holbach, Rudolf. *Frühformen von Verlag und Grossbetrieb in der gewerblichen Produktion (13.–16. Jahrhundert)*. Stuttgart: Franz Steiner Verlag, 1994.

Hont, Istvan. *Jealousy of Trade: International Competition and the Nation-State in Historical Perspective*. Cambridge, MA: Belknap, 2005.

Ingham, Geoffrey. *Capitalism Divided? The City and Industry in British Social Development*. London: Macmillan, 1984.

———. "Commercial Capital and British Development: A Reply to Michael Barrat Brown." *New Left Review* 1, no. 172 (1988): 45–65.

Israel, Jonathan I. *Dutch Primacy in World Trade, 1585–1740*. Oxford: Clarendon Press, 1989.

Kardasis, Vassilis. *Diaspora Merchants in the Black Sea: The Greeks in Southern Russia, 1775–1861*. Lanham: Lexington Books, 2001.

Kellenbenz, Hermann. *Die Fugger in Spanien und Portugal bis 1560. Ein Großunternehmen des 16. Jahrhunderts*, 3 vols. Munich: Verlag Ernst Vögel, 1990.

Kriedte, Peter. *Peasants, Landlords and Merchant Capitalists: Europe and the World Economy, 1500–1800*. Leamington Spa: Berg, 1983.

Levine, David. *Family Formation in an Age of Nascent Capitalism*. New York: Academic Press, 1977.

Lis, Catharina and Hugo Soly. *Poverty and Capitalism in Pre-Industrial Europe*. Atlantic Highlands, NJ: Humanities Press, 1979.

Liu, Tessie P. *The Weaver's Knot: The Contradictions of Class Struggle and Family Solidarity in Western France, 1750–1914*. Ithaca: Cornell University Press, 1994.

Marler, Scott P. *The Merchants' Capital: New Orleans and the Political Economy of the Nineteenth-Century South*. Cambridge: Cambridge University Press, 2013.

Miller, Michael B. *Europe and the Maritime World: A Twentieth-Century History*. Cambridge: Cambridge University Press, 2012.

Misra, Maria. *Business, Race, and Politics in British India, c.1850–1960*. Oxford: Clarendon Press, 1999.

Molà, Luca. *The Silk Industry of Renaissance Venice*. Baltimore: John Hopkins University Press, 2000.

Nash, R. C. "The Organization of Trade and Finance in the British Atlantic Economy, 1600–1800." In *The Atlantic Economy during the Seventeenth and Eighteenth Centuries*, edited by Peter A. Coclanis, 95–151. Charleston: University of South Carolina Press, 2005.

Moutafidou, Ariadni. "Greek Merchant Families Perceiving the World: The Case of Demetrius Vikelas." *Mediterranean Historical Review* 23, no. 2 (2008): 143–64.

Noordegraaf, Leo. "The New Draperies in the Northern Netherlands, 1500–1800." In *The New Draperies in the Low Countries and England, 1300–1800*, edited by N. B. Harte, 173–195. Oxford: Oxford University Press, 1997.

Oakes, James. "Capitalism and Slavery and the Civil War." *International Labor and Working-Class History*, 89 (2016): 195–220.

Ormrod, David. "R. H. Tawney and the Origins of Capitalism." *History Workshop Journal* 18, no. 1 (1984): 138–159.

Ouerfelli, Mohamed. *Le sucre. Production, commercialisation et usages dans le Méditerranée médiévale*. Leiden: Brill, 2008.

Owen, Thomas C. *Capitalism and Politics in Russia: A Social History of the Moscow Merchants 1855–1905*. New York: Cambridge University Press, 1981.

Poni, Carlo. "Fashion as Flexible Production: The Strategies of the Lyons Silk Merchants in the Eighteenth Century." In *World of Possibilities: Flexibility and Mass Production in Western Industrialization*, edited by Charles F. Sabel and Jonathan Zeitlin, 37–74. Cambridge, 1977.

Prange, Sebastian R. *Monsoon Islam: Trade and Faith on the Medieval Malabar Coast*. Cambridge: Cambridge University Press, 2018.

Ray, Rajat Kanta. "The Bazaar: Changing Structural Characteristics of the Indigenous Section of the Indian Economy Before and After the Great Depression." *Indian Economic and Social History Review* 25 (1988): 263–318.

Rediker, Marcus. *Between the Devil and the Deep Blue Sea: Merchant Seamen, Pirates and the Anglo-American Maritime World, 1700–1750*. Cambridge: Cambridge University Press, 1987.

Rudner, David West. *Caste and Capitalism in Colonial India: The Nattukottai Chettiars*. Berkeley, etc.: University of California Press, 1994.

Sewell Jr., William H. "The Empire of Fashion and the Rise of Capitalism in Eighteenth-Century France." *Past and Present*, no. 206 (2010): 81–120.

Shenton, Robert W. *The Development of Capitalism in Northern Nigeria*. London: James Currey, 1986.

Smith, S. D. *Slavery, Family, and Gentry Capitalism in the British Atlantic: The World of the Lascelles, 1648–1834*. Cambridge: Cambridge University Press, 2006.

Stromer, Wolfgang von. *Die Gründung der Baumwollindustrie in Mitteleuropa. Wirtschaftspolitik im Spätmittelalter.* Stuttgart: Anton Hiersemann, 1978.

Tawney, R. H. "A History of Capitalism." *Economic History Review*, 2nd series, 2 (1950): 307–316.

Tripathi, Amales. "Indo-British Trade between 1833 and 1847 and the Commercial Crisis of 1847–8." In *Trade and Finance in Colonial India, 1750–1860*, edited by Asiya Siddiqi, 265–289. Delhi: Oxford University Press, 1995.

Webster, Anthony. *The Richest East India Merchant: The Life and Business of John Palmer of Calcutta, 1767–1836.* Woodbridge, Suffolk: Boydell, 2007.

Wilson, C. H. "Trade, Society and the State." In *The Economic Organization of Early Modern Europe*. Vol. 5, *The Cambridge Economic History of Europe*, edited by E. E. Rich and C. H. Wilson, 487–575. Cambridge: Cambridge University Press, 1977.

Wong, Roy Bin. *China Transformed: Historical Change and the Limits of European Experience.* Ithaca: Cornell University Press, 1997.

Xu, Dixin and Wu Chengming. *Chinese Capitalism, 1522–1840.* New York: St. Martin's Press, 2000.

Zahedieh, Nuala. *The Capital and the Colonies: London and the Atlantic Colonies, 1660–1700.* Cambridge: Cambridge University Press, 2010.

Zubaida, Sami. "Economic and Political Activism in Islam." *Economy and Society* 1, no. 3 (1972): 308–338.

INDEX

ABOUT THE AUTHOR

Jairus Banaji spent most of his academic life at Oxford. He has been a research associate in the Department of Development Studies, SOAS, University of London, for the past several years. He is the author of *Agrarian Change in Late Antiquity*, *Theory as History*—for which he won the Isaac and Tamara Deutscher Memorial Prize—and numerous other volumes and articles.